COOKING FROM A COUNTRY FARMHOUSE

ALSO BY SUSAN WYLER

·———·

Cooking for a Crowd
Tailgate Parties

Cooking from a Country Farmhouse

By SUSAN WYLER

ILLUSTRATIONS BY BARBARA REMINGTON

HarperPerennial

A Division of HarperCollinsPublishers

HarperCollins books may be purchased for educational, business, or sales promotional use. For information, please write: Special Markets Department, HarperCollins Publishers, Inc., 10 East 53rd Street, New York, NY 10022.

FIRST EDITION

DESIGNED BY JOEL AVIROM

Library of Congress Cataloging-in-Publication Data

Wyler, Susan.
Cooking from a country farmhouse / Susan Wyler.—1st ed.
p.   cm.
Includes index.
ISBN 0-06-055344-8—ISBN 0-06-096976-8 (pbk.)
1. Cookery, American.   I. Title.
TX715.W97   1993
641.5973—dc20   92-53415

93 94 95 96 97 DT/RRD 10 9 8 7 6 5 4 3 2 1
93 94 95 96 97 DT/RRD 10 9 8 7 6 5 4 3 2 1 (pbk.)

FOR MOLLY

•——•

Many thanks to Susan Lescher, who encouraged me to write the book that came from my heart; to Rick Kot, whose encouragement and editorial sensitivity polished it; to Joseph Montebello, who understood the look; to Joel Avirom, who contributed a beautiful design; and to Dolores Simon and Dot Gannon, who both have a fine eye for detail.

Thanks especially to Barbara Remington, who loves this place as much as I do and whose charming illustrations bring my words to life. To Jeanette Brownell and Don Rintz for their invaluable help with research. And to all my friends and neighbors, acknowledged within, who so generously shared their recipes and stories.

C · O · N · T

E · N · T · S

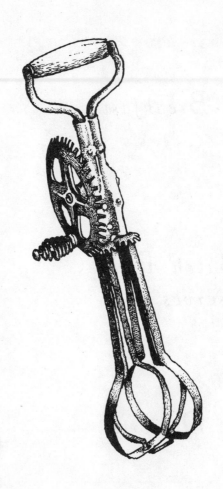

·INTRODUCTION·

I take it as no coincidence that my country farmhouse is located in a tiny town whose official historian is the niece of the man who popularized the mechanical eggbeater. For my life's work is concerned with food— the ways people produce, prepare, and serve it, how they relate to it— and fate has a way of placing us where we belong, whether we recognize it or not at the time.

Almost a century ago, about a decade after my plank house in northeastern Pennsylvania was built, Ed Johnson came East from Missouri and settled in the city closest to my obscure adopted hamlet. In 1909, he bought the patent for an improved mechanical eggbeater for thirty dollars and put it into mass production. Many fine young cooks of our time, raised on electric mixers and pampered with the efficient genius of the food processor, may never have seen this device: twin skeletal beaters formed of flat metal strips, with colorful wooden holding handles on top and a rotary turner on the side, essentially a double whisk hand-powered with a ratchet wheel.

This simple gadget took the elbow grease out of whipping egg whites and cream and effortlessly inflated air into everything from puddings to omelets. Since before the First World War, the eggbeater has made life significantly easier for decades of home cooks. In fact, while the electric mixer with a small home motor was introduced as early as 1920, it wasn't until Sunbeam came out with its classic two-bowl "Mixmaster" for under twenty dollars in 1930 that the appliance reached a significant number of American homes. And the inexpensive hand-operated mechanical eggbeater, which needs no electrical outlet, remained a favorite gadget well into the Fifties. Some people still use one, often an heirloom handed down, or borrowed and never returned, from a bottom drawer of their mother's or grandmother's kitchen.

I remember using an eggbeater at the age of four to mix the batter for my very first cake, a surprise for my grandmother Nettie's sixty-eighth birthday.

Although the recipe promised a double-layer vanilla cake, mine came out one and a half inches tall, tasting pasty; its chocolate glaze was gritty and burnt. No matter—the undue praise lavished upon me was sweet enough to last a lifetime, and the memory of that painless failure was probably responsible for my incurable fondness for flat, European-style confections.

With countless cooks before me having had a great deal more success, Ed Johnson's eggbeater became the foundation for the Ashcroft & Johnson kitchen equipment company in Binghamton, New York, which remained in business until 1929, when it was sold for a goodly sum to Edward Katzinger. He subsequently moved it to Chicago, where it became Ekco Housewares.

A & J's success was well deserved, for its products were sturdy and practical. Almost anyone who collects vintage cooking utensils must have among their treasures at least a couple of A & J gems. One of my favorites is the "Kitchamajig," a slotted, slightly curved, shell-shaped spatula with a cherry-red wooden handle. As the original label promised, it's great for whisking, skimming, draining, and turning. I picked mine up several years ago at a Memorial Day auction in the white clapboard community hall at the edge of town, and despite over three decades of good use, it looked almost new.

Before the auction, 75 percent of the town, at least one hundred people, turned out for the annual Memorial Day chicken and biscuit dinner in the social hall of the Baptist church. These communal meals—fund-raisers, covered-dish suppers, celebrations—are advertised weekly in local mailers all over this region. They are held in the little towns almost every week in the warm months and around holidays, and they take the place of coffee shops and restaurants, which are sparse in rural areas. They offer the companionship of neighbors and old friends, and mountains of familiar food: pancakes and sausages, waffles and bacon, chicken and biscuits, barbecued chicken, roast beef, spaghetti and meatballs, turkey, ham. Occasionally, there are special events—a strawberry festival, blueberry festival, clambake, or pig roast. Often the meals are accompanied by bake sales, the long tables piled high with breads, cakes, pies, cookies, brownies, and muffins.

On this Memorial Day, lunch consisted of a lumbering plate of food heaped high with baked chicken, mashed "patatas" with pan gravy, cabbage salad (aka coleslaw) laced with celery seed, canned green beans, pickle chips, cranberry sauce, and, of course, biscuits. In the old days, I am told, biscuits were always made from scratch, but as the ranks of volunteers diminished, they had to resort to a mix. The biscuits were good, anyway, crusty brown on the outside, crumbly and buttery soft inside.

For a modest set price, you devoured this feast, plus a beverage, plus the best part—homemade pie for dessert. I hadn't been around long enough to tell who made which pie, but of the three—apple, rhubarb, and cherry (I somehow managed to taste the triumvirate)—cherry was the hands-down winner, even though the fruit had to be from a can. The crust was light, flaky, crisp, and just this side of a honey-brown color. The others had tasty sweet fillings, but the crusts were, in one case, flabby, and in the other, soggy, wet, and heavy. Not that it mattered much after all that food.

For me, that Memorial Day was the beginning. Though I'd come to live in the place in the middle of winter, I'd hibernated through the cold, and only toward the end of that first May did I venture out and begin to know my new home. I'd found my country farmhouse literally potluck by calling an 800 number in a realty guide. An escape valve from the city, where I worked as food editor of *Food & Wine* magazine, seemed a necessity. Despite my ongoing passion for food and intense commitment to spreading the word, as it were, the excitement of dining out nine times a week and breathlessly keeping pace with my chock-full appointment book had lost its allure. I was tired of being such a public person. When the real estate agent called back, the name of the town mentioned was not familiar (I had no map of Pennsylvania at the time), but when I told her exactly what I was looking for, she said, "Well, dearie, I think I have just what you want," and she was right. It was the first time in my life that I fell in love with a place at first sight. The *gestalt* of the house, situated halfway up a hill, with its steep gabled roof watched over by towering maple trees, struck a chord deep within me.

For a while it was the perfect weekend place to use as a getaway. But when not long after I left my job to start my own business and began working at home, the pull of the country became stronger. I sold my spacious loft in New York and took a small but chic pied-à-terre as an outpost in the city. There was no need. After six months, I gave up my paid-for parking spot, noticing I'd used it once in the previous thirty days. A week later, it occurred to me that the apartment, too, was an unnecessary appendage. There was no decision made; it was an organic move, determined simply by preference—the call of the wild, if you will. I have been a full-time resident now for almost four years.

Sometimes it seems that everything up here occurs in a kind of time warp. Because of the rural isolation, it's easy to forget about modern concerns: traffic, pollution, noise. The ongoing calm, broken only by certain seasonal confrontations with nature, creates a perception of timelessness enhanced perhaps because the *New York Times* is only sold here on Sundays. Perhaps that's part of what drew me so inexorably and effected such a tranquil transition. What ought to have been a jarring migration from the cosmopolitan glamour and bustle of the city to the stillness of the countryside was instead a homecoming. There is great charm, after all, in the romance of yesteryear.

Day-to-day existence in these parts follows a different rhythm. People drop by with important news instead of calling. Neighbors are always there when you need them to hoist your car out of a culvert, feed the dogs, come on over for dinner. The old farmers still follow *The Old Farmer's Almanac* and predict the changing of the seasons from the lunar cycle. Potatoes are planted in the last quarter of April or May. Small garden vegetables are put in the ground when the moon is full.

The land grows rocks. The soil is poor in most places. Late in the last century, lumber mills and gristmills and tanning factories sprouted miniature boom towns in this water-rich region, before they polluted their own backyards, literally poisoning the wells, and the populations quickly faded. Small dairy farms are now the backbone of the area. There is some lumbering, and until recently, not a few of the locals supplemented their farming or carpentry incomes with fur trapping.

The streams are dense with trout, the ponds full of perch, pickerel, sunnies, bullheads, and both largemouth and brown bass. In April and early May, the shad come swimming up the Delaware. Wild turkeys are hunted in the morning twice each year for one month, from the end of April to the end of May and again in October. We dig wild leeks in the woods in May, and find morels after the rains in late spring when we're lucky. For the hunters, besides the turkeys, there are deer, ruffed grouse, pheasant, quail, squirrels, and rabbits.

Partly because of the area's elevation, two thousand feet, and partly because of its situation, just west of the Delaware River, on the eastern edge of the Endless Mountains, the weather is not often kind. An old-timer explained to me that this was one of the few sites in the Northeast that was never inhabited by the Indians except as a temporary summer campground. Because of a peculiarity of the microclimate, the area is noticeably colder than its close surroundings, and while the cool mountain nights are a blessing in summer, the winters are so harsh that until recent years the snowfalls were notorious. Tall tales still abound.

In the dead of winter, when the north wind surges up over the hill, it howls like a locomotive, powerful and relentless. More than once, I've

Introduction

caught myself turning toward the engine, it sounds so close. Snow whips around, blinding, and the locals say, "Oh, this is nothing. You haven't seen any weather yet." The kindly warmth of the kitchen stove makes me understand why farm wives all over this country bake and bake and bake. The oven is on almost all the time. Here pie is spelled with a capital P it tastes so good, and everyone has her own special cookies, muffins, and breads. Cake is the all-American kind—simple and sky high.

Most of my adult life was spent in New York City, where in addition to my dining out daily at the trendiest restaurants because of my work, I entertained frequently with that particularly urban desire to astound. With everything available all the time, no dishes were too exotic, too witty, or too complicated for the palates of my guests.

The food I cook at the farmhouse is different. While country as a genre of popular music, faux-rustic style of home decoration, or rugged form of fashion may be just a state of mind—or marketing hype—true country is a way of life, dictated by an almost umbilical connection to the land. It holds people close to home.

Local markets cater to traditional tastes. They stock buttermilk, graham flour (coarsely ground whole wheat), buckwheat flour, smoked ham hocks, pickled sausages, and a very few good-keeping vegetables. Some part of the chicken is almost always on sale. Steaks are cut to order. Delicacies that come in once in a blue moon, like fresh oysters or clams, are heralded with handwritten signs in the window and on the door.

Though I retain a stock of imported Parmesan cheese and good pasta, I rely largely on the products in the local markets, augmented by the garden and my neighbors' gardens in season, which I suspect is how the majority of nonurban Americans eat. This country food is predictable, as it is intended to be. After traveling the world in our dining room chairs, startling our guests and challenging our children with virtuoso creations reproduced from the genius of starred chefs, whose dazzling plates are, in fact, produced in their restaurants by batteries of underlings, we are returning home, making time for the basics and learning, perhaps, that there is pleasure in simple comfort. This country food follows the seasons in a reassuring way, and it suits the weather as well as the level of activity.

When it's cold, there are huge breakfasts, with hash and eggs, oatmeal, homemade biscuits, and bacon. In the evening, we warm ourselves with good company, animated conversation, and hearty dishes—potpies, chowders, lentils with fresh kielbasa made by the butcher in the next town over, roast chicken with browned root vegetables and pan gravy, spaghetti with meat sauce. When we have turkey, it goes a long way: First it's roasted, served perhaps with mashed rutabagas, buttered broccoli, and cranberry muffins. Then it divides its remains between a very fine turkey soup with wild rice and carrots and my favorite, barbecued turkey hash with potatoes, lots of browned onions, and an egg apiece on top.

While spring comes late, its arrival heralds a hectic season. When the ramps (wild leeks), dandelions, sorrel, and wild turkeys appear, then the trout, shad, rhubarb, peas, and potatoes are close at hand. In April, as soon as the ground is soft enough to fork, Jerusalem artichokes are dug up before the tubers sprout, sweet after their icy sleep. Before you know it, the tiger lilies raise their stalks, which look like young ginger plants, and the wild leeks, with their dark green leaves shaped like lily-of-the-valley, pop out in the woods. Wild turkeys are mating; you can hear them gobbling just over the hill. The ground is prepared early, planted late, but always something is ripening, tantalizing you with its evanescent moment in time before it disappears.

For me spring officially begins as early as possible with the return of the phoebe, a small, plain bird, whose sweet voice calls its own name. For others, it comes with the first cry of the peepers, tiny brown frogs the size of your thumbnail, who hibernate in the mud all winter and awake and sing when it's almost truly spring. To the uninitiated, they sound like crickets, but their song is not so constant. No matter how warm or cold the weather, many townspeople predict there will be three more snowfalls after you hear the first peepers.

Overnight the apple trees flare into bloom. Bobolinks twang in the meadows, bluebirds flicker in and out of their nests, yellow-throated warblers sing their hearts out, and high up in the skies kestrels, red-tailed hawks, and huge turkey buzzards circle on the drafts. From my window, I see the heifers—virgin cows—let out to pasture, their winter black-and-white coats shiny and clean. Startled with their freedom, they gambol like goats in the green fields.

My first garden was and still is right next to the house. I spent three entire days preparing the beds for this kitchen plot, an herb garden on one side of the walk and a small vegetable patch on the other, both just below the porch. They are each only about eight by three feet, on either side of the steps, but because the earth hadn't been cultivated in many years it was hard work picking out the rocks and pulling up the tangles of quack grass roots that stretched deep into the ground. I lined the beds with rocks. At first it was bare, like a little cemetery. How, I wondered, would I bring this place to life?

Miraculously, my herb garden became an unexpected success—even the thyme survived the winter, and each year I add to the variety. Now there is bee balm, English lavender, lemon thyme, common fragrant thyme, unruly spearmint, winter savory (one of my culinary favorites), oregano, sage, French tarragon (another pet), two kinds of rosemary, chives, anise hyssop, and chervil, which, though an annual, reseeds itself. Each year I plant basil, sweet marjoram, and pineapple sage.

At first the locals laughed at my kitchen garden, situated as it is right up against the house. It never occurred to me at the time, but, of course, those strips of ground were for flowers. All I could think of was grow and eat, grow and cook, grow and cook and eat. Later, when I had first pick of the baby lettuces and the neighbors saw how the animals would avoid that place, they nodded their heads and acknowledged my practicality.

Soon after, I put in a real vegetable garden in the field across the driveway, modest but manageable. Most years, I've had good luck with tomatoes and zucchini. I share my apples and peas with the critters. They usually leave me at least half the bean crop. I may or may not get a taste of my kale, cauliflower, chard, and peppers. Onions are safe in the ground. The birds and I compete for the huckleberries. There are plenty of wild raspberries to go around.

As the days warm up, food becomes lighter, often served cold or at room temperature, and color becomes more dominant. Vegetable soups, salads, and simply cooked meats are the order of the day, with less time spent over the stove. Once fishing season begins, there are trout and bass and fried sunfish for breakfast. The grill comes out, and smoke is added to my list of spices.

The very first barbecue I threw in this place was for last-minute guests. It consisted of grilled chicken legs and marinated pork chops; potato salad with lots of egg and Dijon mustard; and a zucchini-based pistou, spicy with hot sauce and vinegar, served room temperature and Americanized with corn. For dessert, I made lemon pie, sunny yellow and tart-sweet. My guests devoured the vegetables along with two pieces of chicken and two or three pork chops each. They all had seconds on dessert. People eat a lot in the country, I've learned.

❊ ❊ ❊

Cooking from a Country Farmhouse is an homage to my new home, a celebration of the warm, casual entertaining and tasty, wholesome home cooking that is typical of the twin tiers of northern Pennsylvania and southern New York State. Many of the recipes in the book came, either directly or as adaptations, from members of my small community; some of my favorites have been passed down for generations. The majority of dishes were developed in my own farmhouse kitchen with easy-to-find local ingredients—the kinds of stock ingredients found all over America—with seasonal fruits and vegetables, a few wild delicacies, but not much exotic fare. All were devised with modern nutritional values in mind.

These are the favorite recipes that I cook often and enjoy sharing frequently with good friends. While this food emanates from a rural setting, it is, I believe, universally American, appropriate in town or country, city or suburb, anywhere people gather at table to dine.

In these pages you'll also meet my neighbors and get a taste of some of the local animals, plants, and characters, and some of the humor. It is a book written from the heart in the language that I understand best: that of the kitchen, or as it once was more poetically called—the hearth.

COOKING FROM A COUNTRY FARMHOUSE

FARMHOUSE SOUPS AND CHOWDERS

Will Rogers, one of the most famous country personalities there ever was, is well known for his kindly quote "I never met a man I didn't like." Being much less sociable than Will and far more fixed on food, I would rephrase the sentence slightly: I never met a bowl of homemade soup I didn't like. Less altruistic, perhaps, but we all have our own truths.

Cool and silky; hot and chunky; thick and creamy; flavored with vegetables, chicken, fish, or meat; piquant, salty, sour, even sweet, each soup has its own individual character and special merits. The appeal of soups and chowders (their stewlike counterparts) knows no bounds; that is, a sophisticated bisque spoons up just as smooth and velvety from an old earthenware porridge bowl on a plain pine table as it does from a Limoges tureen on an etched silver tray. Yet there is something about the comforting assurance of a big pot of soup bubbling away on the stove that belongs, in spirit at least, to the province of country living. Accordingly, I offer in this chapter the soups I ladle up regularly in my rural farmhouse.

Like all soups, they are satisfying and nourishing. Unlike more temperamental types of recipes, they don't mind waiting for you patiently on the stove, in the refrigerator, even in the freezer, until you are through working, gardening, or cross-country skiing, and rush in hungry and in a hurry to eat fast. Because of this, they are marvelous for entertaining. One friend of mine who always serves soup as a main course at her seemingly effortless Sunday lunches sets a gleaming stainless steel stockpot, brimming with far more than would fill a tureen, right in the middle of the table. She ladles out the first serving into large stoneware bowls, and then guests help themselves to seconds and thirds.

I love the variety soup affords. Of course, choices change with the seasons. In summer, light chowders and vegetable soups, often cool, seasoned delicately with fresh herbs, boast flavors fresh from the garden. Sweet red tomatoes, tender purple beets, fragrant green basil, dill, and chives, sugary golden corn, crisp cucumbers, mild ivory-fleshed zucchini all go into the pot.

As the weather cools, the pot gets fuller and heavier, with cabbage and kale, beans, pasta, lentils and potatoes, pumpkin and eggplant, beef and barley. Tomatoes now come from a can; bones are added to the kettle. Longer-simmering broths, with their steam rising in white wisps across the winter kitchen, are welcome for their warmth.

I envy my neighbors who have wood-burning cookstoves, so perfect for soups and stews. Every time I see one at a country auction, I consider selling my cozy farmhouse and moving to bigger digs with room for a humongous "Home Comfort" range, with its massive iron maze of shelves and cupboards and ovens all designed to cook food the old-fashioned way, gently and evenly, keep it warm for hours and at the same time heat the house. But then I remind myself of two things: what I went through to renovate my kitchen, and how long it would take to make a cup of coffee in the morning if I let the fire go out. Mollified, I settle for my efficient gas stove and console myself by bidding on a wonderful antique cast-iron spider I can use for soups, stews, or frying and some floral-patterned Homer Laughlin soup plates, which were sold through the Sears, Roebuck catalogue in the Thirties.

Some people shy away from homemade soups because they think they take a lot of time. In fact, except for bean soups made with dried beans and stocks made from meat with bones, most soups take half an hour at most, from start to finish. You can always speed things up by slicing, chopping, or shredding in your food processor, though I usually reserve that machine for pureeing.

Vegetable-broth soups as well as soups or chowders based on water and/or milk are quick and easy. Meat stock–based soups require a longer-simmered, flavorful liquid, but that is not as complicated as it may seem. To create a tasty broth, you don't need an industrial-sized stockpot permanently planted on your back burner. Any raw or cooked chicken carcass, with the bits of meat and skin attached, giblets, neck, heart, perhaps an onion and carrot, thrown into a large saucepan with water to cover and simmered for an hour or so—or even boiled for thirty minutes, if that's all the time you have—

will give you a fine base for any soup that calls for chicken broth. If you feel like it, you can add an onion, a stalk of celery, a pinch of thyme, a few sprigs of parsley, a clove or two of garlic. But I even save the plain water from poached chicken breasts and use that as a soup base. It's tastier than water and better than canned.

Of course, if you don't have a chicken carcass lying about, and if you don't feel like running out and buying a bunch of backs and necks, it's much better to use canned broth and make the rest of your soup from scratch than to serve up a commercially manufactured brand. Since I frequently find myself in this position, I purposely developed most of these recipes with reduced-sodium canned chicken broth. (You'll notice all such recipes in the book call for either unsalted homemade chicken stock or reduced-sodium canned broth.) Even if I end up adding salt to the recipe, I prefer the lighter, less tinny taste of the reduced-sodium variety. In these cases, the amount of broth called for is kept to a minimum, so that the essences of the other ingredients dominate and the flavor of the soup remains fresh and vibrant.

Cold Buttermilk
Beet Soup

4 to 6 servings

When it's too hot to work in the garden, and underneath the haze in the fields even the heifers are lying down, this is the cooling tonic I turn to. If the beets in your garden aren't ready, if they're long gone, or if you have no garden and your market is out of fresh, canned beets provide a satisfactory substitute.

To save time and energy, I grate all the vegetables for this soup in the food processor; a hand grater, of course, works just as well. Remember, despite its name, cultured low-fat buttermilk contains only 1.5 percent fat, just a shade above that of skim milk, so if you opt for the yogurt garnish, this soup is exceptionally lean.

1 large cucumber
6 to 8 small fresh beets, or 1 can (16 ounces)
  canned whole baby beets, drained
3 scallions
1 can (14¹/₂ ounces) reduced-sodium chicken broth
¹/₂ to 1 teaspoon sugar
Dash of cayenne
2 cups buttermilk
Salt and freshly ground pepper
¹/₃ to ¹/₂ cup sour cream or nonfat plain yogurt
1 to 2 tablespoons minced fresh dill

1. Peel the cucumber, cut in half lengthwise, and scoop out the seeds. Using the fine slicing blade in a food processor or the side of a square hand grater, thinly slice the cucumber. Transfer to a 2¹/₂- to 3-quart nonreactive saucepan.

2. If you're using fresh beets, peel them with a swivel-bladed vegetable peeler or small knife. Using the shredding disk of the food processor or large holes in the hand grater, shred the beets. If they're fresh, add them to the cucumber; if canned, set them aside.

3. Mince the scallions, keeping the white and green separate. Add the minced scallion bulb to the saucepan.

4. Add the chicken broth, sugar, and cayenne. (Fresh beets will require the lesser amount of sugar.) Bring to a boil, reduce the heat, and simmer until the cucumber and beets are just tender, 15 to 20 minutes. If you're using canned beets, add them during the last 5 minutes of cooking.

5. Remove the soup from the heat and let cool to room temperature. Stir in the buttermilk and season with salt and pepper to taste. Cover and refrigerate for at least 3 hours, or overnight, until well chilled. I think the soup tastes better after a day or two. To serve, ladle into soup plates, top with a dollop of sour cream or yogurt and garnish with the minced scallion green and dill.

CREAMY BUTTERMILK BROCCOLI SOUP

4 servings

Here again, buttermilk contributes its silky richness and delightful tang without the fat of heavy cream. While broccoli is an exceptionally common vegetable, I've noticed that different strains have decided differences in flavor. Some are too cabbagey; others too bland. The best have an almost sweet, distinctly "broccoli" green taste, which I am sure also has something to do with freshness. With its renewed popularity, I fear broccoli may turn into one of those vegetables, like winter tomatoes, that become homogenized to fill the demand. When you plant your spring garden, consider putting in an heirloom variety of broccoli, staggering the plantings so you have a fresh supply over several months. And when you buy it in the supermarket, look for bunches with crisp, dark green leaves and tops that are moist and intact and have not yet begun to flower. If the broccoli consistently smells too strong or tastes too bland, complain to the head of the produce department.

1 bunch of broccoli, about 1 pound
2 tablespoons unsalted butter
1½ tablespoons olive oil
2 medium leeks (white and 2 inches of green), well
    rinsed and coarsely chopped
¼ cup all-purpose flour
1 can (14½ ounces) reduced-sodium chicken broth
3 cups water
½ teaspoon salt
¼ teaspoon freshly ground pepper
⅛ teaspoon cayenne
Dash of freshly grated nutmeg
1 cup buttermilk

1. Cut off and discard the bottom inch or so from the broccoli stems. Peel the stems by slipping the tip of a paring knife just under the skin at the bottom, holding it against the knife with your thumb and peeling it back; the skin will come off in a strip. Repeat all around the stem. Cut the thick stems into 1/2-inch pieces. Separate the tops into 1-inch florets.

2. In a large flameproof casserole, melt the butter in the oil over moderately low heat. Add the leeks, cover the pan, and cook, stirring once or twice, until the leeks are very soft but not brown, about 10 minutes. Add the flour and cook, stirring, for 1 to 2 minutes, without allowing the flour to color.

3. Whisk in the broth and bring to a boil. Whisk in the water and again return to a boil. Add the broccoli stems, salt, pepper, cayenne, and nutmeg. Cook uncovered over moderate heat 10 minutes. Add the florets, partially cover the pan, and cook until the broccoli is very soft but the tops are still bright green, 10 to 12 minutes longer.

4. Transfer the soup to a food processor and puree until smooth. (You may have to do this in batches.) Return to the pot, whisk in the buttermilk, and simmer for 1 to 2 minutes. Season with additional salt and pepper to taste. Serve hot.

VARIATION

Cheddared Buttermilk Broccoli Soup: Prepare the Creamy Buttermilk Broccoli Soup as described above, but stir in 3/4 cup grated sharp (preferably extra-sharp) Cheddar cheese just before serving.

CHICKEN-CORN CHOWDER

4 to 6 servings

Depending on how much you ladle out, this chunky chowder can serve as a first course or as a meal in a bowl. Since, like most soups, it is even better made ahead, I love to have a batch on hand on days when I know there will be long hours of chores or when company is coming and I don't wish to spend much time in the kitchen. Savory, aromatic, and steaming in its pot, the chowder brightens up the room even before it reaches the tureen.

This is one of my favorite late-summer, early-fall soups because it is exceptionally good made with corn and tomatoes right out of the garden. However, its heartiness is more than welcome after a day of cross-country skiing as well, so in winter, I resort to canned, frozen, or Florida corn and plum or canned tomatoes.

> 3 tablespoons unsalted butter
> 1 tablespoon olive or other vegetable oil
> 2 medium onions, cut into ½-inch dice
> 3 tablespoons all-purpose flour
> 3 cups milk (I use 2 percent)
> 1 can (14½ ounces) reduced-sodium chicken broth
> ½ teaspoon savory, preferably winter savory
> 1½ cups diced (½-inch) potatoes
> 2 cups corn kernels
> 2 large ripe tomatoes, cut into ½-inch dice
> 1 teaspoon salt
> ¼ teaspoon freshly ground pepper
> ¼ to ½ teaspoon Tabasco, to taste
> ½ leftover roasted (3-pound) chicken or 1 large
>   whole chicken breast on the bone (1 to 1¼ pounds),
>   skinned and cut in half
> Juice of ½ lime

1. In a large flameproof casserole or soup pot, melt the butter in the oil over moderate heat. Add the onions, cover, and cook 3 minutes. Uncover and cook, stirring occasionally, until pale golden brown, 5 to 7 minutes longer.

2. Add the flour and cook, stirring, 1 to 2 minutes. Gradually stir in the milk, increase the heat to moderately high, and bring to a boil, whisking until thickened and smooth. Add the chicken broth and savory and reduce the heat to moderate. Add the potatoes and cook 10 minutes.

3. Add the corn, tomatoes, salt, pepper, and Tabasco. If using roasted chicken, pull off and discard most of the skin. Add the chicken to the soup. Reduce the heat to moderately low and simmer, partially covered, 10 minutes; if using raw chicken breast, cook 5 minutes longer. Remove the pieces of chicken to a plate.

4. As soon as the chicken is cool enough to handle, pull the meat off the bones and tear into large shreds. Return the chicken to the soup. Add the lime juice and simmer 5 minutes. Season with additional salt and pepper to taste before serving.

Rich Corn Soup with Spicy Basil Lime Butter

Serves 6 to 8

Corn ripens in late August and early September at these heights, and its arrival gives summer a last buoyant bounce. When I've gotten over the thrill of fresh-picked sweet corn its best way—boiled plain with butter—I start putting it in soup. My travels in Mexico years ago taught me the affinity of corn for lime, and since basil is also abundant this time of year, the combination seemed like a natural.

> 12 ears of sweet corn
> 8 tablespoons (1 stick) unsalted butter
> 1 tablespoon light olive or corn oil
> 3 medium onions, chopped
> 1 tablespoon flour
> 5 cups milk
> 1 can (14½ ounces) reduced-sodium chicken broth
> 1½ teaspoons sugar
> ½ teaspoon salt
> Dash of cayenne
> Zest of ½ lime
> 1 tablespoon fresh lime juice
> 2 tablespoons chopped basil leaves
> 1½ tablespoons chopped chives
> 1 large or 2 small canned hot chiles, seeded

1. Cut the kernels from the ears of corn with a sharp knife and set aside in a medium bowl. Using the back side of the knife, scrape off all the "milk" remaining on the cobs; add to the bowl.

2. In a large flameproof casserole, melt 2 tablespoons of the butter in the oil over moderate heat. Add the onions, cover, and cook for 7 to 10 minutes, stirring once or twice, until translucent. Uncover and cook, stirring occasionally, until the onions are golden, about 10 minutes longer.

3. Add the flour to the pot and cook, stirring, for 1 to 2 minutes. Gradually whisk in the milk and chicken broth and bring to a boil. Boil, stirring, for 2 minutes. Add the corn, sugar, salt, and cayenne. Cook for 10 minutes, or until the corn is very tender. Puree the soup, in batches if necessary, in a blender or food processor. Return to the pot; taste and correct the seasonings. The soup can be prepared to this point up to a day in advance.

4. To make the basil lime butter, soften the remaining 6 tablespoons butter by letting it stand at room temperature for an hour or two or by zapping it in the microwave on 50-percent power for 40 to 60 seconds. In a food processor, combine the butter, lime zest, lime juice, basil leaves, chives, and chile(s). Puree until smooth. Cover and refrigerate until shortly before serving time.

5. To serve, reheat the soup if necessary. Ladle into soup plates and garnish with a dollop of the basil lime butter, to be swirled into the soup.

DOUBLE CHICKEN NOODLE SOUP

4 to 6 servings

This is one recipe that really demands a homemade chicken stock. I make up a large batch when the local market has a sale on backs and necks and freeze it in several containers, so it's there when I need it. The extra carrot and leek add a lovely touch of sweetness, as well as a bit of color to this nourishing and comforting brew.

> *2 quarts chicken stock (page 15)*
> *1 whole chicken breast on the bone (about 1¼*
> *pounds), skin and excess fat removed*
> *2 medium carrots*
> *1 medium leek, white and tender part of green*
> *6 ounces thin egg noodles*
> *Salt and freshly ground pepper*

1. In a large saucepan or flameproof casserole, bring the stock to a simmer. Add the chicken breast and simmer over low heat for 25 minutes, or until the chicken is tender and white to the bone. Remove the chicken to a plate and set aside until the meat is cool enough to handle.

2. While the chicken is cooling, peel the carrots and cut them into thin matchstick strips about 1½ inches long. Thoroughly clean the leek and cut it into thin matchstick strips about 1½ inches long. To be sure all the grit is out, swish the strips of leek around in a bowl of cold water, then lift them out into a sieve to drain.

3. Pull the chicken meat off the bone and tear it into good-sized strips; discard the bones. Place the chicken in a small bowl and ladle about 1 cup of the chicken stock over the meat to keep it moist.

4. Bring the chicken stock to a boil over moderate heat. Add the carrots, leeks, and noodles. Cook, stirring occasionally, 10 minutes, or until the noodles are just tender. Reduce the heat to low. Add the chicken with broth to the pot and simmer 2 minutes. Season with salt and pepper to taste.

CHICKEN STOCK

Makes about 4 quarts

4 to 5 pounds chicken backs, necks, wings, gizzards, etc. (but not livers)
2 medium onions, cut in half, each half stuck with a clove
3 medium carrots, thickly sliced
2 celery ribs with leaves, quartered
1 small turnip, peeled and quartered
$^1/_3$ to $^1/_2$ cup mushroom stems and trimmings (optional)
8 to 10 parsley stems
2 garlic cloves, smashed
Pinch of thyme leaves
1 teaspoon whole black peppercorns
1 small bay leaf

1. Rinse the chicken parts well under cold running water. Place in a stock-pot and add cold water to cover by at least an inch. Bring to a boil over moderate heat, skimming off the foam as it rises to the top.

2. Add all the remaining ingredients, reduce the heat to moderately low, and simmer, partially covered, $1^1/_2$ to 2 hours, depending on how much time you have.

3. Strain the stock through a fine-mesh sieve. Let cool, then refrigerate. Lift the congealed fat off the stock and discard. If not using the stock within 2 days, freeze it in tightly covered containers.

COOL CUCUMBER SOUP
WITH SORREL AND CHIVES

4 to 6 servings

When I serve a bowl of this cool, pale lime-colored concoction to new guests, I always call it green soup and ask them to guess what's in it. As a rule, no one can, but they love the mild, slightly tart, secret garden flavors. Be sure to make the recipe several hours before serving, so it has plenty of time to chill.

 2 large or 3 medium cucumbers
 2 tablespoons unsalted butter
 1 tablespoon olive oil
 1 medium onion, coarsely chopped
 2$^1/_2$ tablespoons all-purpose flour
 3$^1/_2$ cups unsalted chicken stock or reduced-sodium chicken broth
 $^1/_2$ teaspoon salt
 $^1/_8$ teaspoon freshly ground pepper
 Dash or two of cayenne
 1 cup (loosely packed) sorrel leaves
 $^1/_3$ cup minced chives
 $^1/_2$ cup sour cream or plain low-fat yogurt

1. Peel the cucumbers. If they are from your garden, or you know they are unwaxed, leave on a couple of thin strips of skin to deepen the color of the soup. Cut off and discard the ends and cut the cucumbers in half lengthwise. Using a tablespoon, scoop out and discard the seeds. Thickly slice the cucumber halves.

2. In a large saucepan, melt the butter in the oil. Add the onion, cover, and cook over moderately low heat, stirring once or twice, until softened, about 3 minutes. Uncover, add the flour, and cook, stirring, 1 to 2 minutes, without allowing the flour to color.

3. Gradually whisk in the chicken stock and bring to a boil over high heat, stirring until thickened. Add the cucumbers and season with the salt, pepper, and cayenne. Reduce the heat to moderately low and simmer, partially covered, until the cucumbers are soft, 15 to 20 minutes. Remove from the heat and let cool slightly.

4. Remove the stems from the sorrel by bending each leaf lengthwise in half, grasping the end of the stem, and pulling back the leaf. Tear the sorrel into pieces. In a blender or food processor, puree the soup with the sorrel, in batches if necessary, until the soup is smooth and the sorrel is finely minced. Stir in the minced chives. Season with additional salt and pepper to taste. Cover and refrigerate until very cold, at least 3 hours.

5. Serve the soup ice cold, with a spoonful of sour cream or yogurt in the center.

· S O R R E L ·

The nicest thing about sorrel, if you are an iffy gardener, as I am, is that, like rhubarb, its sturdy relative, it reappears reliably every year. Sorrel is the first green to appear in my little kitchen garden. Cut back and used regularly before it flowers, it returns time and time again and remains edible long after more delicate lettuces and seasonal vegetables have disappeared.

Sorrel's fresh color is a bright spring green. When cooked, it quickly darkens and mutes, turning grayish, almost khaki, probably because of the prodigious amount of oxalic acid it naturally possesses. This acid gives it a flavor that is tart to the point of sour, which is sorrel's gift, but overcooking can blanch it to a mere shadow of itself. Sorrel disintegrates into a puree almost as soon as it hits the heat. The leaf without the tang tastes like a very dull spinach indeed.

Though it resembles a leafy vegetable, sort of an immature Swiss chard, sorrel loses so much of its volume when cooked that it is really more practical to view it as an herb—to be used, it is true, in very large amounts. Sorrel shows off best in soups and sauces, but I've found it furnishes an interesting substitute for lemon juice in stuffings and spreads as well. Its sprightliness provides a lively counterpoint to the relative blandness of potatoes, rice, and pasta; it enlivens anything creamy, such as scrambled eggs; and its citrusy character gives it an affinity to seafood.

SAVORY CREAM OF ONION SOUP

Serves 6 to 8

Winter savory is an old-fashioned herb, not frequently called for in modern recipes. I cannot imagine why it fell out of favor, because it has a delightful, subtle peppery taste that works particularly well with beans and creamy dishes. It winters over beautifully in my herb garden, which is probably another reason I am so fond of it. White onions are milder, and often sweeter, than the yellow variety, so choose them if you can. Otherwise use whatever onions you have on hand.

> 3 pounds large white onions
> 6 tablespoons unsalted butter
> 1½ tablespoons light olive oil
> 2 teaspoons coarse (kosher) salt
> 3 tablespoons all-purpose flour
> 2 cans (14½ ounces each) reduced-sodium chicken
>   broth or 4 cups unsalted homemade chicken stock
> 4 cups water
> 1 small branch or several sprigs of fresh winter savory or
>   ½ teaspoon dried
> ½ cup heavy cream
> Dash of cayenne

1. Peel the onions, cut them in half, and thinly slice them. In a large flame-proof casserole, combine the onion slices, butter, olive oil, and salt. Cover and cook over moderately low heat, tossing frequently, until the onions are very soft and just beginning to color, 30 to 35 minutes.

2. Add the flour and stir to mix. Increase the heat to moderately high and cook, stirring, for 2 to 3 minutes without allowing the flour to brown. Gradually stir in the broth and water. Bring to a boil, stirring frequently. Reduce the heat to moderate, add the savory, and cook at a low boil for 25 minutes. Remove the savory if you've used fresh.

3. In batches, puree the soup in a blender or food processor until smooth. Return to the pot and add the cream and cayenne. Simmer for 5 minutes. Season with additional salt to taste.

Smoky Eggplant and Lentil Soup

6 servings

*E*ggplant is a naturally lean vegetable, but when roasted to a creamy pulp and added to soup, it surprisingly acts as an enrichment. This is a deep, dark soup with a heady full flavor, perfect for a very cold winter's night.

1 medium eggplant (about 1¼ pounds)
2½ tablespoons extra-virgin olive oil
2 medium leeks, white and all but dark green part,
   well rinsed and diced
1 medium onion, diced
3 to 4 garlic cloves, minced
½ medium green bell pepper, finely diced
   (¾ to 1 cup)
2 plum tomatoes, finely diced
2 cups unsalted homemade chicken or veal stock or
   1 can (14½ ounces) reduced-sodium chicken broth
4 cups water
¾ cup lentils, picked over and rinsed
1 pound smoked ham hocks
1 bay leaf
½ teaspoon salt
¼ teaspoon freshly ground pepper
⅛ teaspoon cayenne
2 teaspoons sherry wine vinegar or red wine vinegar

1. Prick the eggplant in several places with the tip of a small knife. (If you don't, it can explode on you, plastering the oven wall with eggplant—not a happy experience, and one that only has to happen once, as it did to me, before you *never* forget to prick the eggplant.) Either roast in a covered grill over a medium fire or bake in a 475 degree oven, turning once or twice, until the eggplant skin is blackened all over and the meat is meltingly tender and creamy, 30 to 40 minutes. Let stand until cool enough to handle, then cut in half and scrape the eggplant into a bowl, avoiding the juices if they are bitter. Discard the skin.

2. In a large flameproof casserole, heat the oil over moderately high heat. Add the leeks and onion and cook, stirring occasionally, until softened but not browned, 5 to 7 minutes. Add the garlic, bell pepper, and tomatoes and cook until the pepper is softened, about 3 minutes longer.

3. Add the stock, water, lentils, ham hocks, bay leaf, salt, pepper, and cayenne. Bring to a boil, reduce the heat to moderately low, and simmer, partially covered, until the lentils are tender, 30 to 40 minutes. Remove the ham hocks and bay leaf.

4. Puree the eggplant with about 2 cups of the soup; if I'm in the mood for a cream soup, sometimes I puree the whole thing. Return to the pot and stir in the vinegar. Simmer 3 minutes and serve.

NOTE: An excellent vegetarian version of this soup can be made by using vegetable stock or all water, omitting the smoked ham hocks and cayenne, and adding instead a couple of dried chipotle chiles. Puree no more than half of a fiery chipotle with the eggplant, however, and discard the other 1½ chiles, or the soup will be too hot to eat.

COOKING FROM A COUNTRY FARMHOUSE

·JERUSALEM ARTICHOKES·

The really beautiful thing about Jerusalem artichokes is that you can recycle them two ways: you can eat them or you can plant them. Their Native American name, sun roots, perhaps more graphically conveys the spirit of the vegetable, which is an easily grown tuber related to the sunflower, a kinship obvious from its long stalks topped by large, bright yellow fringed flowers. Commercially, they are sometimes marketed as "Sun Chokes."

The humblest of vegetables, like potatoes and peas, are serviceable at all times, but are sublime when superbly fresh, and this is certainly true of Jerusalem artichokes. Cooked just after harvesting, the ivory tubers taste like very delicate potato mixed with the sweetness of hearts of globe artichoke. They are also remarkably versatile. Jerusalem artichokes can be baked, boiled, roasted, stir-fried, or pickled. They can be eaten whole, sliced, mashed, or pureed in soups. Raw, they are refreshingly crisp and, to my palate, a dead ringer for fresh water chestnut. Cut into thin rounds or sticks, they make an excellent addition to a basket of crudités.

If you have any ground to plant in at all, there is no excuse for not having your own supply of fresh Jerusalem artichokes, because if you can't grow anything else, you are guaranteed success with this prolific plant. A friend told me how she once paid an ungodly sum to a gourmet greenhouse to purchase a single tuber, which within one year of being planted in the back of her posh suburban home invaded two yards on either side. One neighbor of advanced years was so incensed by the startlingly aggressive encroachment that he took a 12-gauge shotgun to the flowers—needless to say, to no avail.

The whole root, or any chunk of it with a protruding nodule, is planted in springtime in a well-composted hole one to two inches deep. Once established, the tubers are harvested after the flowers have died and the stalks are withered. They are sweetest and crispest after they've rested in the cold ground for a bit. In more forgiving climates, they are harvested in late October or early November. Because here icy winds swoop down so fast and freeze the ground solid seemingly overnight, many farmers wait for the first thaw of spring to dig their Jerusalem artichokes, but to be palatable, the tubers must be unearthed before they begin to darken and sprout.

Jerusalem Artichoke and Allium Soup

4 to 6 servings

This soup is subtle but somehow addictive. Its savory flavor blends the nutty sweetness of the Jerusalem artichokes with the aromatic potency of the alliums—onion, garlic, and chives—in a delicate way that keeps your spoon on the move. I particularly enjoy this soup before a simple roast of lamb, beef, or chicken.

> 1¼ to 1½ pounds Jerusalem artichokes
> 1½ tablespoons unsalted butter
> 1½ tablespoons light olive oil
> 1 medium onion, sliced
> 2 small to medium celery ribs with leaves, sliced
> 5 large garlic cloves, coarsely chopped
> 2 tablespoons flour
> 4 cups unsalted homemade chicken stock or
>   reduced-sodium canned broth
> 2 cups water
> 2 sage leaves, crumbled
> ⅛ teaspoon mace
> Dash of cayenne
> ¼ cup heavy cream
> Salt and freshly ground pepper
> 1 to 2 tablespoons minced fresh chives

1. Peel the Jerusalem artichokes with a swivel-bladed vegetable peeler, cut into 1-inch pieces, and drop into a bowl of salted water to prevent them from discoloring.

2. In a large nonreactive saucepan or flameproof casserole, melt the butter in the olive oil over moderately low heat. Add the onion and celery and stir to coat with the oil. Cover the pan and cook, stirring once or twice, for 10 minutes, or until the vegetables are softened. Add the garlic and cook, covered, until soft, 3 to 5 minutes longer.

3. Add the flour to the pan, increase the heat to moderate, and cook, stirring, for 2 minutes. Gradually whisk in the chicken stock and add the sage, mace, and cayenne. Bring to a boil, reduce the heat to moderately low, and cook, partially covered, 20 minutes. Remove from the heat, cover, and let stand 10 minutes longer.

4. Puree the soup in a food processor or blender until smooth. Return to the pot, add the cream, and season with salt and pepper to taste. It may also need another dash of cayenne. Simmer, uncovered, for 5 minutes. Stir in the chives and serve hot.

GINGER-MAPLE PUMPKIN BISQUE

6 servings

Almost everyone taps his maple trees in these parts. Some do it the old-fashioned way with buckets and spigots hanging off each trunk; others link their trees with arterial-looking plastic tubing that snakes through the woods and collects the sap here and there in large tubs. The subtle sweetness of the maple along with the bite of ginger complement pumpkin beautifully in this delightfully lush, creamy soup.

> 1 sugar pumpkin, 4 to 4½ pounds
> 4 tablespoons (½ stick) unsalted butter
> 1 medium-large onion, chopped
> 1½ tablespoons peeled and chopped fresh ginger
> 5 cups unsalted homemade chicken stock or
>   reduced-sodium canned broth
> 6 tablespoons heavy cream
> 3 tablespoons pure maple syrup, preferably
>   dark or amber
> ⅛ teaspoon cayenne

1. Preheat the oven to 375 degrees. Cut open the top of the pumpkin and scoop out the fibers and seeds (roast the seeds separately if you like—I always do). Put the top back on the pumpkin and bake it in the oven for 30 minutes. Let stand until cool enough to handle.

2. Cut the pumpkin into wedges and peel off the skin; it will come off easily. Cut the pumpkin into 1-inch cubes. Measure out 6 cups. Reserve any leftover pumpkin for another use.

3. In a large flameproof casserole, melt the butter over moderate heat. Add the chopped onion, cover, and cook for 3 minutes. Uncover and continue to cook, stirring occasionally, until the onion is golden, about 10 minutes longer.

4. Add the ginger and cook for 1 to 2 minutes, until fragrant. Add the pumpkin cubes and the chicken stock. Bring to a boil, reduce the heat to moderately low, and simmer, partially covered, for 15 to 20 minutes, or until the pumpkin is very soft. Puree the soup, in batches if necessary, in a blender or food processor.

5. Return the soup to the pot. Stir the cream and maple syrup into the soup. Season with the cayenne. Simmer for 5 minutes. Serve hot.

Mashed Potato Soup

6 servings

*F*or me the absolute simplicity of this soup and the warm comfort it carries epitomize the best of country cooking. It's a dish whose ingredients are almost always on hand, and it takes little more than half an hour from start to finish. The lavish amount of butter is a must in this recipe, if you want the full effect.

8 tablespoons (1 stick) unsalted butter
1 large onion, chopped
1 can (14^1/$_2$ ounces) reduced-sodium chicken broth
4 large Idaho potatoes (2^1/$_2$ to 3 pounds total),
    peeled and cut into 1^1/$_2$-inch chunks
3 cups water
^{1}/$_2$ cup milk
1 teaspoon salt
^{1}/$_4$ teaspoon freshly ground pepper
Dash of grated nutmeg
Dash of cayenne
Minced chives or parsley, for garnish

1. In a large saucepan or flameproof casserole, melt half the butter over moderate heat. Add the onion and cook, stirring occasionally, until the onion is golden and starting to brown at the edges, 8 to 10 minutes.

2. Add the chicken broth, potatoes, and water. Bring to a boil, reduce the heat to a simmer, and cook, partially covered, until the potatoes are soft, 20 to 25 minutes.

3. With a potato masher or the back of a large spoon, mash the potatoes just enough to thicken the soup, but leave plenty of chunks intact.

4. Add the milk and the remaining butter. Season the soup with the salt, pepper, nutmeg, and cayenne. Serve piping hot, garnished with a sprinkling of minced chives.

TURKEY SOUP WITH CARROTS AND WILD RICE

6 to 8 servings

I make this soup once a year—after Thanksgiving, when I have a nice turkey carcass left over from the roast, along with more turkey meat than I know what to do with.

1 roast turkey carcass
2 onions
2 whole cloves
4 medium carrots, peeled
2 celery ribs
4 parsley sprigs
1 bay leaf
1/2 teaspoon thyme leaves
1 teaspoon whole black peppercorns
1/2 cup wild rice
1 1/2 to 2 cups diced leftover turkey
Salt and freshly ground pepper

1. With a cleaver or large sharp knife, hack up the turkey carcass and put it in a kettle. Stick one of the onions with the cloves and halve the other onion. Put them both in the pot.

2. Quarter 2 of the carrots and the celery ribs and add them to the pot along with the bay leaf, thyme, peppercorns, and enough water to cover, about 3 1/2 to 4 quarts. Bring to a boil, reduce the heat, and simmer, partially covered, until the liquid is reduced by half, about 1 1/2 hours. Strain the soup and return the broth to a clean pot.

3. In a medium saucepan of boiling salted water, cook the wild rice until tender but still slightly chewy, 20 to 25 minutes; drain. Meanwhile, cut the remaining 2 carrots into 1/4-inch dice, add to the broth, and boil until barely tender, about 5 minutes.

4. Add the wild rice and diced turkey to the soup and season with salt and pepper to taste.

Winter Vegetable Chowder

8 servings

Here's a great hearty soup that can be made in the dead of winter, when the pickings at the grocery are lean indeed. The beans are optional, but they can turn this into a main-course soup.

1/4 pound lean bacon, cut crosswise into 1/4-inch strips
1 tablespoon olive oil
1 pound onions (about 3 medium), cut into 1/2-inch dice
1/2 teaspoon sugar
1 pound cabbage (1/2 medium head), cut into 1/2- to 3/4-inch dice
1 pound rutabaga (1/2 medium), peeled and cut into 3/4-inch dice
1 pound red potatoes (3 medium), peeled and cut into 3/4-inch dice
2 large carrots (1/2 pound), peeled and sliced
10 cups water
1 tablespoon white wine vinegar
1 tablespoon salt
1/2 teaspoon freshly ground pepper
3 sprigs of winter savory or 1 teaspoon dried
2 whole cloves
1 can (16 ounces) Great Northern white beans or cannellini (optional)

1. In a large flameproof casserole, cook the bacon in the olive oil over moderate heat until the bacon is lightly browned. Remove the bacon with a slotted spoon and set aside. Pour off all but 2 tablespoons of fat from the pan.

2. Add the onions to the pan and cook 2 minutes. Sprinkle on the sugar and continue to cook, stirring occasionally, until the onions are softened and beginning to brown, 5 to 7 minutes. Add the cabbage and cook, stirring frequently, until translucent, about 5 minutes.

3. Add the rutabaga, potatoes, carrots, water, vinegar, salt, pepper, savory, and cloves. Bring to a boil, reduce the heat to a simmer, and cook, partially covered, until the vegetables are tender, about 20 minutes.

4. Drain the beans into a colander. Rinse well under cold running water and drain again. Add the beans to the soup and simmer 5 minutes longer.

CREAM OF FRESH TOMATO SOUP WITH RICE

4 to 6 servings

It's astonishing how good this childhood favorite tastes when you make it with fresh ripe tomatoes just off the vine. I like to cook with unpasteurized milk, thick and sweet as new-mown hay. The milk and light cream make a safer and more accessible substitute.

> 2$\frac{1}{2}$ tablespoons unsalted butter
> 1 tablespoon olive oil
> 1 large onion, sliced
> 1 tablespoon flour
> 3 cups milk
> 1 cup light cream or half-and-half
> 6 large, very ripe tomatoes (2$\frac{1}{4}$ pounds), peeled,
>   seeded, and coarsely chopped
> 1 teaspoon sugar
> 1 teaspoon salt
> $\frac{1}{8}$ teaspoon cayenne
> 1 cup cooked white rice

1. In a large nonreactive saucepan, melt the butter in the oil over moderate heat. Add the onion and cook, stirring occasionally, until softened and beginning to color, about 5 minutes. Add the flour and cook for 1 to 2 minutes without allowing the flour to color.

2. Gradually whisk in the milk and bring to a boil, whisking until the liquid is thickened and smooth. Add the cream, tomatoes, sugar, salt, and cayenne. Return to a boil, reduce the heat to moderately low, and simmer, partially covered, for 20 minutes.

3. Puree the soup in a blender or food processor, in batches if necessary, until smooth. Return to the saucepan, add the rice, and simmer for 5 minutes. Season with additional salt and cayenne to taste.

Winter Borscht

8 servings

Borscht signifies some kind of beet soup, usually with cabbage—in this case, also with beef. Another winter warmer, this meal-in-a-pot is distinctly sweet and sour in flavor. Serve with a good bread, if you have one—rye, sourdough, pumpernickel, or even whole wheat.

1½ to 2 pounds beef shank, center-cut, 1 to 1½ inches thick
8 cups cold water
1 can (13¾ ounces) beef broth
2 tablespoons olive oil
2 medium-large onions, thinly sliced
1 small cabbage (about 1¼ pounds), shredded
2 bunches of beets, peeled and cut into ¾-inch dice,
    or 2 cans (15 ounces each) whole baby beets,
    drained and diced
3 medium-large carrots, peeled and sliced
3 large boiling potatoes, peeled and cut into ¾-inch dice
1 can (14 ounces) Italian peeled tomatoes,
    drained and chopped
1 bay leaf
1½ teaspoons coriander seeds
½ teaspoon thyme leaves
3 whole cloves
3 tablespoons lemon juice
2 tablespoons white wine vinegar
¼ cup sugar
1 tablespoon salt
½ teaspoon freshly ground pepper
3 tablespoons minced fresh dill
¾ cup sour cream

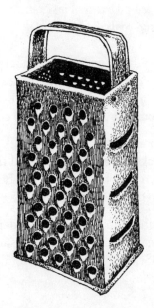

1. Place the meat in a large pot with the water and the beef broth. Bring to a boil, skimming the foam off the top. Reduce the heat to a simmer, and cook for 2 hours, or until the beef shreds easily. Remove the beef to a plate. Strain the broth into a large bowl through a double thickness of cheesecloth and skim any fat from the top.

2. In a large flameproof casserole, heat the oil. Add the onions and cook over moderately high heat until the onions begin to color, 5 to 7 minutes. Add the cabbage and cook, tossing, for 2 minutes. Add the beets, carrots, potatoes, and tomatoes. Pour in the strained broth. Tie the bay leaf, corian-der seeds, thyme, and cloves in a cheesecloth bag and add to the soup. Bring to a boil, reduce the heat to moderately low, and simmer until the vegetables are tender, about 20 minutes.

3. Meanwhile, shred the beef shank, discarding any bone, fat, or connective tissue. Add the shredded beef along with the lemon juice, vinegar, sugar, salt, and pepper to the soup. Simmer 10 minutes longer. Remove and discard the cheesecloth bag.

4. To serve, mix together the dill and sour cream. Ladle the hot borscht into soup plates and garnish with a big dollop of the dilled sour cream.

Farmhouse Vegetable Beef Soup

8 to 12 servings

*O*ne of my most memorable farmhouse meals took place in Illinois. Lorna Lee and Vernon Virgin are the parents of my friend Craig, and on a visit to see their farm in Lebanon, where they raise cattle and wheat, I was served this soup along with a dusky smoked venison sausage, made from deer Craig and Vernon hunted on their own land, and a local Cheddar cheese.

Lorna claims to have raised her three children on homemade soups. The recipe for this oxtail soup with mixed vegetables changes from month to month, she says, depending upon what is in the garden, and Lorna thinks it's a great way to introduce children to new vegetables. She must be doing something right, because Craig grew up to become World Cross-Country Running Champion, the first American to win that title and only the second man in history to hold it two years in a row.

On their farm, Lorna makes this soup—with their own meat and homemade tomato juice—in huge batches, because as she says, "It's just as much trouble to make a lot as a little." Whatever isn't eaten the first night goes into the freezer. This version uses store-bought oxtail and chopped canned tomatoes with their juice. If you cannot find oxtail, you can substitute beef plate or chuck along with some bones, but the flavor will not be as rich.

> 5 to 6 pounds beef oxtail, cut into 2-inch-long pieces
> 1 tablespoon salt
> ½ teaspoon freshly ground pepper
> 12 large sprigs of parsley with stems plus ½ cup
>   chopped parsley leaves
> 1 bay leaf
> 1 can (28 ounces) Italian peeled tomatoes, coarsely
>   chopped, with their juices
> 2 medium onions, chopped
> 5 celery stalks with leaves, chopped
> ⅔ cup barley
> 6 carrots, diced

10 ounces green beans, cut into 1/2-inch pieces
2 cups corn kernels
3/4 pound white turnips, peeled and cut into 1/2-inch dice
2 garlic cloves, crushed through a press
1 1/2 pounds potatoes, peeled and cut into 1/2-inch cubes
3 cups chopped cabbage
2 tablespoons lemon juice
1 to 2 teaspoons sugar (optional)

1. On day one, preheat the oven to 400 degrees. Arrange the oxtails in a single layer in a shallow roasting pan and bake them, turning once, until nicely browned, 30 to 45 minutes. Transfer the oxtails to a large stockpot. If there are browned bits on the bottom of the roasting pan, add some water and scrape them up with a wooden spoon. Add to the stockpot. Add 6 to 8 quarts of cold water, or enough to cover by at least 2 inches. Bring to a boil, skimming as needed. Add the salt, pepper, parsley sprigs, and bay leaf. Reduce the heat to low, cover, and simmer 4 to 6 hours, until the meat is falling from the bone. Remove from the heat and let cool. (If desired, let stand in a cool place overnight.)

2. Remove the oxtails to a large container or bowl. When they are cool enough to handle, pick the meat off the bone; discard the bones. Strain the stock through a fine sieve. Ladle enough stock over the meat to cover it; return the remaining stock to the pot. Refrigerate the meat and stock separately.

3. On day two (or three), remove the congealed fat from the top of the stock and any on top of the meat. Add the tomatoes with their juices, onions, celery, and barley to the stockpot. Bring to a boil, reduce the heat to moderately low, and simmer, partially covered, 30 minutes. Add the chopped parsley, carrots, green beans, corn, turnips, and garlic. Simmer slowly for 1 hour.

4. Add the potatoes, cabbage, and meat with broth to the soup. Cook until the potatoes are tender and the cabbage is softened but still crisp, about 20 to 30 minutes. Add the lemon juice to the soup and season with additional salt and pepper to taste. If the soup is too acidic, add up to 2 teaspoons sugar to balance the flavor. Serve piping hot.

CURRIED ZUCCHINI BISQUE

6 to 8 servings

They say you can never be too rich, too thin, or have too many zucchini, but we country gardeners know that's not the case. Early in summer, the smug pride of a successful harvest wears off after you realize that *anybody* can grow zucchini and that, unlike the water tap, these plants can't be turned off when you think you've had enough; the vegetables just keep coming and coming and coming. Nagging at you always is the knowledge that if you miss one day's picking, a colossus the size of a football will appear overnight, and all your friends will make jokes about the mysterious radioactive force in your garden. Consequently, it's my firm belief that no one can have too many recipes for zucchini.

This one is easy and just as appropriate in the middle of winter, when zucchini is one of the only decent fresh vegetables in the produce department. The soup is subtle, with—as its name suggests—a wonderfully smooth, creamy texture. The blend of curry and lemon is extremely compatible and works well against the softness of the zucchini base. Madras-style curry powder, which is an earthy gold color, is much subtler than the ordinary bright yellow turmeric-laden curry powder, and I urge you to look for it. If you're not fond of curry flavor, this may change your mind. Sun brand is sold in tins in many supermarket chains, and you can certainly find it in Indian markets.

Onions work well here, but leeks are better because they have a more interesting flavor. If you do use leeks, quarter them lengthwise almost to the root and rinse them well under cold running water before cutting them up. I throw the chopped leeks into a bowl of cold water, swish them around, and lift them out. This is an easy way to get rid of any hidden sand, and the extra moisture that clings to them will help the initial covered cooking.

2 nice-sized leeks (white part and about 4 inches
    of tender green, well rinsed), or 2 large onions,
    coarsely chopped
4 tablespoons (1/2 stick) unsalted butter
Salt
2 tablespoons all-purpose flour
1 tablespoon curry power, preferably Madras-style
4 cups unsalted homemade chicken stock or 2 cans
    (14 1/2 ounces each) reduced-sodium chicken broth
2 cups water
1 1/2 pounds zucchini, thickly sliced
Dash of cayenne
1 tablespoon fresh lemon juice
2/3 cup heavy cream
Finely diced tomato and minced chives, for garnish

1. In a large enameled cast-iron casserole or a heavy soup pot, combine the leeks and butter. Season lightly with salt, cover, and cook over moderately low heat, stirring occasionally, 10 minutes. Uncover and continue to cook over moderately low heat, stirring often, until the leeks are very soft and the white part is beginning to brown, about 10 minutes longer.

2. Add the flour and curry powder to the pan. Cook, stirring, 1 minute. Add the chicken stock and water and bring to a boil, stirring until slightly thickened. Add the zucchini and cayenne. Reduce the heat to medium and cook, partially covered, 15 minutes, or until the zucchini is very soft. Remove from the heat and let cool slightly.

3. Puree the soup in batches in a blender or food processor. Return to the saucepan. Season with 1/4 teaspoon salt and stir in the lemon juice; then blend in the cream. Heat over moderate heat until the soup just simmers, reduce the heat to low, and cook at a bare simmer, stirring occasionally to avoid scorching the bottom, 5 minutes. Ladle into bowls and serve topped with a spoonful of diced tomato and a sprinkling of minced chives.

COUNTRIFIED MAIN COURSES

The difference between what we eat in the country and city food is less a matter of content than of style. City dwellers may sample in a single meal a dizzying assortment of dishes designed to set the imagination and intellect reeling: food that is surprising, witty, unfamiliar. We country folk prefer to take fewer chances. When the weather outside the window is howling in our ears, most of us would rather hunker down over a big bowl of spicy red chili; spoon up a savory potpie, tucked away hot and steaming under its flaky golden crust; or dig into a zesty sausage and mashed potato loaf, attended by a cinnamony sauce made with apples picked from our own trees last fall.

One-pot dishes are popular, but so are simple roasts—roast chicken, roast pork, roast turkey, wild if possible. We prefer reliable food that is familiar and easy to anticipate. It's also food made with ingredients you can find in your local market. People out here don't care to purchase their groceries through the mail. Good thing, or Hank the postman would have to buy a bigger truck.

Country-style food is hardly ever plated. Generous platters of sliced meats, casseroles brimming with saucy stews, oversized bowls loaded with mashed and buttered vegetables, baskets of biscuits and breads, smaller bowls of colorful pickles and relishes, sauceboats filled with pan gravy are all spread out across the center of the table. The head of the household dishes everything out, or folks can just help themselves to whatever they like. It is not considered rude to pass dishes around the table.

When there are guests, we push more leaves into the table; the longer it grows, the more bounteous the groaning board becomes. Larger serving bowls are pulled off the top shelves, and we add more dishes to the menu, perhaps an extra relish, another vegetable, or a rice, corn, or macaroni dish in addition to potatoes. Dessert may be dressed up a tad—pie rather than poached fruit, a platter of cookies along with the ice cream, or ice cream on top of the pie.

Beyond that, there is little difference between everyday family food and what is served to company. Any guest will be delighted with meat loaf and mashed potatoes or a dark, richly flavored stew. Don't get me wrong: Country cooks pride themselves on their culinary skill. We are as vain as any chef and as proud of our original creations, but rural needs and expectations are different. Satisfaction and comfort are the primary goals of fine dining on the farm.

While the palette of ingredients in a rural place like this is more limited, nutritional concerns are much the same as they are in urban areas. Some people I know have given up red meat. Many of us are attempting to cut down on cholesterol and saturated fats, though I've noticed farmers in general enjoy all cuts of pork, and they do eat beef. (For obvious humanitarian reasons, I've never met a dairy farmer who is comfortable eating veal.) Our local market carries fine chicken, and you'll often see fresh young turkeys, whole, cut up, and in parts. Just as good cooks enjoy their own cooking best of all, our hunters take exceptional pleasure in the game they bring home, and the fishermen love fish. Vegetables are highly prized, especially in season when they come out of our own gardens.

It seems to me, though, that dining out here in general is a more wholesome, less analytical experience. Except among teenage girls, the fetish with slimness is not constantly discussed. Perhaps it comes from judging all those 4-H contests, but even in people, healthy is considered more attractive than scrawny, a sensible aesthetic, if you ask me. It creates attractive muscular men who age lean and allows women to assume their natural, God-given shape. Hauling rocks, chopping wood, lifting, carrying, milking, hiking out to the back forty to find that heifer—all take the place of high-priced health clubs. People are sturdy, but not fat. Physical labor sanctions heartier eating.

Maybe because there are fewer distractions and less excess in this remote region, more of a fuss is made over small pleasures. Where there is less overabundance, greater appreciation thrives. A wedge of good cheese or a loaf of real bread—with a hard crust and chewy crumb—generate as much excitement as a pound of beluga caviar or a white truffle might in more sophisticated surroundings. This simple joy of reveling in the smallest delights lends an immediacy to the moment. Every humble thanks contains an unspoken grace.

In *Wuthering Heights,* speaking of rural locales, Emily Brontë, who spent her entire brief life secluded in the country, describes what I believe to be this same phenomenon in Lockwood's words:

"I perceive that people in these regions . . . *do* live more in earnest, more in themselves and less in surface change and frivolous external things. . . . One state resembles setting a hungry man down to a single dish on which he may concentrate his entire appetite and do it justice—the other, introducing him to a table laid out by French cooks; he can perhaps extract as much enjoyment from the whole, but each part is a mere atom in his regard and remembrance."

Roast Chicken with Root Vegetables and Pan Gravy

8 servings

*T*he technique used here to roast an unstuffed chicken until it has the crispest skin and most succulent meat possible must be credited to Marcella Hazan and her Lemon Roast Chicken (in *More Classic Italian Cooking*), which provides ongoing inspiration. If you have a convection oven, by all means use it for this recipe; the all-around cooking makes by far the best roast chicken, juicy and moist with crisp brown skin. Set the oven temperature 25 degrees lower and cook about 15 minutes less.

I serve this dish often for special family meals and informal entertaining, which is most of what I seem to do now. Because a large roasting chicken takes almost two hours to cook, all the work is done by the time your company arrives. Buttermilk Mashed Potatoes (page 144) and Broccoli au Gratin (page 124) are particularly nice accompaniments. If there are any leftovers, be sure to save them for the Country Style Chicken Potpie with Buttermilk Biscuit Crust on page 44.

1 roasting chicken, 6½ to 7 pounds
Coarse (kosher) salt and freshly ground pepper
Several sprigs of fresh rosemary or ½ tablespoon
    dried, or use another herb of your choice, such
    as tarragon or thyme
2 large shallots, halved, or 1 small onion, quartered
1 lemon, well washed, dried, and pricked all over
    with a toothpick
6 to 8 carrots, peeled and cut with a rolling cut (see Note) into 1½-inch
    lengths
6 small turnips, peeled and quartered
4 medium onions, peeled and cut through the root
    end into 6 wedges each
2 tablespoons flour
1 cup reduced-sodium chicken broth or water
1 teaspoon lemon juice
1 tablespoon butter

1. Preheat the oven to 375 degrees. Rinse the chicken well inside and out; pat dry with paper towels. Season the inside of the chicken liberally with salt and pepper. Stuff the rosemary, shallots, and lemon inside the large cavity; truss closed, tying up the legs as well. Skewer the neck skin to the back. Season the top of the chicken with salt and pepper. Set breast side down on a rack in a large roasting pan. Season the back side of the chicken with salt and pepper. Place in the oven and roast 45 minutes.

2. Turn the chicken over. (I do this by inserting a long-handled fork into the large cavity and lifting it over; do not pierce the meat.) Scatter the carrots, turnips, and onions in the bottom of the roasting pan around the chicken. Turn to coat them with the drippings in the pan. Roast 30 minutes.

3. Stir up the root vegetables to turn them over. Increase the oven temperature to 425 degrees and roast 15 minutes longer, or until the skin is browned and crisp and the juices run clear when the thigh is pricked with a fork at the thickest point. Transfer the chicken to a carving board. With a slotted spoon, remove the vegetables to a serving dish; cover with aluminum foil to keep warm.

4. Remove the rack from the roasting pan. Tilt the pan and scoop off most of the fat on top of the drippings. Set the pan over moderate heat. Whisk in the flour and cook, whisking, 2 to 3 minutes to make a roux. Whisk in the chicken broth. Bring to a boil, whisking until thickened and smooth. If the gravy is too thick, thin with a little water to the desired consistency. Add the lemon juice and season with salt and pepper to taste. Add the butter and stir until melted. Pour into a warmed gravy boat.

5. Carve the chicken and serve it with the roasted root vegetables. Pass the gravy on the side.

NOTE: To carve up a carrot—or any long cylindrical vegetable—with a rolling cut: trim off both ends. Make a cut crosswise on a diagonal about 1½ inches from the end, or however long you want the piece to be (the first and last pieces will be slightly irregular). Roll the carrot over and cut crosswise on the diagonal again to make another segment. Continue rolling and cutting. Depending on how far apart you make your cuts and how sharply you angle them, you will end up with triangular or lozenge-shaped pieces. I like the rolling cut as an alternative to slices; it produces a more attractive shape than a plain chunk, and its large cut surface area encourages even cooking.

COUNTRY-STYLE CHICKEN POTPIE WITH BUTTERMILK BISCUIT CRUST

6 servings

Potpies are designed for leftovers. If you don't have any, poach or bake 1½ pounds of skinless, boneless chicken breasts or buy a barbecued chicken and take the meat from that; and use canned reduced-sodium chicken broth for the gravy.

1 leftover roast chicken, preferably Roast Chicken
    with Root Vegetables and Pan Gravy (page 42)
1 carrot, thickly sliced, plus 1 cup diced carrots
1 onion, quartered
1 teaspoon peppercorns
2 garlic cloves, smashed
3 sprigs of parsley
1 sprig of rosemary or thyme
Handful of leek greens, if you have them
1 cup leftover roast onions or 2 medium onions, cut into wedges and
    sautéed in 1½ tablespoons olive oil until golden and soft
2½ tablespoons unsalted butter
3 tablespoons flour
1 teaspoon salt
½ teaspoon freshly ground pepper
⅛ teaspoon cayenne
½ teaspoon lemon juice (optional)
1 cup diced green beans
2 cups diced potatoes
1 cup diced turnips (optional; use leftover roast turnips if you have them)
1 cup frozen peas, thawed
1 can (12 ounces) corn kernels, drained
1 recipe Buttermilk Drop Biscuits (page 200)

COOKING FROM A COUNTRY FARMHOUSE

1. Pull as much chicken meat as possible off the bones. Cut into ¾-inch dice. There should be at least 1 cup, and preferably 1½ to 2 cups. With a cleaver or large heavy knife, hack up the carcass into large pieces. Discard most of the skin and any excess fat.

2. In a large saucepan, combine the chicken carcass, sliced carrot, onion, peppercorns, garlic, parsley, rosemary, leek greens, and enough cold water to cover—at least 6 cups. Bring to a boil, reduce the heat, and simmer, partially covered, for 1 to 1½ hours (longer is better). Strain, discarding the solids, and measure the liquid. If there is more than 3 cups, boil until reduced to 3 cups. If there is less, add water or chicken broth.

3. In a blender or food processor, puree half the chicken stock with the cooked onions. Set aside.

4. In a medium saucepan, melt the butter over moderate heat. Add the flour and cook, stirring, for about 2 minutes, until the roux is white and the bubbles are small. Whisk in the remaining chicken stock and bring to a boil, whisking until thickened and smooth. Season with the salt, pepper, cayenne, and lemon juice. Stir in the pureed onions, reduce the heat, and simmer 5 minutes. Season the sauce with additional salt and pepper to taste.

5. Bring a large saucepan of salted water to a boil. Add the diced carrot, green beans, potatoes, and turnips. Boil 3 to 5 minutes, or until just barely tender. Drain and rinse briefly; drain well.

6. Preheat the oven to 425 degrees. In a large bowl, combine the chicken meat, diced carrots, green beans, potato, turnips, peas, and corn. Add the sauce and stir gently to combine. Turn the chicken and vegetables into a 3-quart casserole or baking dish no more than 3 inches deep. Cover with the buttermilk biscuit batter, spreading lightly into an even layer. Bake uncovered 25 minutes, or until the crust is golden and cooked through. Let stand 5 minutes before serving.

Chunky Chicken Potpie

6 to 8 servings

This is a classic potpie, with its big pieces of chicken, chunks of hearty root vegetables, colorful dots of green peas, and crisp, flaky crust. I try to pack in as much flavor as possible by using the cooking liquid from the vegetables and juices from stewed mushrooms along with chicken stock to make the sauce. Nothing makes a better winter supper.

While the instructions look long and complicated, the dish is simple; there are just a lot of steps. If you follow them one at a time, the preparation of the dish will take thirty to forty-five minutes. You can do this a day ahead if you like and prepare the pastry the next day. Or the dish can be completely assembled a day ahead and refrigerated or frozen before baking. What's great about it is that it requires no work at the last minute, and it is an incredibly tasty dish that can feed six to eight people generously with only a pound of chicken.

To my mind, a potpie is designed as a single-dish main course. It is the star of the meal, so decorate the crust as nicely as you can, with leaves and twigs, geometric shapes, or whatever strikes your eye. As a starter, I frequently make an iceberg lettuce and tomato salad, dressed up with olives, peppers, and thin slices of marinated white onion; see House Salad, page 154. For dessert, choose another American classic, such as the Chocolate Chocolate Chip Pudding with Chopped Walnuts on page 262.

1 pound cooked chicken meat, preferably from half of a 6- to
   7-pound roasted chicken (see page 42)
1³/₄ teaspoons salt
1 pound boiling potatoes (3 medium), peeled and cut into 1- to 1¹/₂-
   inch cubes
¹/₂ pound carrots (3 or 4 medium), peeled and cut with a rolling cut into
   1-inch pieces (see Note on page 43)
1 pound turnips (3 or 4 medium), peeled and cut into 1- to 1¹/₂-inch cubes
1 tablespoon lemon juice
¹/₂ plus ¹/₈ teaspoon thyme leaves
¹/₂ pound medium mushrooms, quartered
3 medium onions
3 tablespoons light olive oil
1 large celery stalk with leaves, sliced
4 tablespoons (¹/₂ stick) unsalted butter
¹/₃ cup all-purpose flour
1 can (14¹/₂ ounces) reduced-sodium chicken broth
¹/₂ teaspoon winter savory, crushed
1 small bay leaf
³/₈ teaspoon freshly ground pepper
¹/₃ cup heavy cream
Savory Flaky Pastry (page 49)
1 egg yolk, beaten with 1 tablespoon water to make a glaze

1. With your fingers, tear the chicken into large pieces. By large, I mean perhaps 3¹/₂ × 1¹/₂-inch strips of meat from the breast and 3 × 2-inch strips from the thigh. Be sure to remove the skin and any gristle or pockets of fat. Place the meat in a fairly large bowl.

2. In a medium saucepan, bring 6 cups of water to a boil with ³/₄ teaspoon of the salt. Add the potatoes and cook over moderately high heat for 7 minutes, until barely tender, with some resistance left in the center. Lift out the potatoes with a slotted skimmer or spoon and transfer to the bowl with the chicken.

(continued)

3. Add the carrots to the saucepan and cook for 8 minutes, or until crisp-tender. Lift out and transfer to the bowl. Add the turnips to the boiling water and cook for 7 minutes, or until just barely tender. Lift out and add to the chicken and other vegetables. Measure out and reserve 2 cups of the cooking liquid. Discard the remainder.

4. In a small saucepan, combine 1 cup of water with the lemon juice, 1/8 teaspoon thyme, and a sprinkling of salt. Bring to a simmer over moderate heat. Add the mushrooms, reduce the heat to moderately low, and simmer, stirring occasionally, for 10 minutes. Drain the mushrooms, reserving the cooking liquid. Add the mushrooms to the chicken and vegetables.

5. Cut the onions through the root ends into 6 or 8 wedges each. In a large heavy saucepan or flameproof casserole, heat 1 1/2 tablespoons of the olive oil over high heat. Add the onions and cook, stirring frequently, for 5 minutes. Add the celery and continue to cook, stirring, until the onion wedges are lightly browned and the celery is slightly softened, about 5 minutes longer. Transfer to the bowl with the chicken and vegetables.

6. In the same pan, melt the butter in the remaining 1 1/2 tablespoons olive oil over moderate heat. Add the flour and cook, stirring, until the flour is just beginning to color; it should be a light beige. Gradually whisk in the chicken broth, reserved vegetable cooking liquid, and mushroom juices. Bring to a boil, whisking until thickened and smooth. Reduce the heat to a simmer. Add the remaining 1 teaspoon salt, 1/2 teaspoon thyme, the savory, bay leaf, and pepper. Stir in the cream and simmer for 5 minutes.

7. Gently toss the chicken and vegetables to mix them. Turn into a 4-quart casserole 2 1/2 to 3 inches deep. A 12-inch oval works well. Pour the sauce over the chicken and vegetables. Cover and refrigerate about 30 minutes, or until cool.

8. Roll out the pastry a little less than 1/4 inch thick and about 1 inch larger than the dish. Set over the top and trim to 1/2 inch overhang. Fold the edge under and crimp to seal. Cut several slits around the crust or put a steam vent in the center. Brush with the egg glaze. Use the pastry scraps to make leaves or flowers or what-have-you to decorate the top. Brush again with egg wash.

9. Preheat the oven to 425 degrees. Bake the potpie for 45 minutes, or until the sauce is bubbling up and the crust is a light golden brown.

Cooking from a Country Farmhouse

SAVORY FLAKY PASTRY

The poultry fat or lard in this recipe adds extra flavor and flakiness, while the butter helps keep it crisp, even with the steam from the potpie underneath.

> 2 cups all-purpose flour
> ³/₄ teaspoon salt
> 7 tablespoons cold unsalted butter, cut into
>   small cubes
> 3 tablespoons cold rendered goose, duck, or
>   chicken fat, lard, or solid vegetable shortening
> ¹/₃ cup very cold water

1. In a food processor, combine the flour and salt. Pulse briefly to mix. Add the butter and fat and pulse until the mixture resembles very coarse meal (12 to 16 spurts on my machine).

2. Drizzle on the water and process until blended, but do not mix so long that the dough forms a ball around the blade; at that point it would be overworked. Turn out the dough, press together into a ball, and flatten into a ¹/₂-inch-thick disk. Wrap and refrigerate at least 30 minutes before rolling out.

Chicken Chili with Black Beans, Zucchini, and Corn

6 to 8 servings

Chili is a cold-weather favorite out here, but so many of my friends don't eat red meat that I felt compelled to come up with a "white meat" option. This recipe is chunky and colorful, and it doubles easily to become a terrific party dish. The chili base, which is packed with flavor, can be made a day or two ahead, but to keep the chicken moist, it is best to finish the cooking shortly before serving.

While some people are purists, I obviously am not, and especially for a party, I love to serve my chili with every fixing imaginable: steamed brown rice, shredded sharp Cheddar cheese, minced pickled jalapeño peppers, minced white onion, sour cream, sliced black olives, corn tortilla chips. Take your pick.

3 tablespoons olive oil
2 medium onions, chopped
3 garlic cloves, finely chopped
2¹/₂ tablespoons chili powder
2 teaspoons ground cumin
1 teaspoon dried oregano
¹/₄ teaspoon cayenne, or more to taste
1 can (14¹/₂ ounces) reduced-sodium chicken broth
1 can (28 ounces) Italian peeled tomatoes, coarsely
    chopped, juice reserved
1 bottle (12 ounces) amber beer
1 teaspoon sugar
1 teaspoon salt
1 bay leaf
1 tablespoon yellow cornmeal
2 medium zucchini (1 to 1¹/₄ pounds), cut into
    1-inch chunks

2 pounds skinless, boneless chicken breasts, cut
   into 1-inch chunks
1 can (15 to 16 ounces) black beans, rinsed and
   drained
1 can (11 ounces) corn niblets, drained

1. In a stockpot or large flameproof casserole, heat the olive oil over moderately low heat. Add the onions, cover, and cook for 5 minutes. Uncover and continue to cook, stirring occasionally, until the onions are pale golden and just beginning to brown, 8 to 10 minutes longer.

2. Add the garlic, chili powder, cumin, oregano, and cayenne. Cook, stirring, 1 to 2 minutes to toast the spices lightly, but do not let them burn. Stir in the chicken broth until well blended. Add the tomatoes with their juice, the beer, sugar, salt, and bay leaf. Bring to a boil over high heat, reduce the heat to low, and simmer, partially covered, 40 minutes. Remove and discard the bay leaf. (The dish can be prepared ahead to this point up to 2 days in advance and refrigerated; reheat before proceeding.)

3. Return the chili base to a gentle boil. Slowly sprinkle the cornmeal over the sauce so that it just dusts the surface, then stir it in so that it blends with the liquid without forming lumps. Add the zucchini and cook for 5 minutes. Add the chicken, reduce the heat so that the mixture just simmers, and cook for 5 minutes. Add the black beans and corn and cook 5 minutes longer.

LEMON-SAGE CHICKEN CUTLETS

4 servings

There's always a special on some part of the chicken's anatomy at the local market, and I keep a look out for skinless, boneless chicken breasts, which can be pricey. I like them best for Chinese stir-frying, for grilling, and for sautéeing quickly, as in this easy dish, which is fine enough for company.

My own sage has grown from a small plant into what looks like a wild bush—with very little encouragement. Silvery green leaves and purple flowers make the hardy herb as attractive as it is fragrant. Do not be tempted to substitute dried sage; it won't work in this recipe. Fresh or dried tarragon or rosemary is an alternative. Just eliminate the sautéeing of the leaves at the end.

The amount of chicken here will serve four if you include a first course and some substantial vegetables. Big eaters might insist on two chicken breast halves each, in which case you should increase the recipe accordingly.

4 skinless, boneless chicken breast halves, 5 to 6
    ounces each
Salt and freshly ground pepper
1 medium onion, thinly sliced
1 bunch of fresh sage
4½ tablespoons lemon juice
3½ tablespoons extra virgin olive oil
3 tablespoons unsalted butter
Lemon wedges or slices

1. Trim any external fat or gristle from the edges of the chicken. Pound the thicker end gently with the side of a large knife to flatten evenly. Season lightly with salt and pepper.

2. Scatter half the onion slices and 8 to 12 sage leaves or small sprigs of sage evenly over the bottom of a glass or ceramic dish just large enough to hold the chicken breasts in a single layer. Drizzle about 1½ tablespoons of the lemon juice and ¾ tablespoon olive oil over the chicken and rub it lightly to

coat. Invert the chicken breasts in the dish and coat the tops with another 1½ tablespoons lemon juice and ¾ tablespoon olive oil. Top each breast half with 2 or 3 sage leaves and scatter the remaining onion slices on top. Cover with plastic wrap and let marinate at room temperature for 1 to 3 hours or refrigerate for up to 6 hours. (If the chicken is refrigerated, let it stand at room temperature in its marinade for at least 1 hour before cooking.)

3. In a large heavy nonreactive skillet, heat the remaining 2 tablespoons olive oil over moderately high heat. Remove the chicken from the marinade, wipe off the sage and onion, and pat dry with paper towels. Add the chicken to the hot oil in the pan and sauté for 2½ minutes, or until nicely browned on the bottom. Turn over and cook 2 to 3 minutes, until browned on both sides and white but still juicy in the middle. Remove the chicken to a platter and cover with foil to keep warm.

4. Pour out all the oil from the pan. Add the butter to the skillet and melt over moderate heat, stirring with a wooden spoon to scrape up any brown bits from the bottom of the pan. Add about a dozen sage leaves to the melted butter and cook, stirring gently and turning the leaves over if you can, until they are lightly browned and crisp and the butter is lightly browned, about 3 minutes. Stir in the remaining 1½ tablespoons of lemon juice and pour the sauce and sautéed sage leaves over the chicken breasts. Garnish the platter with lemon wedges or slices to squeeze over the chicken. Serve at once.

SHERRIED CHICKEN WITH OLIVES

4 servings

When the weather dips into the single digits, this easy and irresistibly savory sauté seems to taste twice as good. It's saucy enough to cry out for mashed potatoes or white or wild rice, depending on whether you want to dress the meal up or down. Begin or follow with a salad sprinkled with blue cheese and walnuts.

> 2½- to 3-pound chicken, cut into 8 pieces
> Salt and freshly ground pepper
> 2 tablespoons olive oil
> 1 medium onion, thinly sliced
> 2 garlic cloves, minced
> 1 tablespoon capers, rinsed, drained, and coarsely
>   chopped if large
> ½ cup medium-dry sherry
> 2 tablespoons sherry wine vinegar or white wine
>   vinegar
> 1 small can (14 ounces) Italian peeled tomatoes,
>   drained and coarsely chopped
> ½ teaspoon marjoram
> ½ bay leaf
> Dash of cayenne
> ½ cup pitted or pimiento-stuffed green olives

1. Rinse the chicken under cold running water and dry well with paper towels. This is a bothersome step, but it really does freshen the bird. Season the chicken pieces generously with salt and pepper.

2. In a large nonreactive skillet or flameproof casserole, heat the olive oil. Add the chicken and cook over moderately high heat, turning once or twice with tongs, until the pieces are nicely browned, 7 to 10 minutes. Remove the chicken to a plate.

3. Pour off all but 2 tablespoons fat from the pan. Add the onion and cook, stirring occasionally, until golden, 5 to 7 minutes. Add the garlic and capers and cook 1 minute longer. Pour the sherry and vinegar into the pan and boil, scraping up any brown bits from the bottom of the pan, until the liquid is reduced by about half.

4. Return the chicken to the pan. Add the tomatoes, marjoram, bay leaf, cayenne, olives, and ¼ teaspoon each salt and pepper. Cover, reduce the heat to moderately low, and simmer 20 to 30 minutes, or until the chicken is white throughout but still juicy. Remove the chicken to a serving platter. If it seems necessary, boil the juices in the pan for 2 to 3 minutes to thicken slightly. Pour over the chicken and serve.

EASY ENCHILADA CASSEROLE

6 servings

If Mexican food sounds like an anachronism in northeastern Pennsylvania, keep in mind that these days, salsa outsells ketchup in supermarkets. When my neighbors' lovely daughter Carly was chosen as Dairy Princess of Wayne County, she asked me for an appropriate recipe, and this is the one I gave her.

1 pound skinless, boneless chicken breasts
½ medium white onion
½ lime
Salt and freshly ground pepper
12 corn tortillas
¾ to 1 cup jalapeño salsa or green taco sauce
(depending upon the hotness of the salsa and
how spicy you like your food)
1 can (11 ounces) corn niblets, drained
8 ounces sharp white Cheddar cheese, shredded
(2 cups)
1½ cups sour cream
¾ cup milk
Sliced olives or slivers of red bell pepper,
for garnish

1. Trim any fat and gristle from the chicken. Rinse under cold running water and place in a medium saucepan of lightly salted water. Bring to a simmer, reduce the heat to moderately low, and poach the chicken breasts for 12 minutes, or until just white in the center but still juicy. Remove from the heat and let stand in the hot liquid for 10 minutes longer. Remove to a plate and let cool.

2. Preheat the oven to 375 degrees. As soon as the chicken is cool enough to handle, tear it into large shreds into a medium bowl. Cut the onion half

lengthwise in the center, then cut crosswise into very thin slices. Add to the chicken along with the juice from the lime and salt and pepper to taste. Toss to mix evenly.

3. Wrap 6 of the tortillas together in microwave-safe paper towels and microwave on High for 45 seconds to heat through and soften. Repeat with the other 6 tortillas. (Or wrap 2 batches of 6 separately in aluminum foil and heat in the oven for 10 to 15 minutes.)

4. In a 14-inch oval gratin or shallow baking dish, arrange 4 of the tortillas, overlapping the edges as necessary to cover the bottom of the dish. Scatter half the chicken and onion over the tortillas. Drizzle half the salsa over the chicken. Sprinkle on half the corn and then about ¾ cup of the shredded cheese. Combine the sour cream and milk, and with a large spoon drizzle about ¾ cup over all. Cover with 4 more tortillas and repeat. Top the casserole with the last 4 tortillas. Lightly coat the top with the remaining sour cream mixture. Sprinkle on the remaining ½ cup cheese and garnish decoratively with the sliced olives or pepper strips.

5. Bake the casserole for 25 minutes, or until steaming hot throughout.

Baked Chicken Breasts with Garlic and Oregano

4 servings

These are so quick and easy I usually make them for a last-minute dinner during the week, though they are tasty enough for entertaining. Steamed broccoli and pasta tossed with a generous amount of chopped garlic sautéed briefly in olive oil, a dash of hot pepper flakes, and some good Parmesan cheese make perfect accompaniments.

> 4 chicken breast halves on the bone (about 8
>   ounces each)
> Coarse salt and freshly ground pepper
> 1 teaspoon oregano
> 3 garlic cloves, crushed through a press
> 1 1/2 tablespoons fresh lemon juice
> 1 tablespoon extra virgin olive oil
> 3/4 cup dry white wine

1. Trim off any excess fat from the chicken. Season the breasts generously on both sides with salt and pepper. Sprinkle 1/4 teaspoon oregano over each piece and rub with the crushed garlic. Squeeze the lemon juice over the chicken and coat lightly with the olive oil.

2. Pour the wine into a 12-inch oval gratin or baking dish. Place the chicken breasts in the wine, skin side down, and marinate at room temperature for 20 to 30 minutes. Meanwhile, preheat the oven to 375 degrees.

3. Set the gratin in the oven and bake the chicken 30 minutes. Turn skin side up and bake, basting with the pan juices every 10 minutes, for 25 to 35 minutes longer, until the skin is lightly browned and the chicken is cooked through but still juicy. Serve with any remaining pan juices spooned over the chicken.

Sweet-and-Sour Chicken Spiedies

6 servings

Unlike tougher meats, chicken should not be marinated for too long, or it can turn mushy. Mildly tangy, with an Asian-influenced orange-and-lemon marinade, these chicken kebabs go particularly well with the Barbecued Bean Salad on page 122 and Lemon Tarragon Potato Salad on page 146. And don't forget the corn on the cob.

1½ pounds skinless, boneless chicken breasts, trimmed
    of any fat and gristle and cut into 1½-inch chunks
3 tablespoons olive oil
1 tablespoon Asian sesame oil
¼ cup orange juice
1 tablespoon fresh lemon juice
1 tablespoon rice wine vinegar or white wine vinegar
1 tablespoon soy sauce
1 tablespoon honey
1 teaspoon minced fresh ginger (optional)
1 garlic clove, crushed through a press
¼ teaspoon freshly ground pepper
Salt

1. In a medium bowl, combine the chicken with all the remaining ingredients except salt. Toss to coat well. Marinate at room temperature, tossing occasionally, for 1 hour.

2. Prepare a moderately hot fire in your grill. Remove the chicken from the marinade and thread loosely onto long metal or wooden skewers. (If using wooden skewers, be sure to soak them in cold water for at least 30 minutes to prevent charring.) Season the spiedies with salt to taste.

3. Grill 4 to 6 inches from the heat, turning frequently and basting with the marinade for the first 3 minutes, until the chicken is browned outside and white throughout but still moist, 5 to 7 minutes.

OVEN-BARBECUED CHICKEN WINGS

4 to 6 servings

Barbecue is just as good indoors as out. I make these tangy wings in my oven all year round. They are great for a party, picnic, or family supper.

3 pounds chicken wings
Salt and freshly ground pepper
Tangy Barbecue Sauce (recipe follows) or 2 cups
*   of your favorite barbecue sauce*

1. Preheat the oven to 375 degrees. Bend the wings and tuck the tips under the large joint to form a triangle. Season the chicken wings on both sides with salt and pepper. Set them in a single layer in a large roasting or baking pan. Use 2 pans if you have to. Bake the chicken wings, turning once, until browned, about 45 minutes.

2. Remove the wings from the oven and pour off all the fat from the pan. If necessary, blot the wings with paper towels. Return the wings to the pan. Pour the barbecue sauce over the chicken wings and return to the oven. Bake for 10 minutes. Turn the wings over and bake 10 minutes longer. Serve hot, at room temperature, or cold.

TANGY BARBECUE SAUCE

Makes about 2 cups

You won't actually taste the beer, but it lends a nice, slightly more complex overtone to this all-purpose barbecue sauce.

1 medium onion, minced
1½ tablespoons olive oil
2 tablespoons chili powder
2 teaspoons ground cumin
⅔ cup cider vinegar
½ cup beer
¼ cup ketchup
2 tablespoons Worcestershire sauce
2 tablespoons packed dark brown sugar
1 teaspoon powdered mustard
2 garlic cloves, crushed through a press
¼ to ½ teaspoon Tabasco, to taste
½ teaspoon salt
¼ teaspoon freshly ground pepper

1. In a medium stainless-steel saucepan, cook the onion in the olive oil over moderate heat until softened, about 3 minutes. Add the chili powder and cumin and cook, stirring, for 1 minute.

2. Stir in the vinegar, beer, ketchup, Worcestershire sauce, brown sugar, and mustard. Add the garlic, Tabasco, salt, and pepper. Bring to a boil, reduce the heat to moderately low, and simmer for about 15 minutes, or until the sauce is slightly thickened.

Golden Barbecued Chicken

8 to 10 servings

This recipe is a hometown classic. The original recipe, which makes a gallon and a half of barbecue sauce—enough to baste one hundred chickens—is attributed to Stanley Carpenter, who passed away several years ago, before I had a chance to meet him. His recipe is still used for every holiday, wedding, graduation, and church fund-raiser that decides to serve barbecued chicken. Long pits are built of custom metal siding or concrete blocks, and the racks are laid on top about three feet above a thick bed of coals. The birds are cooked slowly, turned and basted regularly, for at least an hour and a half.

This version offers enough sauce for four or five chickens, which I thought might be more useful for the mainstream. If you're having a really large party, though, feel free to double, triple, or otherwise multiply the recipe.

> 4 to 5 chickens (about 2½ pounds each), split
>   lengthwise in half
> 1½ cups cider vinegar
> ¾ cup light olive oil
> 1½ tablespoons coarse (kosher) salt
> ½ teaspoon freshly ground pepper
> 1 small onion, quartered
> 1 egg

1. Rinse the chickens well under cold running water and pat dry with paper towels.

2. In a blender or food processor, combine the vinegar, oil, salt, pepper, onion, and egg. Whirl to blend well and puree the onion.

3. Brush the chickens with the barbecue sauce and set over a moderately low fire as far from the coals as you can get them. Grill, turning and basting every 10 minutes, until the chickens are well browned outside and tender and juicy inside. The timing will vary according to your grill: 45 to 55 minutes on a gas or charcoal grill, up to 1½ hours on a setup such as that described in the headnote.

· WILD TURKEY ·

I ordered my first wild turkey through the mail. It was absolutely delicious, but, I worried, perhaps too tame, and I hankered after a taste of the real free-flying bird. You know, of course, that wild turkeys are a completely different variety from the domestic dum-dum that graces most Thanksgiving tables. For one thing, wild turkeys are smart. For this reason, as well as their indigenous claim to the land and their handsome earthy brown appearance, Benjamin Franklin wanted the wild turkey, rather than the eagle, to be our national bird. It is said that they are so alert and sharp-sighted they can spot the glint of a gun barrel at five hundred yards.

Wild turkeys can fly, though not far. Occasionally, if a car goes by while they are crossing the road, they will lift off one after the other, forming an arc, like a Japanese bridge, from one side of the road to the other. I am told they actually roost in trees at night; I've heard them take off with a clatter.

The meat of cooked wild turkey with the skin removed looks just like vanilla and chocolate ice cream. The white meat is that white and the dark meat that dark-brown color exactly. The light meat, in particular, is densely textured, and the dark parts have a lot of very tough tendons. There is hardly any fat under the skin; this bird leads a very active life, after all. The flavor of the light meat is surprisingly more delicate than that of domestic turkeys. It lacks that distinctive taste that we think of as "turkey," and possesses instead a fine, clean flavor that is extraordinarily appealing. The dark meat is sublime—much stronger, slightly gamey, but not at all challenging. It is unctuous without being fatty, and requires significantly longer cooking time than the breast.

The shooting of wild turkeys is one of the most sportsmanlike types of hunting there are. Let me add that good game management has brought back the wild turkey from near extinction to comfortably large clans in many Northeastern states. It is said there are more wild turkeys in Pennsylvania today than there were when the Pilgrims landed. One April, I counted one hundred and fourteen of them on the hill across from my house. That season you could set your clock by them as they strolled across the fields every day at the exact same time, nodding and gobbling and nibbling on the grass as they lurched down the incline like dod-

(continued)

dering old men. Ordinarily these birds travel in groups of eleven to fourteen, a harem of nine or ten females with the dominant male and perhaps another young male or two. You can spot the males because they are usually larger, are bearded, and have wattles that are normally a luminous light blue but turn bright red when they are courting seriously. That day they must have been having a convention. Actually, the smaller groups cluster together in fall and spring, probably to discuss where they are going to spend their next vacation.

Wild turkeys are hunted only with shotguns, and their dark brown feathers provide such good armor that only a direct hit above the neck will do any damage. Only mature males with full beards may be taken. (The first time I saw a turkey beard tacked over a bar I thought with horror it was a human scalp.) Since they must be killed cleanly, there is not usually much problem with buckshot in the meat. And only the very best and luckiest hunter will get a wild turkey. It is a trophy to be prized.

So how did I end up with one? After my first sample of the farm-raised wild turkey, I was hooked, but I wanted more. Not only was I curious about what a true turkey sauvage would taste like; mail order is expensive. My greed was so great that I went out and bought a shotgun, but while beer-can practice was fun, I quickly came to the honest realization that I was a hypocrite when

Cooking from a Country Farmhouse

it came to meat. I can cook it and I love to eat it, but I cannot kill it.

One day, my favorite carpenter, Carl, and his assistant, Eddie, the handsomest stock car racer in three counties, were working on my kitchen when spring turkey season began. The next day I asked politely if either of them had gotten a turkey. Eddie said he had, just by luck—it had snuck up behind him when he wasn't looking and run right into the barrel of his shotgun. I asked him what he was going to do with it. Eddie said, "Shucks, I don't know. The last one I cooked tasted like shoe leather."

This crime, I thought, could not be repeated, so I said, "Well, Eddie, if you ever want, I'll be glad to cook it up for you." Eddie got a little flustered, so I just let it drop. . . .

Until a week later, when I was taking a long walk with Carl's wife, Gina. She mentioned Eddie's wild turkey, and wondered what he was going to do with it. I sighed and said how I'd love to cook a real wild turkey to put it in the book I was working on. When she just pursed her lips and looked thoughtful, I knew I had a fighting chance. Sure enough—two days later Eddie showed up with the turkey, frozen hard as a rock, cradled in his arms. It's against the law to sell wild game, and I couldn't even get Eddie to accept a present for the bird, but I'll be forever grateful. It was absolutely delicious!

Wild Turkey with Lemon-Buttermilk Madeira Gravy

6 to 8 servings

Don't think there's no stuffing at this meal. When I make wild turkey with the cavity filled with aromatics and herbs to flavor the bird, as is done here, the dressing is baked in a separate dish, moistened with some of the extra turkey stock.

> 1 wild turkey, 8 to 10 pounds
> 2 lemons
> 1½ teaspoons coarse (kosher) salt
> ½ teaspoon coarsely ground pepper
> 3 garlic cloves, bruised
> 1 medium onion, peeled and quartered
> 3 large sprigs of fresh winter savory or ¾ teaspoon dried
> 3 large sprigs of fresh thyme, preferably lemon thyme,
>   or ¾ teaspoon dried thyme leaves
> 11 tablespoons (1 stick plus 3 tablespoons) unsalted butter
> 2 cups turkey stock or homemade chicken stock or
>   reduced-sodium canned broth
> 3 tablespoons all-purpose flour
> ½ cup dry Madeira
> ¾ cup buttermilk

1. Preheat the oven to 375 degrees. Rinse the turkey well until no blood runs from the cavity and blot it dry inside and out with paper towels. Quarter one of the lemons; cut the other lemon in half. Rub the outside of the turkey with one lemon half, then use the same half to rub the inside of the bird, squeezing to release the juice. Season the bird generously inside and out with salt and freshly ground pepper. Stuff the cavity with the lemon

quarters, garlic, onion, savory, and thyme. Set the remaining lemon half aside. Truss the large cavity closed and tie the legs together.

2. Set the turkey breast side down on a rack in a large shallow roasting pan. Roast for $1/2$ hour. Meanwhile, in a small saucepan, melt 1 stick of the butter in 1 cup of the stock. Turn the turkey over and baste the breast with the stock-and-butter mixture. Tent the breast with aluminum foil, shiny side up. Reduce the oven temperature to 325 degrees and roast for $1^{1}/_{4}$ hours, basting every 15 to 20 minutes. Remove the foil and continue to roast, basting every 20 minutes, for 1 hour longer, or until there is no trace of pink when the thigh is pierced near the bone. Remove the turkey to a carving board and let it rest for 10 to 15 minutes.

3. Meanwhile, pour the pan drippings into a bowl or a gravy separator. Skim off or pour off as much fat as possible. Add the remaining 3 tablespoons butter to the roasting pan and set over moderate heat. Sprinkle on the flour and cook, stirring with a wooden spoon, for 2 minutes. Whisk in the Madeira and bring to a boil, scraping up the brown bits from the bottom of the pan. Whisk in the degreased pan drippings and the remaining turkey stock and bring to a boil. Cook, whisking, until the gravy is smooth and thickened, about 2 minutes. Whisk in the buttermilk and return to a boil, whisking until smooth. Squeeze the juice from the remaining $1/2$ lemon into the gravy and season with additional salt and pepper to taste.

4. Carve the turkey and pass the gravy on the side.

TURKEY SHEPHERD'S PIE WITH BUTTERMILK MASHED POTATO TOPPING

4 servings

Casseroles that can be made ahead and baked at the last minute, after an afternoon of hard work or cross-country skiing, are especially welcome. This one is particularly appropriate for a casual, relaxed Sunday supper. It uses ground turkey, which is now available in practically every market. To my delight, meat eaters didn't realize the switch, and nonmeaters loved it.

1½ tablespoons olive oil
2 medium onions, cut into ¾-inch dice
2 medium carrots, halved lengthwise and cut into 1-inch pieces
½ red bell pepper, cut into ¾-inch dice
1 pound ground turkey
1 teaspoon salt
½ teaspoon freshly ground black pepper
½ teaspoon marjoram or thyme
1 small bay leaf
¼ pound green beans, trimmed and cut into 1-inch lengths
1 cup reduced-sodium chicken broth
¼ cup tomato paste
1 tablespoon soy sauce
1 tablespoon lemon juice
1½ teaspoons Worcestershire sauce
¼ teaspoon Tabasco
1 can (11 ounces) vacuum-packed corn niblets
Buttermilk Mashed Potatoes (page 144)
1 tablespoon unsalted butter, melted

1. In a large skillet or flameproof casserole, heat the olive oil. Add the onions and cook over moderate heat, stirring occasionally, until they just begin to color, 7 to 10 minutes. Add the carrots and bell pepper and cook, stirring, 3 minutes longer.

2. Add the turkey and season with the salt, black pepper, and marjoram. Cook, stirring to break up any large lumps of meat, until lightly browned, about 5 minutes. Add the bay leaf, green beans, chicken broth, tomato paste, soy sauce, lemon juice, Worcestershire sauce, and Tabasco. Reduce the heat to moderately low and simmer, partially covered and stirring occasionally, 25 minutes. Remove and discard the bay leaf. Stir in the corn.

3. Turn the turkey mixture into a 3-quart casserole or baking dish no more than 3 inches high. Spread the mashed potatoes over the top. Score with the tines of a fork into a decorative pattern if you like. Brush with the melted butter. (The recipe can be prepared ahead to this point. Let stand at room temperature for up to 1½ hours, or cover and refrigerate for up to 6 hours. Remove from the refrigerator 1 hour before baking.)

4. Preheat the oven to 400 degrees. Bake the shepherd's pie 20 to 25 minutes, or until the meat and vegetables are bubbling and piping hot and the mashed potatoes are lightly browned on top.

TURKEY PAPRIKASH

4 to 6 servings

*F*resh turkey is easy to come by in our local markets. Wherever you live, you can find designer cuts of turkey in any supermarket. The moistness of dark thigh meat works best in a stew preparation like this. Serve with white rice or noodles to sop up the gravy.

3 to 3½ pounds turkey thighs or 2½ pounds boneless turkey thighs
1 tablespoon plus 1 teaspoon lemon juice
2 tablespoons sweet Hungarian paprika
1 tablespoon hot Hungarian paprika or ⅛ teaspoon cayenne
¾ teaspoon thyme leaves
1 small onion, minced
3 tablespoons olive oil
Salt and freshly ground pepper
5 tablespoons unsalted butter
2½ tablespoons all-purpose flour
¾ cup dry white wine
1½ cups chicken stock or reduced-sodium canned broth
¾ pound medium-size fresh mushrooms, preferably Italian brown
   (cremini), quartered
½ cup sour cream, or more to taste

1. Remove the skin from the turkey, cut out the bone if there is one, and cut the meat into 1½- to 2-inch chunks. Place the turkey in a bowl and season with 1 tablespoon of the lemon juice, ½ tablespoon each of the sweet and hot paprika, ¼ teaspoon of the thyme, the onion, ½ tablespoon of the olive oil, ½ teaspoon salt, and ¼ teaspoon pepper. Marinate at room temperature 1 hour.

2. In a large skillet or flameproof casserole, melt 2 tablespoons of the butter in 1½ tablespoons of the olive oil. Add the seasoned turkey and onion and cook over moderate heat, turning, until lightly browned all over, about 5 minutes. Sprinkle the flour and remaining 1½ tablespoons sweet and ½ tablespoon hot paprika into the pan and cook, stirring, for 1 to 2 minutes.

3. Add the wine and bring to a boil, scraping up the browned bits from the bottom of the pan. Add the chicken stock and $1/4$ teaspoon thyme and bring to a simmer. Reduce the heat to moderately low, partially cover the pan, and simmer 45 minutes, or until the turkey is tender.

4. Meanwhile, in a large skillet, melt the remaining 3 tablespoons butter in the remaining 1 tablespoon olive oil over moderately high heat. Add the mushrooms and sauté until they give up their juices and the liquid evaporates, 5 to 7 minutes. Season with the remaining 1 teaspoon lemon juice, $1/4$ teaspoon thyme, and a sprinkling of salt and pepper. Add the mushrooms to the turkey and simmer 5 minutes.

5. With a slotted spoon, remove the turkey and mushrooms to a warmed serving bowl. Boil the sauce until reduced to the consistency of heavy cream and intense in flavor, 2 to 3 minutes. Remove from the heat and stir in the sour cream until blended. Pour over the turkey and mushrooms and serve at once, with rice or noodles.

Sautéed Turkey Cutlets in Red Currant Cream Sauce with Chestnuts

4 servings

The sweet richness of the chestnuts and tart-sweet creaminess of the sauce provide a lush counterpoint to the leanness of turkey. Served with wild rice and buttered broccoli or Brussels sprouts, this makes a great company dinner. The recipe doubles easily and also works beautifully with veal cutlets, which cook in just 3 to 5 minutes.

> *½ pound chestnuts*
> *1⅓ pounds turkey cutlets*
> *Salt and freshly ground pepper*
> *2 tablespoons unsalted butter*
> *1 tablespoon light olive oil or other vegetable oil*
> *2 large shallots or 1 small onion, minced*
> *⅓ cup dry white wine*
> *1 tablespoon red currant jelly*
> *⅔ cup heavy cream*

1. Preheat the oven to 375 degrees. With a small knife, cut an X into the flat side of each chestnut. Place the chestnuts on a baking sheet and roast for 20 minutes. When they are cool enough to handle, squeeze gently to crack the shells and peel the chestnuts. Remove the inner brown skins. Don't worry if some chestnuts break; they don't all have to be whole. Set the chestnuts aside in a small bowl, or, if you prefer to roast them a day ahead, seal in a plastic bag and refrigerate.

2. Season the turkey cutlets generously with salt and pepper. In a large nonreactive skillet, melt the butter in the olive oil over moderate heat. Add the cutlets and cook, turning once, until lightly browned outside and tender but still juicy inside, 7 to 10 minutes. With tongs, remove the turkey to a plate and set aside.

3. Add the shallots to the fat in the pan and sauté until soft and fragrant, 1 to 2 minutes (if using onion, allow a minute or two longer). Add the white wine and bring to a boil, scraping up any browned bits from the bottom of the pan with a wooden spoon. Boil until the wine is reduced to about 2½ tablespoons.

4. Add the jelly and whisk until melted, about 1 minute. Add the cream and boil for 1 to 2 minutes to reduce slightly. Reduce the heat to a simmer. Return the turkey cutlets to the pan and turn them in the sauce to coat. Add the chestnuts and simmer for 2 minutes, until everything is hot. Serve at once.

POACHED TURKEY BREAST WITH WALNUT–GOAT CHEESE PESTO

12 servings

Okay, you can see the city influence in this one, but turkey breast is one of the most readily available and economical cuts to use for large-scale entertaining, and when fresh basil is in season, this is a truly lovely dish, no matter where you happen to live. To make it easy on yourself, order a whole fresh six-pound turkey breast and ask your butcher to remove the skin and bone and to roll and tie the meat for you into a neat, cylindrical roast. Poach the turkey the night before your party. The pesto takes five minutes at most with a food processor.

> 4 quarts water
> 1 whole clove
> 2 medium onions, halved
> 2 garlic cloves, smashed
> 1 large carrot, thickly sliced
> 1 celery rib with leaves, halved
> 1 medium white turnip, peeled and quartered
> 4 to 6 sprigs of parsley with stems
> 1 bay leaf
> 1 teaspoon black peppercorns
> 1 teaspoon salt
> 1 tablespoon white wine vinegar
> 1 skinless, boneless whole turkey breast, rolled and tied (3½ to 4 pounds)
> Walnut–Goat Cheese Pesto (recipe follows)
> Sprigs of fresh basil and cherry tomatoes, for garnish

1. Pour the water into an 8- to 10-quart stockpot. Stick the clove into one of the onion halves and add it to the pot, along with the remaining onions, the garlic, carrot, celery, turnip, parsley, bay leaf, peppercorns, salt, and vinegar. Bring to a boil, reduce the heat, and simmer for 15 minutes.

2. Add the turkey to the pot, cover and simmer over moderately low heat for 1¼ to 1½ hours, or until the internal temperature of the meat reaches

155 to 160 degrees on an instant-reading thermometer. Adjust the heat so that the liquid bubbles very gently without boiling and skim the foam off the top several times. When the turkey is done, let it cool to room temperature in the liquid; the internal temperature will first increase to about 170 degrees as the turkey sits. Then refrigerate the turkey in the stock overnight, or until thoroughly chilled.

3. Remove the turkey from the stock and cut off the strings. Strain the stock; reserve ½ cup for the pesto sauce that follows. (I always reserve the remainder for soup or sauces.) Carve the turkey into ⅜-inch slices. Arrange them on a platter and spoon some of the walnut–goat cheese pesto down the center. Garnish the platter if you like with sprigs of basil and cherry tomatoes. Serve the remaining pesto in a sauceboat on the side.

WALNUT-GOAT CHEESE PESTO

Makes about 2 cups

Pale green and pungent with basil and garlic, this sauce can also be served as a dip for fresh vegetables. If you make it without the poached turkey, use half a cup of reduced-sodium chicken broth in place of the turkey stock.

½ cup turkey stock (reserved from Poached Turkey, above)
5½ ounces mild white goat cheese, such as Montrachet or Coach Farms
1 large garlic clove, crushed
1 cup walnut halves or pieces
2 cups (packed) fresh basil leaves
⅓ cup extra virgin olive oil
Salt and freshly ground pepper

1. In a food processor, combine the turkey stock, goat cheese, and garlic. Puree until smooth and blended.

2. Add the walnuts and the basil. Process until very coarsely chopped. With the machine on, slowly add the olive oil and process to the desired consistency. Season with salt and pepper to taste.

· SPIEDIES ·

There is no regional American cuisine to speak of in these parts. Church socials advertise the standard preparations—chicken and biscuits, roast beef, pancakes and sausages. Certain ingredients, such as cider vinegar, graham flour, and celery seed in coleslaw are typical. But there is nothing like New England clam chowder, Louisiana Cajun fried catfish, or San Francisco cioppino, recipes that stand as place markers, clearly having been birthed on or about a particular moment in time in a singular place. Nothing, that is, except—spiedies.

Everyone talks about spiedies, they eat them for lunch and supper, serve them at family and company cookouts, enter recipes for them in contests. There are spiedies restaurants and even a bottled spiedie marinating sauce. Every little local market displays the same sign out front: Hoagies/Spiedies. When I first arrived here, my neighbors couldn't believe I'd never tasted a spiedie.

Spiedies are, in fact, heavily marinated grilled cubes of meat, like shish kebab, eaten as a sandwich wrapped in a thick slice of fluffy white or supermarket soft Italian bread. There are pork spiedies, beef spiedies, lamb spiedies, chicken spiedies, even venison spiedies. Before I saw the first sign, I assumed the dish was spelled "speedies," referring to the quick cooking properties of the recipe. While it's probably obvious to everyone else, the origin of the name escaped me until one day when I was leafing through an Italian cookbook and came upon a recipe for spiedini. I'd seen the word in print a hundred times before, but I just never made the connection. Of course, of course. . . .

At the turn of the century, Binghamton, New York, was a flourishing manufacturing city, with a number of shoe factories— Endicott Johnson being the most famous—and cigar factories attracting large numbers of immigrant workers. During the first two decades of the twentieth century, many Italians made their way up the Delaware in search of jobs, and they brought with them the foods and recipes of their homeland. While pizza and spaghetti and meatballs may have caught on elsewhere, it was spiedini that captured the public imagination in the Southern Tier. Locally, a gentleman by the name of Augusto Iacovelli is credited with hav-

ing spread the popularity of the dish to the general public when he put spiedies on the menu of his restaurant, Augie's, in 1945. The rest is history.

Today, spiedies are sold in supermarkets, premarinated in small plastic containers and gargantuan tubs, a testimony to their popularity at big barbecues. Unfortunately, these spiedies are pickled to death, actually beyond—to a mild state of embalmment. A pale gray pallor permeates the meat, and the accepted fashion of cooking often mimics cremation. You need a strong set of choppers to chew on a lean pork spiedie.

Prepared properly in your own kitchen, however, marinated grilled meats, sometimes paired with vegetables, offer limitless creative possibilities and exceptional flavor for the amount of effort, which is minimal. While you can cook spiedies under the broiler, they really do belong on the grill. And while it violates regional tradition, I always take the liberty of omitting the white bread.

STEAK SPIEDIES

4 to 6 servings

Shish kebab by another name. While spiedies are traditionally served wrapped in a thick blanket of soft white bread, this version works well inside a long French or sourdough roll, though I prefer it on a plate, eaten with a knife and fork.

2 pounds boneless sirloin steak, cut 1½ inches thick, trimmed of all excess
  fat and cut into 1½-inch cubes
½ cup dry red wine
3 tablespoons extra virgin olive oil
2 tablespoons red wine vinegar
2 garlic cloves, crushed through a press
1 teaspoon oregano
½ teaspoon salt
¼ teaspoon freshly ground pepper
1 medium white onion, cut into 1½-inch squares about ½ inch thick
1 medium green bell pepper, cut into 1½-inch squares
12 cherry tomatoes

1. In a medium bowl, toss the meat with the wine, olive oil, vinegar, garlic, oregano, salt, and pepper. Marinate at room temperature, tossing occasionally, for 1 to 2 hours, or cover and refrigerate for up to 24 hours. If the meat is chilled, let it stand at room temperature for an hour before cooking.

2. Prepare a hot fire in your grill. Remove the beef from the marinade and thread it onto long metal skewers, alternating the cubes of steak with the squares of onion and green pepper. Stick the cherry tomatoes on a separate skewer. Grill the spiedies about 4 inches from the heat, turning occasionally, until the meat is browned outside but still pink and juicy inside, 8 to 12 minutes. Grill the cherry tomatoes 2 to 3 minutes, turning, until hot but not bursting.

Scotch-Grilled Steaks

4 servings

Scotch whisky makes an exceptionally good pairing with beef. Just a few drops add superb flavor. In summer, I cook these steaks on the outdoor grill. In winter, they are just as good in a cast-iron grill pan.

4 boneless rib steaks, cut 1 inch thick (6 to 8 ounces each)
2 garlic cloves, cut in half
Coarse (kosher) salt and freshly ground pepper
4 teaspoons Scotch whisky
4 teaspoons extra virgin olive oil

1. Trim external fat from the steaks so they are as lean as possible. Place the steaks on a platter and rub the cut sides of one of the garlic cloves over the top of the steaks. Season them to taste with salt and pepper. Sprinkle ½ teaspoon Scotch over each steak; rub it around to cover the meat. Do the same with the olive oil. Turn the steaks over and repeat. Set aside at room temperature for at least 30 minutes and up to 1 hour.

2. Light a hot fire in a grill or preheat your grill pan. Cook the steaks, turning once, 5 to 6 minutes for rare, 6 to 7 minutes for medium rare, or longer as desired. To achieve crisscross grill marks on the meat, rotate the steaks 90 degrees halfway through the cooking on each side.

BEEF STEW WITH CARROTS AND ROASTED ONIONS

6 to 8 servings

All this deep, dark dish needs is an interesting green salad, such as the Baby Beet and Spinach Salad on page 152, for starters, and a big mound of Buttermilk Mashed Potatoes (page 144) as accompaniment. If you have any mushrooms lying around, they make an excellent addition to the dish; quarter and sauté them and add them with the carrots and onions in step 7. Of course, a chewy sourdough whole-grain loaf and a nice bottle of Burgundy will make the meal memorable. Like most stews, this improves if made a day or two in advance.

> $3^{1/2}$ to 4 pounds boneless beef chuck
> 1 teaspoon salt
> $^{1/2}$ teaspoon freshly ground pepper
> $2^{1/2}$ cups dry red wine
> $^{1/4}$ cup Armagnac or Cognac
> $^{1/4}$ cup extra virgin olive oil
> 2 tablespoons red wine vinegar
> 2 tablespoons maple syrup or dark brown sugar
> 6 to 8 sprigs of parsley
> 2 bay leaves
> $^{1/2}$ teaspoon thyme leaves, preferably lemon thyme, or marjoram
> Dash of cayenne
> 4 medium onions—1 thinly sliced, 3 cut into 6 or 8 wedges each
> 6 medium carrots—2 sliced, 4 cut on a sharp diagonal with a
>   rolling cut into 2-inch lengths (see Note on page 43)
> 6 garlic cloves
> 2 slices of bacon, cut crosswise into $^{3/8}$-inch strips
> 3 tablespoons all-purpose flour
> 2 tablespoons tomato paste

1. Trim all excess fat from the chuck and cut the meat into 2-inch chunks. Season with the salt and pepper and place in a large bowl. Pour the wine over the beef. Add the Armagnac, $1^{1/2}$ tablespoons of the olive oil, the

vinegar, maple syrup, parsley, bay leaves, thyme, cayenne, the sliced onion, and the sliced carrots. Crush 1 garlic clove through a press into the bowl. Marinate the meat at room temperature, stirring occasionally, for up to 6 hours, or refrigerate overnight.

2. Strain the marinade into a bowl. Pick out the beef chunks and press them dry with paper towels. Pick out the bay leaves and parsley and set aside. Reserve the sliced onion and carrots.

3. In a large flameproof casserole, cook the bacon over moderately high heat, stirring, until the fat is rendered and the meat just begins to brown. Remove with a slotted spoon and set aside.

4. Add 1 tablespoon of the olive oil to the bacon fat. Cook the beef in batches without crowding, turning, until nicely browned all over, about 5 minutes per batch. As the beef browns, remove it to a bowl. If the fat burns at any point, replace it with fresh oil.

5. When all the beef has been browned, add the sliced onion and carrots to the pot and cook, stirring frequently, until the onion is softened and beginning to brown, about 5 minutes. Sprinkle on the flour, reduce the heat to moderate, and cook, stirring, about 2 minutes, or until the mixture turns a light beige. Whisk in the reserved marinade and the tomato paste. Return the beef to the pan. Tie the parsley together with kitchen string and add along with the bay leaves and enough water to barely cover the meat. Bring to a simmer, cover tightly, reduce the heat to low, and cook at a bare simmer for about 2½ hours, or until the meat is very tender.

6. About an hour before the stew is done, preheat the oven to 450 degrees. Place the onion wedges in a shallow baking or gratin dish along with the remaining unpeeled garlic cloves and toss with the remaining 1½ tablespoons olive oil. Roast, turning once or twice, for 20 minutes. Remove the garlic cloves and set aside. Continue to cook the onions, turning once more, until they are nicely browned, 10 to 15 minutes longer. In a large saucepan of boiling water, cook the carrots for about 10 minutes, until just tender.

7. When the meat is done, add the carrots and roasted onions to the stew. Squeeze the garlic cloves from their skin and pass through a garlic press or mash with a fork. Stir into the stew. Simmer for 10 minutes. Season the gravy with additional salt, if needed, and plenty of pepper. Remove and discard the parsley and bay leaves before serving.

Brisket of Beef
Braised in Ale

8 to 12 servings

This is one of those do-ahead dishes that are infinitely juicier and more tasty if the meat is cooked, sliced, then returned to its cooking juices and left overnight. Simply reheat gently before serving.

    1 first-cut brisket of beef, well trimmed (4½ to 5 pounds)
    1 teaspoon salt
    ½ teaspoon freshly ground pepper
    3 tablespoons olive oil or peanut oil
    2 pounds onions, thinly sliced (about 8 cups)
    1½ tablespoons sweet Hungarian paprika
    1 teaspoon hot Hungarian paprika or ¼ teaspoon cayenne
    1 bottle (11½ to 12 ounces) ale or amber beer
    1 tablespoon soy sauce
    2 garlic cloves, crushed through a press
    1 bay leaf

1. Preheat the oven to 325 degrees. Trim all excess fat from the brisket. Season the meat on both sides with the salt and pepper. Choose a very large flameproof casserole or heavy roasting pan with a lid; the meat will shrink several inches in length as soon as you brown it, so if the pan is a little smaller than the piece of brisket, it should be all right. In the pan, heat 2 tablespoons of the oil over high heat; if necessary, swirl the pan to coat the bottom. Add the brisket and sauté over high heat, turning several times, until nicely browned on both sides, about 8 minutes. Lift up the meat to drain it into the pan and transfer it to a dish.

2. Add the remaining 1 tablespoon oil to the pan and reduce the heat to moderate. Add the onions and cook for a minute, scraping up the browned bits on the bottom of the pan with a wooden spoon. Cover and cook, stirring once or twice, for 5 minutes. Uncover and raise the heat to moderately high.

Cook, stirring occasionally, until the onions are wilted, about 3 minutes. Add the sweet paprika and the hot paprika and cook, stirring frequently, for 2 minutes.

3. Return the meat to the pot. Spoon about half the onions up on top of the meat. Pour the ale and soy sauce around the meat. Add the garlic and bay leaf. Bring to a simmer, cover the pan, and transfer to the oven. Bake for 1½ hours, basting the meat with the liquid in the pan after 45 minutes. Turn the meat over and cook, basting once or twice, 1½ hours longer, or until the meat is fork tender.

4. Remove the meat to a carving board. Skim as much fat as possible off the top of the pan juices. Carve the meat against the grain and serve with the pan juices and onions poured on top. For extra flavor, return the slices of meat to the pot and let stand in the juices for 10 minutes or overnight. Serve warm or at room temperature.

· ROAD KILL ·

Road kill isn't something polite people are prone to discuss. And it isn't a particularly popular topic in cookbooks. It is, however, an ever-present fact of life in any rural region, and more than one cook I know carries an aura of fame because of a recipe that turned an accident into a feast, so I couldn't let it pass without mention.

You should know from the outset that I am an animal lover. My two mutts, Trixie and Beansy, will testify to my kindness toward four-legged creatures. And around here, no one I know is so poor that they scrounge the roadsides looking for meat. But many people, some of whom do not otherwise eat flesh at all, believe it is a crime to kill an animal, even accidentally, and then let it go to waste.

Laws vary from state to state, but at least here, in Pennsylvania, if you report an accident to the proper game authorities, you can claim the road kill and take it home with you. Of course, you should examine the carcass to make sure it is healthy. Rabbits, as all hunters know, can carry a liver disease, highly visible with yellow spots on the organ, which is transmissible to humans. But when the animal is healthy, meat certainly doesn't come any fresher.

If this discussion sounds repugnant to you, here's a mathematical puzzle you should try to solve: If you're driving along a country road at night, and you're going ten miles below the posted speed limit, and in the fifteen minutes it takes to drive home from your friend's house you narrowly miss hitting twenty deer, how many deer are frolicking in the forest? I've never been good at algebra, but even if you cannot compute the exact answer, you must realize that with those odds, if you don't run into a deer while driving home, you're lucky.

Many people think so many deer are hit by cars at night because they're blinded by the headlights. Not true! They'll run right into the side of your car in broad daylight as well. The truth of the matter is that when God was deciding who would become a physicist and who a mechanical engineer, the deer were out decimating the last cornfield in the Garden of Eden. They didn't get back until all knowledge of the physical world had been passed around. So, unlike many of their furry forest friends—such as rabbits, woodchucks, raccoons, and even squirrels—deer lack any concept of velocity and acceleration at all. The herd did get back, however, by the time God was deciding who would become a world-class sprinter. Consequently, a deer will wait until your vehicle is right on top of it before making that split-second decision to charge out of the bushes, race across the road, and blithely smash into the moving car at upward of forty miles an hour, causing thousands of dollars' worth of damage.

Other forms of road kill include 'coons, which do get blinded by headlights at night. Only the old-timers tend to eat them; they say they're very greasy, an acquired taste. Rabbits have an odd zigzag pattern of escape; sometimes when they've zigged away from the car and you think you're safely by them, they make a mad zag toward the back wheels, and there's nothing you can do about it but make hasenpfeffer. Woodchucks can usually hunker out of the way but are sometimes too busy eating, and of course, there are the game birds.

In mating season, ruffed grouse get so distracted that they are frequently seen wandering aimlessly down the roads, staggering first left, then right, like drunks. Given how hard it is to find a grouse, I am tempted to just turn that wheel and . . . but of course I never do, though I know for a fact there are those less scrupulous than I. Two of my friends serendipitously acquired ruffed grouse when the birds executed themselves on their kitchen windows.

One was Eddie, my carpenter's assistant. He told me about it the next day. Actually the grouse flew right through the closed window and dropped with a thud on the hearth of his stone fireplace. Eddie told me he tore off all the feathers, cleaned the bird, and threw it directly into the microwave.

"Tasted like shoe leather," said Eddie. Everything Eddie cooks tastes like shoe leather.

A friend of mine who supplies farm-raised game to many of the top restaurants in the country is an avid game hunter. He tells me that if you find a bird that looks freshly killed, you can tell for sure by looking under the feathers. If the skin on the belly is still pink and the eyes are shiny, he says chances are it's highly edible.

Of course, any sensible cook should be wary of uninspected meat they find lying by the side of the road. For myself, I prefer to examine the package. If the color of the meat looks good and the date on the label has not expired, I assume chances are it's highly edible.

ROAD KILL CHILI

8 to 10 servings

All right, just kidding—For "road kill," read venison, or use beef if you prefer, or a mixture of beef and pork. This chili did originate, however, from a real road kill, which is how it got its name. A local character, who had eaten no red meat in over two decades, was driving home with his son one night in his 1956 Chevy pick-up truck when they were suddenly hit by a deer, who died instantly after destroying the front of the truck. A number of people stopped to help, and a state trooper happened along. It was he who suggested they report the accident to the game authorities and take the meat home, since it was so fresh. His son dressed the animal in the field, and they carted off the meat to be butchered by one of the many local grocers who specialize in venison. When you bring in a whole deer, you end up with several small roasts, a number of steaks, some tiny medallions from the fillet, and six to ten pounds of ground venison, which is actually venison ground up with a substantial proportion of pork or beef fat for moisture. Hence this chili.

½ pound dried pinto beans (use black beans if you want to be trendier),
  picked over and rinsed
3 tablespoons olive oil
3 medium onions, chopped
2 celery ribs with leaves, chopped
1 small green bell pepper, finely diced
5 garlic cloves, minced
3 pounds coarsely ground venison or beef
2 teaspoons salt
1 teaspoon freshly ground pepper
1½ teaspoons oregano, preferably Mexican
¼ cup plus 2 tablespoons chili powder
2 tablespoons ground cumin
1 can (28 ounces) Italian peeled tomatoes, coarsely cut up, with their juices
1½ cups water
1 tablespoon cider vinegar
Cayenne or Tabasco (optional)

1. In a large saucepan, soak the beans overnight in enough cold water to cover them by at least 3 inches. Drain and rinse the beans under cold running water. Return them to the pan and fill it with fresh cold water. Bring to a boil, reduce the heat to moderate, and cook until the beans are tender, about 1 hour. Drain, rinse, and set aside.

2. In a very large flameproof casserole or stockpot, heat the oil over moderately low heat. Add the onions and celery, cover the pot, and cook until softened, 5 to 7 minutes. Uncover, raise the heat to moderate, and continue to cook, stirring occasionally, until the onions are beginning to brown, 5 to 10 minutes. Add the bell pepper and garlic and cook 2 minutes longer.

3. Crumble the venison into the pot. Season with 1 teaspoon of the salt, $1/2$ teaspoon of the pepper, and the oregano. Raise the heat to moderately high and cook, stirring to break up large lumps and to turn the meat over, until the meat is no longer pink, about 10 minutes. Add the chili powder and cumin and cook, stirring, for 2 minutes. Stir in the tomatoes with their juices and the water. Add the remaining 1 teaspoon salt and $1/2$ teaspoon pepper. Bring to a boil, reduce the heat to moderately low, partially cover, and simmer, stirring occasionally, for $1 1/2$ hours. Add the cooked pinto beans and simmer until the chili is thick and the venison is tender, $1/2$ to 1 hour longer. (If the chili thickens too quickly at any time, reduce the heat to low and add additional water.)

4. Add the vinegar and season with additional salt and pepper to taste. If the chili is not as spicy as you'd like—chili-powder blends vary considerably in hotness—add cayenne or Tabasco to suit your palate.

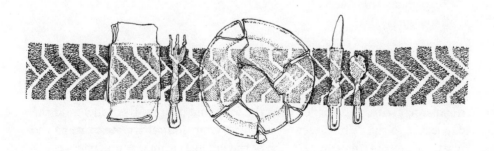

Venison Pot Roast

6 servings

Maple syrup may look surprising here, but the effect is subtle and irresistibly savory, lending the dish a flavor very much like that of a mild sauerbraten. I am grateful to Mary Weatherall, who recently opened her own restaurant, Mary's Kitchen, in a neighboring town, for suggesting it. She explained that their first year in the country, she and her husband lived largely off the land, eating meat only when venison was hunted on their own property and flavored with maple syrup tapped from their own trees.

If there are any leftovers or if you make this dish several hours ahead, store the meat in the gravy and reheat it later or the next day. The flavor will be even better.

1 venison roast, 2½ to 3 pounds
1 teaspoon coarse salt
¾ teaspoon coarsely cracked black pepper
¾ teaspoon dried thyme leaves
2 garlic cloves, minced
¼ cup Armagnac or Cognac
¼ cup maple syrup, preferably amber
⅓ cup red wine vinegar
3½ tablespoons extra virgin olive oil
1 large onion, thinly sliced
1 large carrot, thinly sliced
6 to 8 parsley sprigs with stems
2½ cups dry red wine
2 bay leaves

1. Wipe off the roast and place it in a deep oval dish. Season with the salt, pepper, thyme, and garlic. In the order given, pour the Armagnac, maple syrup, vinegar, and 2 tablespoons of the olive oil over the venison. Scatter the onion, carrot, and parsley over the roast and pour on the wine. Add the bay leaves to the dish. Cover with plastic wrap and refrigerate, turning the roast and re-covering it with some of the onions, carrots, and parsley, every 6 to 12 hours, as you think of it. Marinate the venison at least 24 and preferably 48 hours.

2. Preheat the oven to 325 degrees. Remove the venison from the marinade and pat it dry. In a flameproof casserole just large enough to hold the roast, heat the remaining 1½ tablespoons oil over moderately high heat. Add the venison and cook, turning, until browned all over, 5 to 7 minutes. Pour the marinade over the roast and cover the pot tightly. Place in the oven and cook 2 hours. Turn the roast over and continue cooking, covered, 1½ to 2 hours longer, until the meat is fork tender. Remove to a carving board.

3. Remove and discard the bay leaves from the pot. In a blender or food processor, puree the cooking liquid and vegetables. Season the gravy with additional salt and pepper to taste and reheat if necessary. Slice the venison roast against the grain and arrange on a platter. Ladle some of the gravy over the meat. Pass the remainder in a sauceboat.

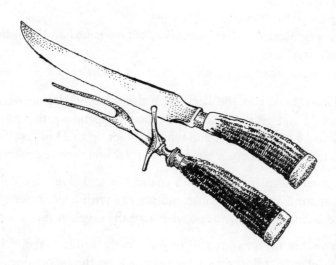

Lamb and Eggplant Spiedies with Garlic and Rosemary

4 to 6 servings

*L*amb is not as popular in markets around here, but it happens to be my favorite red meat, and this treatment is exceptionally tasty. The Plum Tomatoes Roasted with Garlic and Mint on page 160 make a fine accompaniment.

2 pounds lamb steak (from the leg), well trimmed and cut into 1½-inch cubes
⅓ cup extra virgin olive oil
¼ cup fresh lemon juice
3 garlic cloves, crushed through a press
1½ teaspoons rosemary, fresh if you have it
½ teaspoon salt
½ teaspoon freshly ground pepper
1 medium eggplant (1 pound), peeled and cut crosswise into 1-inch-thick slices
Coarse (kosher) salt
1 tablespoon chopped parsley plus a few sprigs of parsley

1. In a large bowl, toss the lamb with the olive oil, lemon juice, garlic, rosemary, salt, and pepper. Marinate at room temperature, tossing occasionally, for 1 to 2 hours, or cover and refrigerate for up to 24 hours. If the meat is chilled, let it stand at room temperature for 1 hour before cooking.

2. Sprinkle the eggplant slices with coarse salt and layer in a colander to drain for about 30 minutes. Rinse and pat dry with paper towels, pressing to remove as much moisture as possible. Cut the eggplant into 1-inch cubes.

3. Prepare a hot fire in your grill or preheat the broiler. About 5 minutes before you plan to grill the meat, remove it from the marinade and thread the lamb onto long metal skewers. Add the eggplant to the marinade left in the bowl and toss to coat. Thread the eggplant onto separate skewers.

4. Grill or broil the lamb and eggplant spiedies about 4 inches from the heat, turning, until the eggplant is tender and lightly browned and the lamb is browned outside and rosy pink inside, 8 to 12 minutes. Slide the spiedies off the skewers onto a platter or individual plates. Sprinkle the chopped parsley over the eggplant for a touch of color and garnish with sprigs of parsley.

PEANUT BUTTER
SPIT-ROASTED LEG OF LAMB

8 servings

My friend Karen Carr, who lived in Indonesia for a time, gave me this easy recipe. It makes an unbelievably tender, juicy, and savory leg of lamb, with just the right edge of nutty flavor to complement the smokiness of the grill. Some of the marinade will fall off the meat in clumps as it rotates on the rotisserie. Scoop up what you can and smear it back on the lamb, but don't worry too much; it won't affect the flavor.

1 leg of lamb, 5 to 6 pounds
1 pound freshly ground peanut butter or 1 jar (16 to 18 ounces)
    peanut butter
1 jar (8 ounces) Dijon mustard
2 tablespoons soy sauce
1 tablespoon fresh lemon juice
3 garlic cloves, crushed through a press

1. Trim the lamb of all excess fat. Insert both ends of a rotisserie skewer in the lamb and tie the leg onto the skewer with butcher's string to secure as snugly as possible.

2. In a medium bowl, combine the peanut butter, mustard, soy sauce, lemon juice, and garlic. Blend well. Smear the peanut butter marinade all over the lamb. Let stand at room temperature for 2 hours.

3. Light the grill and set the fire to medium-hot. Grill the lamb on the rotisserie for 1½ hours, or until medium-rare, 148 to 150 degrees on an instant-reading thermometer. Let stand for 10 minutes before carving.

Oven-Barbecued Pork

6 to 8 servings

This tangy meat, which makes great party food, tastes very much like its Southern inspiration, though it lacks that magic kiss of smoke. The sauce is strong and pungent, so the meat needs a bland counterpoint—mashed potatoes, cornbread, or rice and beans. Or consider shredding the meat and serving it over toasted buns. Coleslaw or braised kale is a perfect accompaniment.

> 5 pounds boneless pork butt (shoulder), well trimmed
> 2 cups water
> ½ teaspoon ground allspice
> ½ teaspoon thyme leaves
> ½ teaspoon freshly ground pepper
> 2 teaspoons salt
> 1 tablespoon fresh lemon juice
> 1 medium onion, minced
> 3 garlic cloves, crushed
> 1¼ cups cider vinegar
> ½ cup ketchup
> 2½ tablespoons packed dark brown sugar
> 1 tablespoon Worcestershire sauce
> 2 teaspoons ground cumin
> 1 teaspoon dry mustard
> 1 teaspoon imported sweet paprika
> ¼ teaspoon cayenne

1. Preheat the oven to 350 degrees. Cut the pork into 2- by 4-inch chunks 1½ to 2 inches thick. Place the meat in a heavy, nonreactive flameproof casserole with a lid. Add the water, allspice, thyme, pepper, 1 teaspoon of the salt, and the lemon juice. Cover and place in the oven. Braise, turning occasionally, 2 to 2½ hours, until the pork is tender.

2. Meanwhile, in a small nonreactive saucepan, combine the onion, garlic, vinegar, ketchup, brown sugar, Worcestershire sauce, cumin, mustard, paprika, cayenne, and remaining 1 teaspoon salt. Bring to a boil, stirring to dissolve the sugar.

COOKING FROM A COUNTRY FARMHOUSE

3. Pour the sauce over the pork. Increase the oven temperature to 375 degrees and bake, uncovered, basting with the sauce in the pan every 10 minutes, until the sauce is thickened and the pork is tender enough to shred with a fork, 35 to 45 minutes.

PORK SPIEDIES

4 to 6 servings

Because pork has to grill for such a relatively long time, I always cook any vegetables separately. Otherwise, they will be overdone and falling apart by the time the pork is ready. While the meat must be white throughout with no trace of pink in the center, it can—and should—remain juicy. Cremation is not required.

2 pounds well-trimmed boneless pork loin, cut into 1½-inch cubes
3 tablespoons olive oil
2 tablespoons sherry wine vinegar or red wine vinegar
2 tablespoons fresh lime juice
2 garlic cloves, crushed through a press
¾ teaspoon marjoram
½ teaspoon ground cumin
½ teaspoon salt
¼ teaspoon freshly ground pepper

1. In a medium bowl, toss the pork with all the remaining ingredients. Marinate at room temperature, tossing occasionally, for 1 to 2 hours, or cover and refrigerate for up to 24 hours. If the meat is chilled, let it stand at room temperature for an hour before cooking.

2. Prepare a hot fire in your grill. Remove the pork cubes from the marinade and thread them loosely onto 4 or 6 long metal skewers. (If you use wooden skewers, soak them in cold water for at least 1 hour to prevent charring.) Grill about 6 inches from the heat, turning occasionally, until browned outside and cooked through but still moist, 10 to 15 minutes.

MAPLE BAKED
PORK AND BEANS

6 to 8 servings

This dish is one of the all-American classics. While salt pork may not be part of your regular diet, it is a great treat once or twice a year, and it contributes a wonderful unctuousness to the beans. Order it from your butcher, if you can, to obtain salt pork with plenty of meat on it. Use a darker, amber maple syrup for more flavor.

> 1 pound small white navy pea beans
> ³/₄ pound meaty salt pork
> 2 large onions, preferably white, finely diced
> ¹/₂ cup ketchup
> ¹/₃ cup pure maple syrup
> ¹/₄ cup (packed) dark brown sugar
> 1 tablespoon Dijon mustard
> ¹/₄ teaspoon cayenne pepper
> 2 whole cloves
> 1 cup boiling water

1. Rinse the beans in a colander under cold running water. Pick them over and discard any grit. Place in a large bean pot or flameproof casserole (a heavy copper pot works well) and add cold water to cover by at least 2 inches. Soak overnight. (You can use the fast method of boiling the beans for 5 minutes and then letting them soak for 1 hour, but the results will not be as even.) Drain the beans.

2. Preheat the oven to 250 degrees. Cut the rind off the salt pork in one piece, leaving about ¹/₂ inch of the fat attached; reserve. Cut the remaining salt pork into strips about 1¹/₂ inches long, ¹/₂ to ³/₄ inch wide, and ³/₈ inch thick. Blanch the salt pork rind and strips in a large saucepan of simmering water for 5 minutes to remove some of the salt. Drain and rinse under cold running water; drain well.

3. In the same bean pot or large flameproof casserole, combine the beans, the salt pork strips, and all the remaining ingredients except the pork rind. Stir to blend well. Lay the rind on top, cover tightly, and bake 3 hours.

4. Remove the rind, cover again, and bake 3 to 5 hours longer, until the beans are tender and the liquid is reduced to a thick sauce. Check occasionally during the last several hours and add a little additional boiling water if necessary to prevent burning.

Farm-Style Sausage and Mashed Potato Loaf

6 to 8 servings

Nothing is more satisfying after a bracing afternoon of bicycling or a hike through the snow than this zipped-up version of meat loaf. Leftovers are great whether cold on sandwiches or sliced and fried with an egg on top for breakfast. How good and wholesome this tastes will depend upon the quality of your sausage. In the country, many local markets have fine butchers who pride themselves on their homemade sausage. Bulk sausage in the supermarket is a little more iffy. My closest country store has an owner/butcher—Freddy Hobbs—who makes excellent sausage, low in fat and light but definite on the seasonings.

The potatoes are baked rather than boiled for this recipe, both for the flavor and to add as little moisture as possible to the loaf. If you have leftover baked potatoes, by all means use them.

Since there are mashed potatoes and bread crumbs in the loaf, I often avoid another starch and instead serve two vegetables—buttered broccoli and steamed carrots, for example, or perhaps Orange Beet Salad (page 125). It's also nice to pass extra tomato sauce on the side. As an alternative flavor combination, omit the tomato sauce on top of the loaf and coat it lightly with a third of a cup of honey mustard instead. Here more mashed potatoes are called for, and a big bowl of Cinnamony Applesauce (page 261).

³/₄ pound baking potatoes
1¹/₂ pounds bulk pork sausage
3 eggs
1 can (8 ounces) tomato sauce
1 tablespoon Dijon mustard
¹/₄ teaspoon freshly ground pepper
¹/₄ teaspoon Tabasco
1¹/₂ cups dried bread crumbs
¹/₂ cup minced onion

1. Preheat the oven to 400 degrees. Prick the potatoes once and bake on the oven rack for 1 hour, until very soft. Cut in half and let cool; then scoop the potato into a large bowl and mash with a fork. There should be 1½ cups. (The potatoes can be baked and mashed up to a day ahead.)

2. Reduce the oven temperature, or preheat again, to 375 degrees. Remove the sausage from the refrigerator and set aside. Add the eggs to the mashed potatoes and beat well until blended. Mix in half the tomato sauce, the mustard, pepper, and Tabasco. Add the bread crumbs and onion and mix well.

3. Add the sausage meat to the bowl and knead with your hands until the ingredients are blended. On a small baking sheet, form the meat mixture into an oblong loaf about 10 inches long, 4 inches wide, and 2½ inches high.

4. Bake the meat loaf for 1 hour 10 minutes. Spread the remaining tomato sauce over the loaf. Bake for 15 minutes longer. Let stand for 5 to 10 minutes before slicing.

POTTED PORK

12 to 16 servings

Country people love this dish, which the French would call *rillettes*. While many of us eschew fatty meats on a daily basis, this is a special dish for entertaining, particularly welcome because it can be made in advance. I think you'll find it a treat. Serve with toasted French bread or crackers.

> 3½-pound boneless pork butt (shoulder)
> 1 tablespoon coarse (kosher) salt
> 1 teaspoon coarsely cracked pepper
> 1 teaspoon thyme leaves
> ¾ teaspoon crushed sage
> ¼ teaspoon ground allspice
> 3 large garlic cloves, crushed through a press

1. Leave all the fat on the pork (it will cook off later). Cut the pork and fat into 1-inch squares about ½ inch thick. Put the pork, all the other ingredients, and 3 cups water into a large, heavy pot with a lid. Bring to a boil, reduce the heat to moderately low, cover, and simmer for 45 minutes.

2. Uncover, increase the heat to moderate, and cook, stirring occasionally, until the water is evaporated and the meat is so tender it is falling apart, about 1½ hours. Increase the heat to moderately high and cook, stirring frequently, until the meat near the bottom starts to brown, about 10 minutes.

3. Drain into a sieve set over a bowl, pressing on the meat with a large spoon to release as much fat as possible; reserve the fat. Put the meat into a medium bowl and mash and tear it apart with two forks until there are no lumps of meat.

4. Beat 3 tablespoons of the reserved liquid fat into the meat paste. Pack tightly into a large crock or several individual ramekins. Cover and refrigerate until the fat hardens, about 1 hour. If the remaining reserved fat has set, melt it in a microwave or over low heat until liquid. Pour over the potted pork to seal. Refrigerate until set, then cover with a sheet of plastic wrap directly on the surface or with a cover. Scrape off the top layer of fat before serving. The pork spread will keep in the refrigerator for 1 to 2 weeks.

BLACKENED RED SHRIMP

4 servings

These were originally called "Orange Barbecued Shrimp," but the first time I made them I left them under the broiler a little too long, and they charred slightly around the edges. It happened that the added smokiness enhanced the flavor, and they were immensely popular. My friend Frank Mroczka rechristened them "Blackened Red Shrimp," and so they've remained.

Use shrimp graded large, which as we all know are really small, if you plan to serve these on toothpicks as an hors d'oeuvre. For a shellfish main course, the jumbo are more practical.

1 pound large (or jumbo) shrimp, shelled and deveined
1 orange
3 tablespoons ketchup
1½ tablespoons soy sauce
1 tablespoon fresh lemon juice
2 teaspoons sugar
1 teaspoon Madras curry powder
1 tablespoon vegetable oil
¾ teaspoon Asian sesame oil

1. Rinse the shrimp, drain, and pat dry. Grate enough of the orange zest (the colored part of the peel) to measure ½ teaspoon. Cut the orange in half and squeeze out 3 tablespoons of juice.

2. In a medium bowl, combine the orange zest, orange juice, ketchup, soy sauce, lemon juice, sugar, curry powder, vegetable oil, and sesame oil. Stir to blend well and dissolve the sugar. Add the shrimp and marinate, tossing occasionally, 2 hours at room temperature or up to 6 hours in the refrigerator.

3. Preheat your broiler so it gets good and hot. Line a broiler pan or baking sheet with heavy-duty aluminum foil. Remove the shrimp from the marinade and arrange on the foil in a single layer. Broil as close to the heat as possible without turning, 2 to 3 minutes for large shrimp, 3 to 5 for jumbo, until the shrimp are just opaque throughout and are beginning to brown on top. If you want to try them "blackened," leave them in for an extra 30 to 60 seconds.

BASS BAKED WITH TOMATOES, WHITE WINE, AND OLIVES

4 to 6 servings

*O*f course this dish is best made with that wide-mouthed bass you caught this afternoon—that's what it was designed for. But if the fishing hole is dry, or you just couldn't get off work, a market-fresh striped bass or whole red snapper will cook up almost as well.

> 4 1/2- to 5-pound largemouth bass, gutted, cleaned, and scaled,
>   head and tail left intact
> 1/2 teaspoon salt
> 1/4 teaspoon pepper
> 1/4 teaspoon hot Hungarian paprika or several dashes of cayenne
> 2 tablespoons fresh lemon juice
> 1/4 teaspoon oregano leaves
> 3 tablespoons extra virgin olive oil
> 1 medium onion, sliced
> 2 large garlic cloves, thinly sliced
> 1/2 cup dry white wine or vermouth
> 1 can (14 ounces) Italian peeled tomatoes, coarsely chopped,
>   with their juices reserved
> 2 tablespoons chopped parsley
> 2 ounces pimiento-stuffed green olives, sliced (about 1/2 cup)

1. Preheat the oven to 425 degrees. Rinse the fish well inside and out. Pat dry with paper towels. Season the outside of the fish and its cavity with 1/4 teaspoon of the salt, the black pepper, paprika, and half the lemon juice. Sprinkle the oregano into the cavity of the fish.

2. In a large oval gratin dish or a flameproof rectangular baking dish, heat the olive oil. Add the onion and cook over moderate heat until softened and almost golden, about 5 minutes. Add the garlic and cook 1 minute longer.

3. Add the wine to the dish and bring to a boil. Add the tomatoes with their juices and 1 tablespoon of the chopped parsley. Place the fish in the dish. (If you use the rectangular pan, you may need to bend the tail of the fish so that it fits inside the dish.) Spoon the sauce up over the fish.

4. Tent the fish with a length of aluminum foil and bake for 30 minutes, basting once or twice. Baste again and add the olives to the dish. Sprinkle the remaining lemon juice over the fish. Bake uncovered for 10 to 15 minutes longer, or until the fish is cooked to the center and opaque white next to the bone. Garnish with the remaining 1 tablespoon parsley and dish out the fish with some of the sauce and olives spooned over each serving.

Herb-Breaded Bass

4 servings

The first fish I ever caught up here was a three-and-a-quarter-pound large-mouth bass. At the request of my fifteen-year-old fishing instructor, I prepared it this way. Children especially seem to find breaded fish more palatable. I make this dish with a crispy crust and very little fat by giving the fish a preliminary browning and then finishing the cooking in the oven.

1 freshly caught 3- to 3½-pound largemouth bass, filleted with the skin
    removed, or 2 pounds firm white fish fillets, such as halibut or snapper,
    cut about 1 inch thick
2 cups fine fresh bread crumbs, made from 4 or 5 slices of firm-textured
    white bread
1 teaspoon savory
¾ teaspoon oregano
½ teaspoon thyme leaves, preferably lemon thyme
½ teaspoon imported sweet paprika
1 teaspoon coarse (kosher) salt or ½ teaspoon table salt
¼ teaspoon freshly ground pepper
⅛ teaspoon cayenne
2 garlic cloves, crushed through a press
½ cup all-purpose flour
1 egg
1½ tablespoons plus 2 teaspoons olive oil
2 tablespoons unsalted butter
Lemon wedges

1. If they need it, soak the fish fillets in a bowl of cold, lightly salted water for 10 minutes to remove most of the blood. Rinse and pat dry with paper towels.

2. In a wide, shallow bowl or pie plate, combine the bread crumbs, savory, oregano, thyme, paprika, salt, pepper, cayenne, and garlic. Mix with a fork until blended. Place the flour on a plate or a sheet of waxed paper. In another bowl, beat the egg with 2 teaspoons of the olive oil until well blended.

3. Dip the fish fillets in the flour, then in the egg, letting the excess drip back into the bowl, and finally in the seasoned bread crumbs to coat. Pat the crumbs lightly to help them adhere. Place the fillets on a plate or baking sheet and refrigerate for 20 to 30 minutes to set the coating.

4. Preheat the oven to 400 degrees. In a large ovenproof skillet or gratin dish large enough to hold the fillets in a single layer, melt the butter in the remaining 1½ tablespoons olive oil over moderately high heat. Add the fish fillets and cook until the bottoms are nicely browned, about 5 minutes. Turn the fillets over with a wide spatula and cook until browned on the second side, about 3 minutes. If the coating seems to be browning too quickly, reduce the heat to moderate.

5. Transfer the pan to the oven and bake for 10 to 12 minutes, or until the fish is opaque throughout, with no translucency or pink in the center. Serve hot, with plenty of lemon wedges to squeeze over the fish.

GRILLED LOBSTER

4 servings

What's this recipe doing in a book entitled *Cooking from a Country Farmhouse*? Well, it's from Corsica, and one could argue that Corsica is rural. And although lobster is a luxury, it is one of the few types of fresh seafood available in supermarkets across the country.

Actually, this recipe was given to me years ago by a colleague, Marlene Swanson, who cooked in a restaurant on the island of Corsica one summer. It's one of my all-time favorite recipes, and I've always wanted to share it. It's for very special, once-in-a-blue-moon occasions with your closest friends.

The grill adds a subtle smokiness to the lobster, which soaks up the Cognac and crème fraîche like a sponge, not only adding extra flavor but acting as a tenderizer. As accompaniment, the butter sauce is an added extravagance, but well worth the extra effort and the calories. Trust me, it's a treat.

> 4 live lobsters, preferably female, 1¼ to 1½ pounds each
> Extra virgin olive oil
> Salt and freshly ground pepper
> ½ teaspoon minced fresh thyme leaves or ¼ teaspoon dried
> ¼ cup Cognac or Armagnac
> ¼ cup crème fraîche or 3½ tablespoons heavy cream mixed with
>   1½ teaspoons buttermilk
> Tarragon Butter Sauce (recipe follows)

1. Preheat a covered charcoal or gas grill to hot. Bring a very large pot of water to a rolling boil. Dunk in the lobsters head first, immediately cover the pot, and boil for 1 to 2 minutes, just until they are red and dead. Remove with tongs and, wearing a mitt to help you handle the hot shells, set the lobsters on their stomachs. Use kitchen shears to snip the tail open down the *back* of each lobster. Pry the shell apart a bit so that the lobster meat is exposed. Brush the tail meat with olive oil. Season lightly with salt, pepper, and a pinch of thyme.

2. Set the lobsters, cut sides down, on the grill and cook covered for 3 minutes. Turn the lobsters right side up (stomach down) and dollop a tablespoon of Cognac and then of crème fraîche onto the tail meat of each. Cover the grill and cook 5 to 7 minutes, until the lobsters are tender and cooked through. Serve hot, with the tarragon butter sauce on the side.

TARRAGON BUTTER SAUCE

Makes about ½ cup

> 2 tablespoons dry white wine
> 2 tablespoons Champagne vinegar or white wine vinegar
> 1 tablespoon minced shallot
> 1 teaspoon minced fresh tarragon or ½ teaspoon dried
> 8 tablespoons (1 stick) cold unsalted butter

1. In a small heavy nonreactive saucepan, preferably enameled, combine the wine, vinegar, shallot, and tarragon. Bring to a boil over moderately high heat and boil 2 to 3 minutes, until the liquid is reduced to about 1½ tablespoons.

2. Remove from the heat and immediately add 3 tablespoons of the cold butter. Whisk until the butter is almost incorporated, then add another tablespoon. Continue until all the butter is added and the sauce is the consistency of a thin mayonnaise. If necessary, return to low heat briefly. Serve at once or set aside over a bowl of hot water for up to 30 minutes.

NOTE: If the sauce breaks or if it cools and congeals completely, reheat gently over low heat, then whisk in another tablespoon or two of butter until the sauce is thickened.

Baked Macaroni and Cheese with Crispy Crumb Topping

6 servings

There is only one secret to great macaroni and cheese: great Cheddar cheese. If you use a bland, mediocre mass-market brand, you'll end up with bland, mediocre macaroni and cheese. There's no way around it. Look for a farmhouse Cheddar, domestic or imported, or a supersharp cheese that has been aged for at least two or preferably three years. In the southern part of Pennsylvania, the Amish make wonderful Cheddar, as do many fine producers in New England and Wisconsin. Other good cheeses come in from England and Canada. I'd make my own if I weren't so lazy.

The crumb topping adds an extra dimension of texture as well as flavor, turning ordinary macaroni and cheese into a dish fit for company. For a special Sunday supper, start with Farmhouse Vegetable Beef Soup (page 34) and serve a lovely salad along with or after the macaroni. Easy Apple Coffee Cake (page 192) would make an especially appropriate dessert.

3/4 pound (3 cups) elbow macaroni
3 tablespoons unsalted butter
2 tablespoons all-purpose flour
1 garlic clove, crushed through a press
2 cups milk
1/4 teaspoon salt
1/8 to 1/4 teaspoon cayenne, to taste
8 ounces Cheddar cheese—the sharpest you can find—shredded
    (about 4 1/2 cups)
2 1/2 teaspoons Dijon mustard
Crispy Crumb Topping (recipe follows)

1. Preheat the oven to 375 degrees. Butter a 14-inch oval gratin or shallow 2-quart baking dish. Bring a large saucepan of salted water to a boil. Add the macaroni and cook until almost tender but still slightly hard in the center, about 7 minutes. Drain into a colander.

2. In a large heavy saucepan, melt 2 tablespoons of the butter over moderately low heat. Add the flour and cook, whisking, about 1 minute, until the

mixture bubbles up whitish in color across the entire bottom of the pan. Stir in the garlic and gradually whisk in the milk, salt, and cayenne. Raise the heat to moderate and bring to a boil, whisking until smooth and thickened. Remove from the heat. Gradually stir in the cheese until melted. Whisk in the mustard.

3. Add the macaroni to the cheese sauce and stir until well mixed. Turn into the buttered dish. Sprinkle the Crispy Crumb Topping evenly over the top. Dot with the remaining 1 tablespoon butter.

4. Bake uncovered 20 to 25 minutes, until the dish is bubbling and the top is golden brown. Let stand for about 5 minutes before serving.

CRISPY CRUMB TOPPING

Makes about 2 cups

> 4 slices of firm-textured white bread
> 1/3 cup chopped shallots
> 1/3 cup coarsely chopped parsley
> 2 garlic cloves, crushed through a press
> 1 1/2 teaspoons imported hot paprika or 1 1/2 teaspoons sweet
>   paprika and several dashes of cayenne
> 1/4 teaspoon salt
> 1/4 teaspoon freshly ground pepper
> 2 tablespoons unsalted butter
> 1 tablespoon olive oil

1. Tear the bread into pieces and place in a food processor. Add the shallots, parsley, crushed garlic, paprika, salt, and pepper. Process, pulsing the machine quickly on and off, until the bread is ground into coarse crumbs and the ingredients are well mixed.

2. In a large skillet, melt the butter in the oil over moderate heat. Add the seasoned crumbs and cook, stirring frequently, until the crumbs are toasted to a light golden brown and the garlic is fragrant, 3 to 5 minutes.

Spaghetti with Fresh Tomatoes and Zucchini

4 to 6 servings

*O*f course we eat pasta in the country. This is one of those lazy summer dishes, for when you really don't feel like doing a lot of cooking and the garden is just reaching its peak. The simplicity of the preparation really extols the glories of vine-ripened tomatoes, and if you have freshly picked zucchini, you'll find the texture of it lightly steamed to be extremely pleasing, a perfect match for al dente pasta. Serve with a little cheese as a first course for six, or a lot of cheese as a meatless main course for four.

3 large ripe tomatoes, cut into 1/2-inch dice
3 to 4 tablespoons shredded fresh basil
1 small garlic clove, finely minced
1/4 cup extra virgin olive oil
1 teaspoon salt
1/4 teaspoon freshly ground pepper
Dash or 2 of crushed hot red pepper flakes
2 medium zucchini
1 pound thin spaghetti or spaghettini
Grated Romano or Parmesan cheese

1. In a large serving bowl, combine the tomatoes, basil, garlic, olive oil, salt, pepper, and hot pepper flakes. Toss to mix and set aside at room temperature for about 15 minutes.

2. While the tomatoes are marinating, scrub the zucchini with a vegetable brush. If they are fat, cut them in half lengthwise. Thinly slice the zucchini and steam them over boiling water until just tender but not mushy, 1 1/2 to 2 minutes. Add the zucchini to the tomatoes.

3. Bring a large pot of salted water to a boil. Add the pasta and cook until tender but still firm to the bite, 8 to 10 minutes for the spaghetti, 6 to 8 minutes for the spaghettini. Scoop out about 1 cup of the pasta cooking water and reserve; drain the pasta.

4. Add the spaghetti to the bowl with the tomatoes and zucchini. Add ½ cup of the reserved pasta cooking water and toss well to mix. If the pasta seems dry (it probably won't), add a little more of the pasta water. Serve at once, with a bowl of grated cheese and a pepper mill passed on the side.

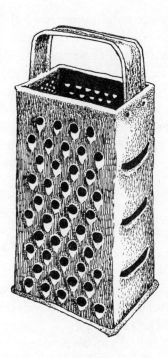

LINGUINE WITH EGGPLANT AND ANCHOVIES

4 servings

This is a more wintry pasta dish, inspired by the classic Italian eggplant *agrodolce*, or sweet-and-sour eggplant. It came about when a couple of friends dropped over unexpectedly, and these were the ingredients I happened to have lying about. We ate it as a main course, with a generous sprinkling of cheese, but it can serve just as well as a first course for six people with or without the cheese.

I find that eggplant browns especially well in a cast-iron skillet, but if you use one, you'll have to switch to a nonreactive pan in step 3.

> 2 medium eggplants
> Coarse salt
> 2 to 3 tablespoons olive oil
> 1/4 cup extra virgin olive oil
> 1 green bell pepper, diced
> 6 garlic cloves, thinly sliced
> 1/2 cup slivered almonds (by all means use pignoli if you have them)
> 1 can (2 ounces) flat anchovy fillets, drained and coarsely chopped
> Dash of crushed hot red pepper flakes
> 1/3 cup currants, plumped in 1/2 cup hot water
> 2 tablespoons balsamic vinegar
> 1/2 teaspoon coarsely ground black pepper
> 8 kalamata olives, pitted and halved or quartered (optional)
> 1 pound thin linguine or spaghettini
> Grated Romano and/or Parmesan cheese

1. Trim off the ends of the eggplants and cut the vegetables crosswise into 1/2-inch slices. Sprinkle the slices with coarse salt and layer in a colander to drain for at least 30 minutes or up to 2 hours. Rinse off the eggplant slices under cold running water and dry well with paper towels, pressing to remove as much moisture as possible.

2. In a large nonreactive skillet, heat 2 tablespoons of the olive oil over high heat. Add as many eggplant slices as will fit in a single layer and cook, turning once, until browned on both sides, about 3 minutes. It doesn't matter if the eggplant is not quite cooked through; it will finish cooking later. If the slices begin to burn, reduce the heat slightly. Remove to a paper-towel–lined platter to drain. Repeat in batches with the remaining eggplant slices, adding the remaining 1 tablespoon olive oil as necessary to prevent sticking. When the eggplant is cool enough to handle, cut into 1-inch chunks.

3. Wipe out the skillet. Add the extra virgin olive oil to the pan and heat over moderate heat. Add the green pepper and garlic and cook, stirring occasionally, for 2 minutes. Add the almonds and cook, stirring often, until the garlic is soft but not brown and the almonds are beginning to color, 2 to 3 minutes longer.

4. Add the anchovies and hot pepper flakes to the skillet and cook, stirring, for about 30 seconds. Add the currants with their soaking liquid, the balsamic vinegar, black pepper, and olives. Return the eggplant to the pan. Reduce the heat to moderately low and simmer, partially covered, until the eggplant is tender and the flavors have blended, 5 to 10 minutes.

5. Meanwhile, in a large pot of boiling salted water, cook the linguine until just tender but still slightly firm to the bite, 6 to 8 minutes. Scoop out and reserve 1 cup of the pasta cooking water. Stir ½ cup into the eggplant sauce. Drain the linguine into a colander and add to the sauce. Toss gently. Add the remaining ½ cup cooking liquid only if needed to coat the pasta. Serve hot. Pass a bowl of grated cheese and a pepper mill on the side.

Gazpacho Pasta

4 to 6 servings

There are moments, when the yellow and black butterflies are toying with the wild purple irises by the stream and the garden has just been planted, which pull me out of the kitchen. Days when the landscape looks like an Impressionist canvas and playing outdoors—canoeing down the river, perhaps—is more appealing than standing over the stove. I'm so hungry that dinner, enjoyed only after the sun has set, has to be thrown together in a flash. That's when I turn to recipes like this one, quick and light but tantalizing. This dish gets better after it sits for a few hours.

> 12 ounces capellini or spaghettini
> 2 cups cut-up ripe tomatoes
> 1 cup (loosely packed) fresh basil
> 3/4 cup cut-up red bell pepper (1/2 large)
> 3/4 cup cut-up yellow bell pepper
> 1/2 cup cut-up Vidalia or other sweet onion
> 1 garlic clove, crushed
> 2 teaspoons balsamic vinegar
> 3 tablespoons extra virgin olive oil
> 1 teaspoon coarse salt
> 3/8 teaspoon freshly ground pepper
> Dash or 2 of hot pepper flakes
> Grated Pecorino Romano cheese

1. Bring a large pot of salted water to a boil. Add the capellini and return to a boil. Cook, stirring occasionally, until just al dente (tender but still firm), about 3 minutes. Drain into a colander.

2. Meanwhile, in a food processor or blender, combine all the remaining ingredients except the cheese. Pulse 6 to 8 times, then let the motor run for 5 seconds. Scrape down the side of the bowl. Pulse again until the vegetables are minced.

3. Turn the pasta into a large bowl. Pour most of the sauce over the pasta and toss. Top with the remaining sauce and serve warm, at room temperature, or chilled. Pass a bowl of grated Romano cheese on the side.

TOMATO RABBIT

4 servings

In some places, this may be called "rarebit," but up here, with all the critters, it is definitely a "rabbit." My mother made a fifties version of it with processed cheese and canned tomato soup when I was a child. Only when I tasted it on a trip to Wisconsin made with a local handmade Cheddar aged in someone's private cellar for five years, did I realize just how good the dish could be. It makes a perfect meatless lunch or supper, comforting both in its taste and texture and in its improvement upon the past.

3 tablespoons butter
1 small onion, chopped
2 1/2 tablespoons flour
1 1/2 cups dark ale, such as Killian's Red, or milk
1/3 cup tomato paste
1/2 teaspoon salt
1/4 teaspoon Tabasco
Dash of Worcestershire sauce
1 egg
6 ounces sharp aged Cheddar cheese, shredded
Toasted white bread or English muffins

1. In a medium nonreactive saucepan, melt the butter over moderate heat. Add the onion and cook, stirring occasionally, until softened, about 3 minutes. Add the flour and cook, stirring, 1 to 2 minutes without allowing the flour to color.

2. Gradually whisk in the ale or milk. Bring to a boil, whisking until smooth and thickened. Stir in the tomato paste, salt, Tabasco, and Worcestershire. Reduce the heat to moderately low and simmer 5 minutes.

3. Whisk in the egg until blended. Add the cheese and whisk until melted and smooth. Serve over toasted white bread or English muffins.

GARDEN VEGETABLES, SALADS, AND STUFFINGS

By all rights this chapter should be entitled "Dining on What the Deer Didn't" or "Eating What the Woodchuck Wouldn't." I'll never forget the August afternoon that I glanced out of the kitchen window and saw a four-point buck big as a truck planted plop in the middle of the garden, blissfully chowing down on my carefully tended crop of just-ripe tomatoes. Or the evening I encountered the Rambo of woodchucks stuffing his fat furry face with my special mail-order Italian chard. Just for spite, I harvested one serving for dinner that night before it all disappeared.

But when you *can* beat the critters to it, eating from the local earth is one of the great pleasures of country living. Rural gardening, however, is not a genteel pastime. With its strategic planning and fortifications, it resembles nothing less than a military campaign. The growing season here embraces only about one hundred reliable days. Planting outside before Memorial Day is risky, and the first frost will easily appear before the middle of September is past. In summer, there may be drought or, alternatively, too much rain.

Forget about the tiny pests and plant diseases that can be mastered with trial and error; try keeping out the largest deer population ever recorded in the Northeastern United States. And then, of course, there are still the woodchucks, rabbits, porcupines, chipmunks, raccoons, opossums, moles and voles, skunks, and squirrels. Having dogs helps; having them in the house doesn't. Some try electric fences. Others swear by raised beds. Most just swear and insist they've had it: Next year they'll buy at the market.

While growing your own vegetables appears at first glance to be an economic enterprise, toting up losses, I reckon last year's zucchini cost me about eighty-five dollars a pound. Of course, as soon as those first seductive seed catalogues show up at the door early in February, we all forget last year's foul weather and four-footed pilfering. The pleasures of the garden are primal.

It was only when I left the city that I discovered many vegetarian delights, from the pleasing idiosyncrasies of the more old-fashioned vegetables, such as dandelion greens and kale, to the exquisite but ephemeral quality of pristine familiar produce. Just-picked peas and asparagus, like corn, are candy-sweet, even tasty raw. Potatoes dug freshly from the ground have a fine texture and a flavor as delicate as that of artichoke. All they need are simple steaming and a slip of butter. Nonetheless, I also like them mashed with buttermilk, which gives them a low-fat, nutty tang. I like them sliced and scalloped in milk and cream with plenty of winter savory to add a peppery punch. I like them in soup, baked and stuffed, sautéed with lots of onions to make hash browns. I even like the skins, roasted in the oven until they are crackling crisp. If you can't tell by now, I like potatoes any which way at all.

Out here, with no market importing exotic produce at romantically inflated prices, I've learned to appreciate the best of each season. First there are the young greens, wild and cultivated: dandelion, sorrel, wild leeks. Then come peas and the other early vegetables. My favorite spring dinner consists of an unadorned but perfectly cooked leg of lamb or fresh chicken accompanied by a spectacular platter of colorful roast vegetables: slender whole carrots, pencil-thin asparagus, turnips and potatoes the size of marshmallows, shallots or small onions, even radishes. A garlicky sweet red pepper and almond sauce dresses both the meat and the vegetables, which are definitely the stars of the meal.

In summer come different kinds of pole and bush beans, each with its own subtle flavor and texture. Picked young, they illustrate how delightful a vegetable cooked until "crisp-tender" can be, and help you understand why this particular cooking direction is so ludicrous in winter, when the only fresh beans are tough and fibrous. Some people grow cauliflower, others broccoli. Lettuce and onions come up for months.

When you're lucky, your pepper plants yield peppers, and when you're even luckier than that, the deer don't eat them. Toward the end of the season, tomatoes, both red and green, separately and together, offer almost boundless possibilities, and everyone smiles when the corn is green. Our growing season is not usually long enough for eggplant, though this year, which was unseasonably warm, gave rise to minor successes and a lot of major bragging. There are always infinite zucchini and, come fall, larger squash and pumpkins. In winter, root vegetables—sweet potatoes, turnips, rutabagas, carrots—save the day. Broccoli travels well, and frozen spinach, in my opinion, is fine for cooking.

Dried beans, those semi-digestible, fiber-rich little nuggets packed with carbohydrates, provide a healthy change of pace all year round. There are a million and one ways you can cook them or toss them in salads, not to speak of soups. And stuffing, of course, is a quintessential country side dish. I've only given two versions here, but they are two of my favorites: a local very traditional bread stuffing, which, if you wish, is designed to be made in industrial quantities; and a rich, more complex chestnut and dried fruit stuffing of my own, which goes particularly well with wild turkey and goose, though it tastes just fine spooned steaming from the insides of a humble supermarket turkey, roasted to a gorgeous mahogany brown.

SNAP BEANS WITH RICE AND TOMATOES

6 servings

Snap beans, which are flatter, thicker, and wider than ordinary green beans, have a sturdier texture and more pronounced flavor, and they are easy to grow. My favorite variety is labeled "Romano beans." This is one way to use in them in summer when they are in abundance, and it is a dish that works well in winter with frozen snap beans as well. If you are using the frozen kind, let them defrost and stir them in during the last five minutes of cooking.

2 tablespoons olive oil
1 medium onion, diced
2 garlic cloves, chopped
1/4 teaspoon dried oregano leaves
1 cup long-grain white rice
1/2 pound snap beans, trimmed and cut into 1-inch lengths (2 cups)
1 can (14 ounces) peeled whole tomatoes, drained and coarsely chopped
1 can (14 1/2 ounces) reduced-sodium chicken broth
1/4 teaspoon salt
1/4 teaspoon freshly ground pepper

1. In a large heavy saucepan or small Dutch oven, heat the olive oil. Add the onion and cook over moderate heat, stirring occasionally, until the onion is softened and the edges are just beginning to brown, about 5 minutes. Add the garlic and cook 1 minute longer.

2. Add the oregano and the rice. Cook, stirring, until the rice is coated with the oil. Add the beans, tomatoes, chicken broth, salt, and pepper. Stir to mix. Bring to a boil. Reduce the heat to low, cover, and simmer for 20 to 25 minutes, until the liquid is absorbed and the rice is tender.

SNAP BEAN SUCCOTASH

4 to 6 servings

While succotash is traditionally made with lima beans and no tomatoes, I don't grow lima beans—and I love fresh ripe tomatoes. I also have a bumper crop of snap beans and other types of green beans that last, if I plant them right, for a couple of months through July and August. Just in time for the tomatoes and corn.

You'll probably notice that most of the recipes in this book are relatively low in fat, and I cook mostly with olive oil. However, a few recipes just cry out for butter and cream. They're so delicious it's worth the splurge. This is one of them. It is particularly good with grilled chicken or pork chops.

1 medium onion, chopped
4 tablespoons (1/2 stick) unsalted butter
3/4 pound snap beans, cut into 1/2-inch lengths (2 cups)
3/4 pound vine-ripened tomatoes, seeded and cut into 1/2-inch dice (1 1/2 cups)
1 cup corn kernels, cut from about 3 ears (or substitute canned or thawed frozen)
2/3 cup heavy cream
1/2 teaspoon fresh lemon juice
Dash of cayenne
1/4 teaspoon salt
1/8 teaspoon freshly ground pepper

1. In a large skillet or flameproof casserole, cook the onion in the butter, covered, over medium-low heat 3 minutes. Uncover and cook, stirring often, until the onion just begins to color, about 3 minutes longer.

2. Add the snap beans and toss to coat with the butter. Cook, stirring occasionally, until the onion is golden brown, 2 to 3 minutes. Add the tomatoes and corn and toss to mix.

3. Add the cream and lemon juice and season with the cayenne, salt, and pepper. Cover, reduce the heat to low, and cook, stirring occasionally, until the beans are just tender and the cream is reduced to a thick sauce, 3 to 5 minutes. Remove from the heat and let stand, covered, for a few minutes to allow the flavors to blend. Serve hot.

Green Beans with Peanut Sauce

6 to 8 servings

While peanuts are not uncommon in Southern country cooking, this recipe was actually inspired by the cooking of another country: Indonesia. The cooked beans are topped with a simplified version of the sauce that graces the Indonesian national salad, *gado-gado*. You'll find this a popular vegetable dish at the table or on the buffet, and it is equally good warm or at room temperature. For extra color, garnish with a few slivers of sweet red pepper.

1 pound green beans, ends trimmed
1/2 cup peanut butter, smooth or chunky (natural is best)
1 tablespoon (packed) dark brown sugar
1 tablespoon soy sauce
1 tablespoon lemon juice
1 large garlic clove, smashed
2 or 3 thin slices of peeled fresh ginger
1/2 cup hot water

1. Bring a large pot of lightly salted water to a boil over high heat. Add the green beans and cook until tender, about 5 minutes. Drain and rinse briefly under cold running water.

2. Meanwhile, in a food processor, combine the peanut butter, brown sugar, soy sauce, lemon juice, garlic, and ginger. Process until smooth. With the machine on, add the hot water and mix until well blended.

3. Transfer the beans to a serving dish. Pour the sauce over the beans and serve. If you prefer the dish hotter, reheat in a microwave oven on High for 50 to 60 seconds, rotating the dish once. (If you do this, be sure the serving dish is microwave-safe glass or ceramic.)

Green and Yellow Beans with Balsamic Vinegar

4 servings

I like to use one pan to minimize cleanup, so I cook these beans in a skillet. This is quick, and good hot, cold, or at room temperature.

½ pound green beans
½ pound wax beans
2 tablespoons olive oil
1 large onion, sliced
1 tablespoon balsamic or sherry wine vinegar
Salt and freshly ground pepper

1. Rinse the beans well and drain in a colander. Trim off the ends and, if the beans are long, break them in half.

2. Bring a large nonreactive skillet of lightly salted water to a boil. Add the green and wax beans and cook until just tender but still brightly colored, about 5 minutes. Drain into a colander and rinse briefly under cold running water. Let drain. Rinse and dry the skillet.

3. In the skillet, heat the olive oil over moderately high heat. Add the onion and sauté, stirring occasionally, until soft and golden brown, 5 to 10 minutes.

4. Return the beans to the pan and toss with the onions to coat and reheat them. Drizzle the vinegar over the beans and season with salt and pepper to taste.

BARBECUED BEAN SALAD

8 to 12 sevings

.

This salad, which is one of my most popular potluck offerings, improves if it stands at room temperature for an hour or two before serving. If you like, make it a day ahead, but crumble the tortilla chips over the top at the last minute so they stay crisp.

1 package (16 ounces) dried pinto beans
1/4 cup ketchup
1/4 cup cider vinegar
1/4 cup light olive oil
3 tablespoons packed brown sugar
1 1/2 tablespoons chili powder
1 tablespoon Worcestershire sauce
1 teaspoon ground cumin
1 teaspoon salt
1/4 teaspoon pepper
1/4 teaspoon Tabasco
1 1/2 tablespoons Dijon mustard
1 medium red bell pepper, diced
1 medium green bell pepper, diced
1 medium white onion, finely diced
1 can (11 ounces) vacuum-packed corn niblets
4 ounces crushed corn tortilla chips or 1/4 pound bacon,
    cooked until crisp and crumbled

1. Rinse the beans and pick over to remove any grit. Place in a large pot with enough water to cover by at least 2 inches. Let the beans soak overnight. (Alternatively, bring them to a boil. Cover, remove from the heat, and let stand for 1 hour.) Drain and rinse the beans. Return them to the pot, add enough fresh water to cover them by at least 2 inches, and bring to a boil. Reduce the heat slightly and simmer 1 to 1½ hours, or until tender but not falling apart. Drain, rinse under cold running water to stop the cooking, and drain well.

2. Meanwhile, make the dressing. In a small nonreactive saucepan, combine the ketchup, vinegar, olive oil, brown sugar, chili powder, Worcestershire sauce, cumin, salt, pepper, and Tabasco. Bring to a boil, reduce the heat to low, and simmer for 10 minutes. Remove from the heat and whisk in the mustard. Set the barbecue dressing aside.

3. To assemble the salad, in a large bowl, combine the cooked pinto beans, the red and green bell peppers, white onion, and the corn. Toss lightly to mix. Pour the barbecue dressing over the beans and toss to coat evenly. Shortly before serving, fold half the crushed tortilla chips into the salad. Sprinkle the remaining chips over the top. Serve at room temperature.

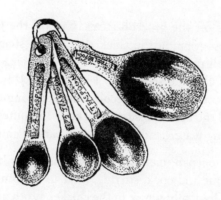

BROCCOLI AU GRATIN

4 to 6 servings

Creamed vegetables may seem old hat, but perhaps we've just forgotten how good they can be. Every time I serve this fine accompaniment to roasted chicken and meats, it is the first side dish to go.

1 large bunch of broccoli (1 to 1¼ pounds)
3 tablespoons unsalted butter
2 tablespoons all-purpose flour
½ cup reduced-sodium chicken broth
1 cup milk (2 percent is fine)
½ teaspoon salt
⅛ teaspoon freshly ground pepper
Dash of grated nutmeg
Dash of cayenne
Few drops of lemon juice (optional but desirable)
1 cup coarsely grated Swiss or Gruyère cheese (4 ounces)

1. Trim the ends off the broccoli stems. Cut off the florets and set aside. Peel the stems by gripping the thick skin at the stem end between your thumb and a small paring knife. Pull and it will come right off. Repeat all around the stem. Cut the stems into 1-inch chunks. In a large saucepan of boiling salted water, cook the broccoli stems for 2 minutes. Add the florets and cook until all the broccoli is tender, about 3 minutes longer. Drain, rinse under cold running water, and drain well. Coarsely chop the broccoli.

2. In the same saucepan, melt 2½ tablespoons of the butter over moderate heat. Add the flour and cook, stirring, for 1 to 2 minutes without coloring to make a roux. Gradually whisk in the chicken broth and the milk. Increase the heat to moderately high and bring to a boil, whisking until thickened and smooth. Reduce the heat to moderately low and boil gently, whisking, for 3 minutes. Season with the salt, black pepper, nutmeg, cayenne, and lemon juice. Remove from the heat and stir in the broccoli and ¾ cup of the Swiss cheese. Stir until the cheese is melted. Turn the broccoli mixture into a buttered shallow 1½- to 2-quart casserole or baking dish. Sprinkle the

remaining cheese evenly over the top and dot with the remaining butter. (The recipe can be prepared ahead to this point.)

3. Preheat the oven to 375 degrees. Place the casserole in the oven and bake uncovered 20 minutes, or until the dish is bubbling hot and lightly browned on top.

ORANGE BEET SALAD

4 servings

This fat-free dish tastes best when there are baby sugar beets dug right out of the kitchen garden, but it is excellent year round. Baking the beets rather than boiling them seals in and intensifies the flavor. In a pinch, you can even use sliced canned beets with a half teaspoon of sugar.

2 bunches of small beets
2 navel oranges
1 to 2 tablespoons orange juice (optional)
2 tablespoons red wine vinegar
1/4 teaspoon ground coriander

1. Preheat the oven to 375 degrees. Cut off the beet leaves, leaving at least 3 inches of the stems attached to the beets. Reserve the leaves for another use. Leave the roots intact. Wrap the beets in a double layer of aluminum foil and bake for 45 to 60 minutes, or until tender. Unwrap and let cool. Then trim off the stems and roots and rub off the skins; they will come off easily. Slice the beets, halving them first if they are larger than 1 1/2 inches.

2. While the beets are baking, cut the peel with all the white pith off the oranges. Holding them over a bowl to catch the juice, cut down on both sides of the membranes to release the orange segments; cover and refrigerate. Squeeze the membranes over the bowl to release as much juice as possible. Pour the juice into a measuring cup. If there is not 1/4 cup, add the additional juice.

(continued)

3. Put the beets in a bowl. Add the orange juice, vinegar, and coriander; toss gently to mix. Set aside at room temperature for up to 3 hours, or refrigerate overnight. Just before serving, drain off the marinade and toss the beets with the orange segments. Serve chilled or at room temperature.

Broccoli Rabe with Summer Squash and Onions

6 servings

Broccoli rabe is an Italian vegetable, but these days you'll find it in supermarkets across the country, and I'm seeing it much more often in my local market. With a slight bitterness adding an interesting note missing from plain broccoli, its tamer cousin, the green cooks up quickly—a boon for busy evenings.

This dish turns out an attractive yellow and green color, and the slight sweetness of the squash, the cooked onions, and the balsamic vinegar provides a lovely counterpoint to the bite of the broccoli rabe.

> 1 bunch of broccoli rabe (about 1 pound)
> 3 tablespoons olive oil, preferably extra virgin
> 1 large onion, sliced
> 2 large garlic cloves, halved and thinly sliced
> ³⁄₄ pound yellow squash, sliced about ¹⁄₄ inch thick

Cooking from a Country Farmhouse

¹/₄ teaspoon salt
¹/₄ teaspoon freshly ground pepper
Dash of crushed hot red pepper flakes, or more to taste
1 tablespoon balsamic vinegar

1. To prepare the broccoli rabe, swish it around in a bowl of cold water and drain in a colander. If you're feeling lazy, just cut the flowery and leafy tops and thin stems into 1-inch pieces. If you have a bit more time and energy—it doesn't take much—peel the thick stems the same way you would celery, by gripping the skin between your thumb and first finger and the edge of a small knife at the bottom and pulling up the skin so that it peels off.

2. In a large saucepan or flameproof casserole, heat the olive oil. Add the onion, cover the pan, and cook over moderately low heat for 5 minutes. Uncover, increase the heat to moderately high, and cook, stirring occasionally, until the onion is just turning golden, about 5 minutes longer.

3. Add the garlic and cook for 30 seconds. Add the squash and cook, stirring often, until the squash is about half cooked, 3 to 5 minutes. Season with the salt, black pepper, and hot pepper flakes.

4. Add the broccoli rabe by handfuls, stirring it in so that it wilts in the hot pan. Cover the pan, reduce the heat to moderate, and cook for 2 minutes. Uncover the pan and cook, stirring occasionally, until the broccoli rabe and the squash are just tender and any excess liquid is evaporated, 2 to 3 minutes longer. Stir in the balsamic vinegar and serve.

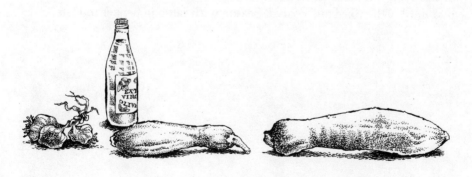

GARDEN VEGETABLES, SALADS, AND STUFFINGS

Brussels Sprouts and Carrots with Dill Butter

6 to 8 servings

Carrots mate sweetly with almost any other vegetable, and this combination is a classic country match. It is best served, I think, with roast turkey or pork.

> 1½ pounds Brussels sprouts
> 1 pound carrots
> 2 tablespoons unsalted butter
> 1 teaspoon sugar
> 2 tablespoons chopped fresh dill or 2 teaspoons dried
> 1 tablespoon lemon juice
> Salt and freshly ground pepper

1. Trim and rinse the Brussels sprouts and cut a small X into the root end of each. If they are very large, cut them in half lengthwise. Peel the carrots and cut them crosswise on the diagonal into ½-inch slices.

2. In a large pot of boiling salted water, cook the carrots for 3 minutes. Add the Brussels sprouts and cook the vegetables together until they are both tender but still firm to the bite, 5 to 7 minutes longer. Drain well. (The vegetables can be prepared ahead up to this point.)

3. Shortly before serving, melt the butter in a saucepan over moderate heat. Add the vegetables and sprinkle on the sugar. Toss over the heat for a couple of minutes, until hot and glazed. Sprinkle on the dill and lemon juice and toss until well mixed and coated. Season with salt and pepper to taste.

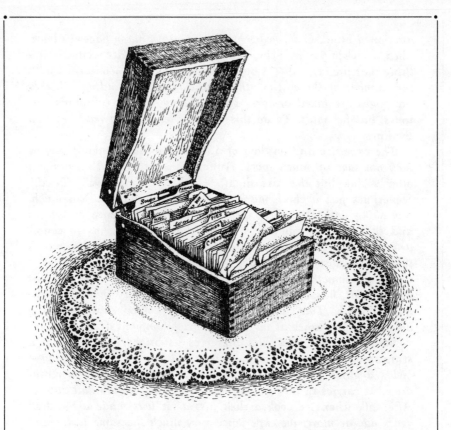

· FARMHOUSE RECIPES ·

Farmhouse recipes are inscribed largely in a language of women. The words they use are deceptively concise. Behind the shorthand lists and directions are years of cooking, feeding, nurturing, making do. Handed down from mother to daughter, aunt to niece, mother-in-law to daughter-in-law, these recipes comprise a priceless maternal legacy. Shared verbally at first, they are edited accidentally or on purpose, embellished, attenuated, and reinterpreted before being recorded in a smudgy penciled hand or spidery scrawled script in the margins of cookbooks, on yellowing paper or neatly lined cards, sometimes hidden in a secret journal.

People do not always value their legacies. I search for these culinary treasures at country auctions, used-book shops, yard sales, antique stores. Sometimes journals are sold as books. Recipes collected over a lifetime may be bundled in an old wooden box and

(continued)

auctioned blind. Old cookbooks often contain blank pages in back, filled in, when you're lucky, with the owner's favorite recipes. Anything that predates 1940 I buy indiscriminately, unconcerned with the number of the edition, the condition of the binding, whether the pages are foxed or torn. I am looking not for collector's volumes, but for souls. To do this involves learning to read between the lines.

The expertise and wisdom of a lifetime of homemaking may or may not take up much space. Annotations on printed recipes can offer a clue, but they are slight: "Good!," "Made this," "Tried." Sometimes just a check mark appears in the margin. Not much, but along with clipped recipes, they provide evidence of choices and taste. In the country, most of the interest seems to center around baked goods, desserts, and preserves. But nothing conjures up kitchen ghosts more vividly than the cook's original script.

There's something about a homey, handwritten recipe that, for me at least, has more intimations of immortality than a monumental tomb. That it was chosen to be copied says something about its importance at the time. A brief comment or explanation —"It's the lemon juice that preserves its bright red color" on a strawberry preserve; "Good with whipped cream" on a pudding— yields a glimmer of personality. Every time that recipe is reproduced it carries in its incarnation the spirit of its familial author. After all, when we cook a dish just as it was made a hundred years ago or more, we experience very much the same tastes and smells and textures. An old recipe allows us, if we wish, to sit down at table for a moment with a long-departed spirit.

One spring day, about six months after I moved here, my nearest neighbor, Marie Soden, invited me over. She knew I was writing this book, and she offered to share any of her old recipes that might be helpful. At the age of seventy, she was a kindly, generous woman, who had raised five strapping sons, helped her husband on the dairy farm, driven the local school bus parttime, and still donated her time to cook for the Baptist church, which was dear to her heart. Since half a dozen women cook on occasion for at least a hundred people for church functions, they pass their recipes around so everyone can help out. They've done it this way for generations. Each dish is always scrupulously assigned to whoever is recognized as its author. I've often wondered how many of these recipes are original and how many claimed through preference and adoption. Nonetheless, in Marie's book, each recipe was at-

COOKING FROM A COUNTRY FARMHOUSE

tributed to a particular name. I sat down with her that day, and we pored through her well-used collection of cooking notebooks and cards.

We came upon one called "Edith Fancher's Scalloped Corn," and I caught my breath. This was the woman who, as her seventy-two-year-old daughter told me, had birthed six children in the southeast corner of my living room. She was the one who had planted five kinds of daffodils all about the yard, who picked out the nine layers of wallpaper that once covered my kitchen walls, who chose the lilac bushes, the umbrella-shaped hydrangea tree, the great silver maple that shelters the front of the house, and the varieties of heirloom apples out back. She was the harbinger of the warmth that graces my home. Giddily, I felt as if I were meeting her at last.

Another recipe was for "Josie Soden's Sweet Green Tomato Pickles." Josie Soden was Marie's mother-in-law. She passed away in 1963, and no one had made her pickles for thirty years. Months later, when the first green tomatoes filled out on the plants, I picked them early, made the recipe, and gave Marie's husband, Bill, a jar, sweet and crunchy, redolent of cinnamon and cloves. He took them without much fuss, but a few weeks later, after he had eaten them, he came up to me with his blue eyes shining and told me how good they were. You could tell by his shy smile the memories were much more effective than the taste.

Marie is gone now. The first person I met in my new home was the first person to depart, and she is greatly missed. But every now and then, when I look over my own handwritten notebooks and come across one with her name, or when I follow one of her recipes, I smile and remember her exactly as she was. For a cook, a person's name on a recipe is not a trivial testament. Next to a poem, a song, or a play, it is one of the warmest, most personal memorials any of us can leave behind.

MARIE SODEN'S
THREE-DAY CABBAGE SALAD

12 to 16 servings

Marie Soden's husband, Bill, is a second-generation dairy farmer, and his son Dave has now taken over the farm, which neighbors mine. Marie was a sweet, down-to-earth woman, who perfected her cooking early on, because her own mother preferred doing "men's chores" outdoors and left the housekeeping to her eldest daughter. Marie was extremely generous with her time, and her interest in my project moved me deeply.

I've seen other versions of this recipe entitled "Endless Coleslaw." The name derives, I believe, more from the longevity of the salad than from our location in the Endless Mountains. One source stated it kept for up to six months, but six to ten days is all I'll give it.

> 3 pounds cabbage (1 medium to large head), shredded
> 1 large green bell pepper, chopped
> 1 large carrot, shredded
> 2 medium onions, chopped
> ¾ cup sugar
> ¾ cup vegetable oil
> 1 cup cider vinegar
> 1½ teaspoons salt
> 1½ teaspoons celery seed

1. In a large ceramic or stainless steel bowl, combine the cabbage, green pepper, carrot, and onions.

2. In a medium nonreactive saucepan, combine the sugar, oil, vinegar, salt, and celery seeds. Bring to a hard boil. Pour the dressing over the cabbage salad and toss well.

3. Let the cabbage salad cool slightly, tossing once or twice. Cover tightly and refrigerate for at least 3 days before serving. (Many local townspeople like this salad after it's sat for up to a week.)

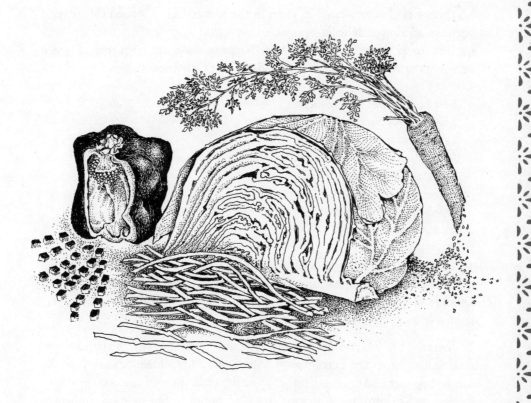

Sautéed Cabbage with Browned Onions and Lemon

4 to 6 servings

Cabbage is always available, even in the hinterlands. Cooked this way, it becomes an almost delicate vegetable that makes a particularly fine accompaniment for pork or chicken. When shopping, look for crisp, bright green leaves and a white stem end as an indication of freshness.

> 2 medium onions, thinly sliced
> 2 tablespoons olive oil
> 2 teaspoons sugar
> 1 small head of cabbage (about 1½ pounds), shredded, tough core
>   discarded (about 8 cups)
> ¾ teaspoon salt
> ½ teaspoon freshly ground pepper
> 3 tablespoons lemon juice

1. In a large Dutch oven, cook the onions in the oil, covered, over moderately low heat, stirring occasionally, until very soft, 5 to 7 minutes. Uncover, sprinkle on the sugar, and cook, stirring frequently, until the onions are golden brown, 15 to 20 minutes.

2. Increase the heat to moderately high and gradually stir in the cabbage, mixing it up from the bottom as it wilts, until all is added. Season with the salt and pepper and cook, stirring frequently, until the cabbage is translucent, tender, and beginning to brown, about 15 minutes. Sprinkle on the lemon juice and serve.

Honey Glazed Carrots

4 servings

If you do live in the country, or if you are a city dweller with access to a good specialty food shop, it's worth looking for goldenrod honey for this recipe. It has a light, delicate, decidedly buttery flavor that goes particularly well with carrots. Of course, any kind of honey will serve nicely.

1 pound carrots (5 or 6 medium), peeled and thickly sliced, or cut
*   with a rolling cut into ³/₄-inch pieces (see Note on page 43)*
2 tablespoons unsalted butter
1 large shallot, minced (about 2 tablespoons)
¹/₈ teaspoon salt
¹/₈ teaspoon pepper
1 generous tablespoon honey

1. In a heavy medium saucepan, combine the carrots, butter, and minced shallot. Season with the salt and pepper and pour in ¹/₃ cup water. Cover tightly and cook over moderately low heat, stirring occasionally, until the carrots are tender, 20 to 25 minutes. (The dish can be prepared to this point up to several hours in advance. Set aside at room temperature.)

2. Add the honey and cook over moderately high heat, stirring gently, until the carrots are hot and glazed, 1 to 2 minutes.

EDITH FANCHER'S SCALLOPED CORN

6 to 8 servings

Creamed corn has fallen out of favor, but I notice that whenever I serve this homey pudding, it quickly disappears. Velvety and easy to eat, it goes well with almost any country food. While scalloped corn is no gastronomic marvel, this recipe has particularly warm associations for me, because it comes down from the mother of the family who lived in my house almost a century ago.

> 3 eggs
> 2 cans (16 ounces each) cream-style corn
> 1/4 teaspoon freshly ground pepper
> Dash of cayenne
> 2 tablespoons unsalted butter, melted
> 1 2/3 cups milk
> 1 cup saltine cracker crumbs (about 28 crackers, finely crushed)
> 1 teaspoon baking powder

1. Preheat the oven to 350 degrees. In a large bowl, beat the eggs until blended. Mix in the corn, pepper, cayenne, melted butter, milk, cracker crumbs, and baking powder. Turn the mixture into a lightly buttered shallow 2- to 3-quart baking dish.

2. Bake 30 to 40 minutes, until the pudding is just set.

CORN OYSTERS

Makes 16 to 20

If you drop the batter into the pan properly—that is, sideways off a spoon —you'll see how these fritters came upon their name. They make an unusual hot hors d'oeuvre or first course, and wouldn't be bad on a brunch table, either. While it never occurs to me to make them except when the corn is green, you can, of course, use 1¼ to ½ cups canned or frozen corn kernels.

> 2 ears of corn
> ¾ to 1 cup peanut oil or other light vegetable oil
> ½ cup all-purpose flour
> ½ teaspoon sugar
> ½ teaspoon baking soda
> ¼ teaspoon salt
> Dash of cayenne
> 1 egg
> ⅓ cup buttermilk
> Maple syrup

1. Bring a large saucepan of unsalted water to a boil. Add the corn and cook 2 minutes, or until the kernels are just tender. Remove the ears with tongs and rinse under cold running water. With a large sharp knife, cut the corn kernels off the cobs. Set aside.

2. Heat ¼ inch of oil in a large heavy skillet, preferably cast iron, over moderate heat. While the oil is heating, in a medium bowl, combine the flour, sugar, baking soda, salt, and cayenne. Whisk to blend. Make a well in the center and add the egg. Beat until blended. Whisk in the milk and stir in the corn kernels.

3. Drop the batter by tablespoons into the hot oil. Fry in batches without crowding until nicely browned on the bottom and about half cooked through, about 3 minutes. Turn over with a wide spatula and cook until the oysters are browned on the second side and cooked through to the center. Adjust the heat as necessary. Drain on paper towels. Serve hot, with a bowl of maple syrup on the side for dipping or a pitcher of syrup for drizzling over the top if you plan to plate them.

· DANDELION GREENS ·

Few people born in Pennsylvania can resist a dandelion salad. In fact, I've seen tears come to the eyes of normally impassive, manly faces when they begin to reminisce about their grandmother's or grandfather's family recipe. While this is particularly true of denizens hailing from the German (i.e., Deutsch, or "Dutch") southern part of the state, I have noticed its effects on northerners, as well. This nostalgia stems, I believe, less from the food itself than from the dandelion's position in the seasonal world of country living. Like the phoebe or the robin, it is one of the very first signs of spring.

Dandelion is definitely a controversial taste, bitter to a fault. Some crave it; others chew it slowly, screw up their faces, and try to be polite. If you are one of those who enjoy Campari, endive, and arugula, dandelion is another vegetable to explore. It is usually eaten in salads, raw, or wilted and warm. Because of its extreme bitterness, it is often balanced, as endive is, with vinegar, sugar, and salt.

Connoisseurs search for infant dandelion leaves before the ground shows any sign of green. They say that if you know where to look, the youngest, tenderest, mildest shoots can be unearthed from beneath dead brown leaves, which shield them from still frost-ridden weather, against embankments and under hedges, as early as April. Once the flowers bloom, the greens become much more bitter.

To harvest dandelion greens, take a good-sized sturdy knife—an old butcher's knife, if you have one. Stick the knife in the ground at an angle so that it cuts off the dandelion plant below the ground level. The leaves will come off in a bunch with some of the root attached. When you are ready to use it, cut off the root, separate the tender leaves, and wash the dandelion well.

City sissy that I am, I planted the French cultivated variety the first year I established my kitchen garden, just down from the porch. This plant is designed to produce a plethora of leaves with fewer and later flowers and to grow back after being cut practically all season long. It tastes fine to me, but Carl, my carpenter, a leader among cognoscenti of the hunted and gathered, turns up his nose at them and prefers stalking the wild dandelion.

WILTED DANDELION SALAD

4 servings

This is an absolutely traditional Pennsylvania Dutch recipe, but I'm sure there are others like me who have never seen it before. My friend Kent, whose family came to America from Germany in 1750 and whose recipe this is, speculates that along with the German sweet-and-sour seasonings, which were familiar to the early settlers, the dish became so popular because it was one of those simple country recipes made with ingredients that would be found on every farm. He remembers with obvious pleasure how often he and his mother would make a meal out of this dandelion salad and boiled potatoes, accompanied sometimes with a slice of fried ham or a pork chop.

6 thick slices of lean bacon
1 egg
2 tablespoons sugar
⅓ cup half-and-half or light cream
3 tablespoons cider vinegar
8 cups tender young dandelion greens
Freshly ground pepper

1. Cut the bacon slices into 1-inch squares. Fry them in a large, well-seasoned cast-iron skillet over moderately low heat until they are cooked but not brown or crisp, 3 to 5 minutes.

2. Meanwhile, in a small bowl, mix together the egg, sugar, cream, and vinegar until well blended. Take the bacon out of the fat and set it aside. Reduce the heat to very low. Pour in the egg mixture and stir it around briskly so that it doesn't scramble. As soon as it begins to thicken, dump in the bacon and the dandelion greens.

3. Immediately remove the skillet from the heat and toss until the greens wilt. Season with pepper to taste and serve at once.

Sautéed Salad of Dandelion Greens and Wild Leeks

4 servings

I love the way the sweetness of wild leeks complements the bitterness of dandelion. If you don't have wild leeks, or ramps, available, substitute scallions and add a crushed garlic clove at the beginning of step 2. Although it sounds as if this recipe calls for a lot of dandelion greens, the measurement is not packed, and you will be surprised at how far down they wilt, much like spinach.

6 thick slices of lean bacon (about ½ pound) cut crosswise into ¼-inch strips
2 tablespoons olive oil
2 cups slivered ramp (wild leek) bulbs, about 2 inches long
2 cups shredded ramp greens
8 cups dandelion greens, well rinsed
1 tablespoon plus 1 teaspoon sugar
2 tablespoons cider vinegar
3 tablespoons water

1. In a wok or large flameproof casserole, cook the bacon strips in the olive oil over moderate heat until they are lightly browned and have given up much of their fat, 3 to 5 minutes. Remove the bacon with a slotted spoon and set it aside.

2. Add the ramp bulbs to the wok, increase the heat to moderately high, and sauté for about 2 minutes, until they soften. Add the ramp greens and stir-fry until wilted, about 1 minute.

3. Add the dandelion greens and cook, tossing, until partially wilted, 1 to 2 minutes. Sprinkle on the sugar and season with salt and pepper to taste. Add the vinegar and water, increase the heat to high, and cook, tossing, about 2 minutes longer, until most of the liquid has evaporated.

4. Add the bacon, toss to mix, and serve warm.

Stir-Fried Jerusalem Artichokes

4 to 6 servings

When the artichokes are fresh, you can just scrub the skins well with a vegetable brush if you like, but I prefer to peel them. If you don't use them at once, be sure to drop them into a bowl of acidulated water—that is, cold water mixed with a little vinegar or lemon juice—to prevent them from turning brown. Here is a very simple way to fix them.

> 2 tablespoons olive oil
> 1 medium onion, sliced
> 1½ pounds Jerusalem artichokes, scrubbed well, peeled if you wish, and sliced
> Salt and freshly ground pepper

1. In a wok or large skillet, heat the olive oil. Add the onion and cook over moderately high heat, stirring often, until softened but still somewhat crisp and pale golden, 3 to 5 minutes.

2. Add the Jerusalem artichokes, reduce the heat to moderate, and cook, again stirring often, until they are tender but still slightly crunchy, 3 to 5 minutes. Season with salt and pepper to taste.

Braised Kale and Leeks

6 servings

Like many greens, kale is very high in calcium and vitamin A. This preparation, which combines it with meltingly tender leeks, is exceptionally savory. I like to serve it with Maple Baked Pork and Beans (page 94) for an almost meatless main course.

> 1½ pounds kale
> 3 large leeks
> 4 tablespoons (½ stick) unsalted butter
> 3 whole garlic cloves, unpeeled
> 1¼ cups unsalted homemade chicken stock or
>   reduced-sodium canned broth
> Salt and freshly ground pepper

1. Rinse the kale well and remove the tough stems. Cut the leaves into 1-inch pieces. There will be 5 to 6 cups.

2. Split the leeks down the center. Rinse very well under cold running water. Cut off the top 2 inches and remove any damaged or excessively thick outer portions. Unlike most recipes that call only for the white and "tender green," this one uses the entire leek. Slice the leeks; there will be about 4 cups. Place the sliced leeks in a large bowl of cold water and swish them around to remove any stubborn dirt. Lift them out into a colander, rinse again under cold running water, and drain. It won't matter if there is some moisture clinging to them.

3. In a large saucepan or flameproof casserole, melt the butter. Add the leeks and the whole garlic cloves, cover, and cook over low heat, stirring occasionally, until tender, about 20 minutes.

4. Add the chicken stock and bring to a boil. Add the kale, in batches if necessary, stirring until it is slightly wilted. Cover and cook over moderately low heat, stirring occasionally, until the kale is tender, about 25 minutes. Season with salt and pepper to taste. Remove the garlic before serving.

BUTTERMILK MASHED POTATOES

4 servings

If you decide to double or even triple this recipe to feed a large party, you may want to cook the potatoes whole in their skins, which saves a lot of fuss and preparation time. Start them off in a large pot of cold water and bring them to a boil. They'll take about fifteen minutes longer to cook, but the skins will just slip off when they're done. Buttermilk adds a wonderful tang, and it has only half a percent more fat than skim milk.

> 2 pounds baking potatoes, peeled and cut into 2-inch chunks
> 3 tablespoons unsalted butter
> 1/2 to 2/3 cup buttermilk
> 3/4 teaspoon salt
> 1/4 teaspoon freshly ground pepper
> Dash of cayenne

1. In a large saucepan of boiling salted water, cook the potatoes until they are very soft, 15 to 20 minutes. Drain into a colander.

2. Put the hot potatoes through a ricer or beat with an electric mixer until mashed. (Do not puree in a food processor or you will end up with wallpaper paste.) Add the butter and beat until melted and smooth. Beat in 1/2 cup of the buttermilk. If the potatoes are still too thick, beat in the remaining milk, 1 tablespoon a time, until they are of the desired consistency. Season with the salt, pepper, and cayenne.

SAVORY SCALLOPED POTATOES

8 servings

Another plug for savory, my favorite old-fashioned herb. While there are a great many recipes for scalloped potatoes, potatoes are so popular that I figured there was room for one more. For everyday eating I make this dish with all milk, but half heavy cream turns it into sumptuous company fare.

6 large baking potatoes
3 tablespoons unsalted butter, melted
Salt and freshly ground pepper
1 large garlic clove, crushed
1½ teaspoons minced fresh savory
1 cup heavy cream or milk
About 1 cup milk

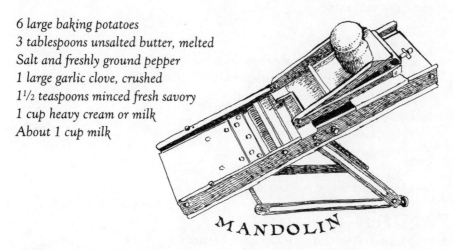

MANDOLIN

1. Preheat the oven to 375 degrees. Peel the potatoes and thinly slice, using a mandolin if you have one.

2. Layer half the potato slices in a buttered 2½- to 3-quart flameproof gratin dish. Drizzle 1½ tablespoons melted butter over the potatoes. Season liberally with salt and pepper and sprinkle half the garlic and savory over the potatoes. Repeat with the remaining potatoes and butter, more salt and pepper, and the rest of the garlic and savory.

3. Pour the cream and 1 cup milk over the potatoes. If the liquid does not cover them, add enough additional milk to almost cover. Bring to a simmer over moderate heat and transfer to the oven.

4. Bake uncovered 1 hour 15 minutes, or until the liquid is absorbed and the potatoes are tender.

LEMON TARRAGON POTATO SALAD

6 to 8 servings

Especially good with more delicate foods, such as chicken, veal, or even a meaty fish, this is a lighter potato salad than either the traditional American mayonnaise or European olive oil and vinegar variety. I tend to make it when the herb garden is at its greenest. This potato salad is best served the same day it is made.

3 pounds red potatoes, scrubbed
2 tablespoons white vermouth or dry white wine
2 tablespoons Champagne vinegar or white wine vinegar
3 tablespoons extra virgin olive oil
1 teaspoon salt
1/4 teaspoon freshly ground pepper
1/3 cup mayonnaise
1/4 cup sour cream
1 teaspoon finely minced lemon zest
2 tablespoons fresh lemon juice
1 to 2 tablespoons minced fresh chives
2 teaspoons minced fresh tarragon or 1/2 teaspoon dried
Sprigs of fresh tarragon or parsley, for garnish

1. In a large saucepan of boiling water, cook the potatoes until tender at the center, 20 to 25 minutes. Drain into a colander, rinse under cold running water, and let stand until cool enough to handle. Then peel and cut into 3/4-inch dice.

2. While the potatoes are still warm, toss them in a serving bowl with the vermouth. Let cool to room temperature; then toss with the vinegar, olive oil, salt, and pepper.

3. In a small bowl, combine the mayonnaise, sour cream, lemon zest, lemon juice, chives, and tarragon. Stir to blend well. Add to the potatoes and toss. Garnish with the sprigs of tarragon. Serve at room temperature or slightly chilled.

COOKING FROM A COUNTRY FARMHOUSE

BAKED POTATO SALAD

8 to 10 servings

My friend Kevin Huffman is a compulsive cook. Nothing pleases him more than when friends drop by in twos and threes on a Sunday afternoon. When a family of four grows into a party of eight or more, he's delighted. Here's a terrific throw-together salad of his. With its roasted potatoes and mint, the flavor is a little different from that of the traditional potato mélange, and if anyone is on a restricted diet, there is no cholesterol. Mint grows like a weed in this climate; I think it grows like a weed everywhere but in the Sahara Desert. In any event, it is a must here.

1 (5-pound) bag red potatoes, scrubbed
2 pounds onions (5 or 6 medium), unpeeled
1/2 cup extra virgin olive oil
2 tablespoons balsamic vinegar
3/4 cup loosely packed mint leaves
1 garlic clove, crushed
1 1/2 teaspoons salt
1/2 teaspoon freshly ground pepper
1 pint cherry tomatoes, cut in half if large

1. Preheat the oven to 400 degrees. Set the potatoes and onions on 1 or 2 large baking sheets and roast at least 1 hour, until the potatoes are very soft throughout and the skins fairly crisp, and the onions are tender and browned on the outside. You may want to remove the onions 10 to 15 minutes before the potatoes, depending upon their size.

2. Let the vegetables stand until cool enough to handle; then halve, quarter, or cut the potatoes into 1 1/2-inch-chunks, depending upon their size. Slip off the onion skins and cut the onions into 1-inch wedges. Put the potatoes and onions in a large serving bowl.

3. In a food processor, combine the olive oil, vinegar, mint, garlic, salt, and pepper. Puree until the mint is finely chopped. Add three-quarters of the tomatoes to the salad. Pour the dressing over the top. Toss gently to coat. Season with additional salt and pepper to taste. Garnish with the remaining tomatoes and another sprig or two of mint. Serve at room temperature.

Oven-Fried Potato Skins

Recycled food is my favorite food. Save the skins whenever you bake potatoes and don't eat the outsides, or when you cook them in the skins but only need the insides for mashed potatoes. These make great snacks, and they are surprisingly popular as hors d'oeuvres.

FOR EACH POTATO:

1/2 teaspoon olive oil
Coarse salt

1. Prepare the potato skins by cutting the cooked potatoes in half, and scooping out the insides, leaving a 1/8- to 1/4-inch shell. Eat the potatoes or reserve them for another use. The skins can be prepared up to a day ahead. Wrap and refrigerate to store.

2. Preheat the oven to 400 degrees. Use 1/4 teaspoon olive oil to coat each potato skin half inside and outside. Sprinkle with coarse salt to taste. Set on an aluminum foil–lined baking sheet and oven-fry for 12 to 15 minutes, turning once, until crisp. Cut in half again to serve.

Oven-Fried
Sweet Potato Chips

4 to 6 servings

Sweet potatoes are good keepers, and while they are not grown in these parts, they are frequently seen in the markets. I prefer them cooked simply, as they are here.

2 pounds sweet potatoes
Peanut oil
Coarse (kosher) salt (optional)

1. Preheat the oven to 450 degrees. Peel the sweet potatoes with a swivel-bladed vegetable peeler and cut them crosswise into ¼-inch slices.

2. Lightly oil 1 or 2 baking sheets, preferably nonstick. Spread out the sweet potato slices on the baking sheets in a single layer. Brush the tops lightly with oil. Bake, turning twice with a wide spatula, until the potatoes are golden brown and crisp on the outside and tender inside, 30 to 35 minutes. Season lightly with salt if you like.

CHILI-CHEESE POTATO SKINS

6 servings

These appetizers are so popular it's impossible to make enough. The chili powder called for in this recipe is ordinary chili powder or chili con carne powder found on supermarket spice shelves.

Skins from 6 large baked potatoes
1½ teaspoons olive oil
1 teaspoon chili powder
1 teaspoon coarse salt
⅛ to ¼ teaspoon cayenne
4 ounces Cheddar or Monterey jack cheese, cut into 24 thin slices

1. Preheat the oven to 400 degrees. Rub the potato skins with the olive oil to coat lightly all over. Set the skins, cut sides up, on an aluminum foil–lined baking sheet.

2. Combine the chili powder, salt, and cayenne. Sprinkle lightly over the potato skins. Bake about 12 minutes, until crisp. Lay the cheese slices over the potato skins to cover to within ⅜ inch of the edges. Return to the oven and bake until the cheese is just melted, about 2 minutes. Serve hot.

Apple, Onion, and Rutabaga Puree

6 to 8 servings

.

Though I have only two mature apple trees, they yield plenty of fruit, and in good growing years I spend lots of time trying to think of new ways to use apples. This puree, with its touch of natural sweetness, gains extra depth of flavor from the browned onions and rutabaga. It goes especially well with roast turkey, pork, and duck.

> 1 medium rutabaga (about 2 pounds)
> 8 tablespoons (1 stick) unsalted butter
> 2 medium-large onions (3/4 pound total), coarsely chopped
> 2 large, flavorful cooking apples, such as Northern Spy (1 pound)
> 1/2 teaspoon salt
> 1/4 teaspoon freshly ground pepper
> 1/8 teaspoon ground allspice
> 1/8 teaspoon ground cinnamon

1. Peel the rutabaga with a sharp knife or swivel-bladed vegetable peeler and cut it into 2-inch chunks. Bring a large pot of salted water to a boil. Add the rutabaga and cook until soft, 35 to 45 minutes; drain.

2. In a medium saucepan or flameproof casserole, melt the butter over moderately low heat. Add the onions, cover, and cook, stirring occasionally, for 15 minutes. Uncover, increase the heat to moderate, and cook, stirring from time to time, until the onions are pale golden brown, about 15 minutes.

3. Meanwhile, peel and quarter the apples. Cut out the cores and cut the apples into 1-inch dice. Add to the onions, reduce the heat to moderately low, and cook, stirring frequently, until the apples are softened to a coarse puree, about 20 minutes.

4. Pass the apples, onion, and rutabaga through the medium blade of a food mill or puree coarsely in a processor. Return the puree to the saucepan and reheat, stirring, over low heat. Season with the salt, pepper, allspice, and cinnamon. Simmer, stirring, for a few minutes before serving.

Baby Beet and Spinach Salad

4 to 6 servings

*L*ate spring is the perfect time for this salad, when the first baby beets and tender leaves of spinach are coming up in your garden. I also make it in late winter, though, when those vegetables are coming up in somebody else's garden—down in Florida or out in California. Whenever you make it, and with whoever's produce, choose the smallest, freshest beets you can find— you can tell by the leaves (they should look bright green and recently picked rather than yellowish and wilted)—and the youngest, most tender spinach, preferably of the flat-leaf variety, which is far superior raw. It doesn't have that gritty residue that coats your teeth the way the curly kind does.

With the Roquefort cheese, this is a fairly substantial salad. While I enjoy it as a separate course after a light supper, you could serve it as a first course, or have it for lunch with a big chunk of whole-grain or sourdough bread.

1 bunch of baby beets (4 or 5 beets, 1½ to 2 inches in diameter)
1 tablespoon orange juice
1 tablespoon red wine vinegar
1 teaspoon sugar
½ bunch of fresh spinach, preferably flat leaf, or 1 (10-ounce)
 bag prewashed spinach
½ bunch of curly green or red oak leaf lettuce
¼ cup slivers of sweet white onion
1 tablespoon fresh lemon juice
½ teaspoon coarse salt
¼ teaspoon freshly ground pepper
3½ tablespoons olive oil
2 ounces Roquefort or other good blue cheese

1. Preheat the oven to 375 degrees. Trim the beets to leave 3 to 4 inches of stem. Wrap them up in a double layer of aluminum foil and crimp to seal tightly. Bake the beets 45 minutes. Remove from the oven and let cool in the foil. Then trim and peel; the skins will rub right off the beets. Slice the beets and put them into a medium bowl. Add the orange juice, 1 teaspoon

of the vinegar, and ½ teaspoon of the sugar. Toss to coat, cover, and set aside or refrigerate until you are ready to assemble the salad.

2. Rinse the spinach well. Remove the stems and tear any large leaves in half. Separate the lettuce leaves, remove any tough ends and tear the leaves into large bite-size pieces. If the spinach or lettuce is not quite as fresh and crisp as it should be, soak in a large bowl of very cold water for an hour. Remove and drain well. Dry spinach and lettuce leaves in a salad spinner or dry with paper towels.

3. Put the onion slivers in a large bowl. Sprinkle the remaining 2 teaspoons vinegar and ½ teaspoon sugar and the lemon juice, salt, and pepper over the onion. Toss to mix. Add 2½ tablespoons of the olive oil and toss again. Just before serving, add the spinach and lettuce and toss gently. Add the remaining 1 tablespoon olive oil and toss lightly.

4. To assemble the salad, make a bed of the greens on a large round or oval platter. About halfway to the edge, make a circle of the beet slices. If there are any juices left in the bowl, drizzle them over the beets. Coarsely crumble the cheese into the center. Serve at once.

House Salad

6 servings

In the city, I almost never threw a dinner party without serving four or five courses—a first course, main course, salad course, cheese plate, and dessert. Of course, it was overkill; that was the point. Anyway, as much as I still enjoy such leisurely dining upon occasion, most dinners somehow come to the point much quicker up here. I rarely offer a first course, except for soup or sometimes a tasty salad, such as this one. P.S.—People who think they don't like anchovies won't know there're in here unless you tell them.

6 flat anchovy fillets (half a 2-ounce tin), chopped
1½ tablespoons Champagne vinegar or red or white wine vinegar
1 tablespoon water
¼ teaspoon dried oregano
¼ teaspoon salt
⅛ teaspoon freshly ground pepper
Several dashes of crushed hot red pepper flakes
½ medium white onion, thinly sliced
1 large tomato, cut into thin wedges or ¾-inch cubes
1 small red bell pepper, cut into ¾-inch squares
½ jar (3 ounces) pimiento-stuffed olives, sliced
1 medium celery rib, sliced
1 medium carrot, peeled and very thinly sliced
1 small cucumber, peeled, seeded, and thinly sliced (optional)
3 to 4 tablespoons extra virgin olive oil
1 small head of iceberg lettuce, cut into 1-inch pieces

1. In a large salad bowl, use the back of a large spoon to mash the anchovies with the vinegar and water. Mix in the oregano, salt, pepper, and hot pepper flakes. Add the onion slices and toss well. Add the tomato, red bell pepper, olives, celery, carrot, and the cucumber if you're using it. Add 1½ table-spoons of the oil and toss to mix. Set aside for half an hour.

2. Shortly before serving, add the lettuce to the bowl, drizzle on another 1½ tablespoons olive oil, and toss. Taste and decide if you need the last tablespoon of oil or not. Serve the salad at room temperature.

GREEN TOMATO RATATOUILLE

6 to 8 servings

There is a time late in August or early in September, especially in good growing years, when the tomato plants lie low with their bounty, each tomato a different shade of brilliant crimson, some still apple green. I am indebted to my friend Pauline Ross for the idea of this intriguing vegetable mélange, which uses both ripe red and tart green tomatoes, as well as zucchini, which are probably still stalking the garden in chilling numbers.

Because of the tartness of the green tomatoes, no vinegar is used, though you can add a few drops of lemon juice if you think it needs it; I don't. Like the classic ratatouille, this one is good hot, at room temperature, or chilled.

1 large onion, cut into ½-inch dice
3 tablespoons extra virgin olive oil
2 garlic cloves, minced
1 small green bell pepper, cut into ½-inch squares
1 small red bell pepper, cut into ½-inch squares
2 large green tomatoes, cut into ¾- to 1-inch dice
2 medium zucchini, cut into ¾- to 1-inch dice
2 large ripe red tomatoes, cut into ½-inch dice
½ teaspoon salt
¼ teaspoon freshly ground pepper
Dash of crushed hot red pepper flakes

1. In a large nonreactive flameproof casserole (I use enameled cast iron), cook the onion in the olive oil over moderate heat until it is softened and just beginning to color around the edges, about 5 minutes. Add the garlic and the bell peppers and cook for 2 minutes.

2. Add the green tomatoes and the zucchini. Increase the heat to moderately high and stir frequently until the zucchini looks coated with oil and is beginning to cook, 2 to 3 minutes. Add the red tomatoes and season with the salt, pepper, and hot pepper flakes.

3. Cover the pan, reduce the heat to moderately low, and cook, stirring occasionally, until the zucchini and green tomatoes are tender and the red tomatoes are reduced to a thick sauce, 20 to 25 minutes.

SPICY FRIED GREEN TOMATOES

4 to 6 servings

Okay, Cajun comes from southern Louisiana, and this is northeastern Pennsylvania, but everyone loves hot food these days. Tart green tomatoes are one of the countryside's seasonal pleasures, and prepared this way, they are downright addicting. It is typical in these parts just to dip the tomato slices in the flour mixture and then fry them, but I find that the egg dip and extra layer of breading create a crisper crust that absorbs less oil and reheats well. Zucchini is also good cut lengthwise into three-by-four-inch slices and prepared this way.

½ cup all-purpose flour
3 tablespoons yellow cornmeal
¾ teaspoon coarse (kosher) salt
¼ teaspoon dried thyme leaves
¼ teaspoon freshly ground pepper
⅛ to ¼ teaspoon cayenne, to taste
1 egg
3½ tablespoons olive oil or other vegetable oil
3 medium-large green tomatoes

1. In a wide, shallow bowl, combine the flour, cornmeal, salt, thyme, pepper, and cayenne. Stir or whisk gently to mix. In another bowl, beat the egg with ½ tablespoon of the oil until well blended.

2. Cut the green tomatoes into ¼-inch slices. Dredge the slices in the seasoned flour to coat lightly; tap off any excess. Dip the slices in the egg mixture and then return them to the flour. Press firmly on both sides to coat nicely.

3. In a large heavy skillet, preferably nonstick, heat 1½ tablespoons of the oil over moderate heat. Add half the tomato slices, or as many as will fit in a single layer. Cook, turning once and adjusting the heat between moderate and moderately low as necessary, until the outside is nicely browned and

the tomato slices are tender, 5 to 7 minutes. (If it's early in the season and the tomatoes are very hard, they may take a couple of minutes longer.) Carefully wipe out the skillet with several paper towels to remove any browned flour and repeat with the remaining oil and tomato slices.

4. Drain well on paper towels before serving hot. If you wish to prepare these up to 2 hours ahead, brown them and set the slices aside at room temperature on a baking sheet. Shortly before serving, reheat them in a 375 degree oven for about 10 minutes, until hot and crisp.

Baked Tomatoes Stuffed with Mushrooms and Sorrel

6 to 8 servings

Served hot, this is a wonderful side dish with roast chicken or beef. At room temperature, it can be set out as part of a buffet. The sorrel adds a pleasing tartness. If it is not available, substitute 1½ to 2 tablespoons fresh lemon juice.

2 tablespoons unsalted butter
2 tablespoons olive oil
2 large shallots or 1 small onion, minced
½ pound mushrooms, finely chopped (I use a food processor)
¾ cup (packed) sorrel leaves, chopped (about ⅓ cup)
2 tablespoons heavy cream
¼ teaspoon salt
¼ teaspoon freshly ground pepper
Dash of cayenne
1 cup fresh bread crumbs
1 large garlic clove, crushed through a press
½ teaspoon thyme leaves (fresh or dried), preferably lemon thyme
1½ tablespoons chopped parsley
4 or 5 medium tomatoes

1. In a large skillet, melt 1 tablespoon of the butter in 1 tablespoon of the olive oil over moderate heat. Add the shallots and cook until softened, 1 to 2 minutes. Add the mushrooms, increase the heat to moderately high, and cook, stirring frequently, until the pieces begin to dry out and separate, 8 to 10 minutes. Add the sorrel and the cream and cook, stirring, 1 to 2 minutes. Scrape into a bowl and season with half the salt and pepper and the cayenne. Set aside.

2. Wipe out the skillet. Melt the remaining butter in the remaining oil over moderate heat. Add the bread crumbs and garlic and cook, stirring frequently, until the crumbs are golden brown, 3 to 5 minutes. Season with the thyme and the remaining salt and pepper. Scrape into a small bowl, stir in the parsley, and set aside.

3. Core the tomatoes as shallowly as possible and cut them horizontally in half. Using a curved, serrated grapefruit knife, hollow out the tomato halves, leaving a ³/₈- to ¹/₂-inch shell. If there is a hole in the bottom of any of the stem-end halves, plug it with a piece of the pulp. (Save the insides of the tomatoes for soup or sauce.) Season the tomato shells lightly with additional salt and pepper. (All the components of this dish can be made several hours ahead.)

4. Preheat the oven to 375 degrees. Add the bread crumbs to the mushroom-sorrel mixture and stir well to blend. Set the tomato shells in a large baking dish and fill each with the mushroom stuffing. Bake 15 minutes. Transfer to a broiler set about 6 inches from the heat and broil 2 to 3 minutes, until the top of the stuffing is lightly browned.

Plum Tomatoes Roasted with Garlic and Mint

4 to 6 servings

These tomatoes are copied after a dish I tasted at a country-style grill restaurant outside of Orvieto in the southern part of Tuscany. Actually, I asked for the recipe in broken Italian, and it was recited to me in fluent Italian, although I don't officially speak the language. Nonetheless, I was confident I had all the ingredients and only worried whether the intensity of flavor would come through with tomatoes not grown in the Mediterranean and not cooked in a wood-burning oven. In fact, I was amazed at how well the dish works in rural Pennsylvania; I hope you agree. These tomatoes are especially good with leg of lamb.

> 6 plum tomatoes, halved lengthwise
> Coarse salt and freshly ground pepper
> 1/4 cup packed fresh mint leaves
> 2 or 3 garlic cloves, chopped
> 2 tablespoons extra virgin olive oil

1. Preheat the oven to 350 degrees. Season the tomatoes generously with salt and give them a grinding of pepper. (I've learned from experience that lightly salting just won't give the same results.)

2. Chop the mint along with the garlic until the mint is finely chopped and the garlic is minced. Sprinkle over the tomatoes. Drizzle about 1/2 teaspoon olive oil over each tomato half.

3. Arrange the tomatoes in a small baking dish, nonstick if available, and bake 20 to 25 minutes, or until the tomatoes are soft but still hold their shape and the garlic is beginning to color. Serve hot or at room temperature.

Cooking from a Country Farmhouse

CASSOULET OF TURNIPS AND ONIONS

8 servings

Root vegetables are a country staple. People brag about how long they've been eating last year's earthy harvest out of their stone and dirt cellars. Easy to understand when you realize how hard—and expensive—it still is to get fresh produce in many sparsely populated rural areas.

This is my favorite turnip dish. It goes beautifully with roast goose or turkey.

1 pound small white boiling onions or shallots, peeled
2 tablespoons olive oil
1½ pounds peeled baby white turnips or quartered medium turnips
⅜ teaspoon salt
¼ teaspoon freshly ground pepper

1. Place the onions and olive oil in a heavy flameproof casserole, preferably enameled cast iron, large enough to hold the onions in a single layer. Cook over moderately high heat, rolling the onions over occasionally, until they are lightly browned, 5 to 7 minutes.

2. Add the turnips, season with the salt and pepper, and toss gently to mix with the onions and coat with the oil. Reduce the heat to moderately low, cover the pan tightly, and cook, stirring once or twice, until the onions are golden and all the vegetables are quite tender, about 25 minutes.

ROASTED RED PEPPER AND ALMOND SAUCE

Makes 3½ cups

I first learned about this Basque sauce, called Romesco sauce, from Paula Wolfert, food writer extraordinaire. While there's nothing distinctly sum-mery about it, I traditionally serve it in the green months, with spring lamb and roasted young vegetables or as a dip with fresh vegetables and big loaves of good bread. It's become one of my favorite potluck standbys, and it always receives raves. Everyone knows about pesto, but not everyone has tasted roasted pepper sauce, and few have a recipe for it. This one is simple and surefire, and it doubles perfectly for a large party.

> *1 pound red bell peppers (2 large)*
> *8 large garlic cloves*
> *2 medium plum tomatoes*
> *4 ounces natural whole almonds (1 cup)*
> *2 teaspoons cumin seeds*
> *1 tablespoon lemon juice*
> *1 teaspoon coarse (kosher) salt or ½ teaspoon table salt*
> *¼ to ½ teaspoon crushed hot red pepper flakes, to taste*
> *¼ teaspoon freshly ground black pepper*
> *3 tablespoons extra virgin olive oil*
> *¾ cup hot water*

1. Preheat the oven to 500 degrees. Cut the peppers lengthwise in half and remove the stems and seeds. Place them skin side up on a baking sheet along with the garlic cloves in their skins. Roast, turning the garlic cloves over once, for 20 minutes, or until the pepper skins are charred and the garlic is soft. Remove and set aside. Depending on the size of the cloves, you may want to remove the garlic a bit sooner than the peppers.) Reduce the oven temperature to 400 degrees.

2. Place the whole tomatoes on the baking sheet. Spread out the almonds on the same sheet and make a pile of the cumin seeds. Roast in the oven for 10 minutes, or until the tomato skins split, the almonds are light brown

inside, and the cumin seeds are crisp and toasted but not burned. The cumin seeds may be done a couple of minutes before the tomatoes and almonds.

3. While the tomatoes are roasting, peel the skin off the peppers, remove any thick ribs, and place the peppers in a food processor. Slip the garlic cloves out of their skins and add to the processor. When the tomatoes are done, peel and seed them and add to the processor along with the toasted almonds and cumin seeds, lemon juice, salt, hot pepper flakes, and black pepper. Puree until smooth.

4. With the machine on, add the olive oil and then the hot water through the feed tube. This sauce holds well at room temperature, but if you're not using it in the next couple of hours, cover and refrigerate for up to 3 days. Let return to room temperature before serving. Thin with a little more hot water if the sauce thickens.

ROASTED SPRING VEGETABLES

4 to 6 or 8 to 12 servings, depending upon how many
   vegetables you offer

Roasted Asparagus: Preheat the oven to 475 degrees. Arrange 2 pounds trimmed asparagus on an aluminum foil–lined baking sheet. Toss with 2 to 3 tablespoons extra virgin olive oil and season with coarse salt to taste. Roast 10 to 15 minutes, turning once with tongs, until the asparagus is just tender. Serve with lemon wedges.

Roasted Turnips: Preheat the oven to 425 degrees. Peel 1 pound baby turnips and halve or quarter them, depending on their size. Place in a shallow baking dish and toss with 2 tablespoons olive oil. Season with salt and pepper to taste. Roast 20 to 25 minutes, turning once or twice, until tender and lightly browned.

Roasted Carrots: Preheat the oven to 425 degrees. Peel 1½ pounds baby carrots, or use regular carrots and cut them on the diagonal into three or four 2- to 3-inch lengths. Place in a shallow baking dish and toss with 2 tablespoons olive oil. Season with salt and pepper to taste. Roast 25 to 30 minutes, turning several times, until lightly browned and just barely tender.

(continued)

Roasted Shallots or Onions: Preheat the oven to 425 degrees. Peel 1 pound shallots or baby onions. Place in a shallow baking dish and toss with 2 tablespoons olive oil. Roast 30 to 35 minutes, turning several times, until browned and just tender.

Roasted New Potatoes: Preheat the oven to 425 degrees. Rinse and scrub 2 pounds new potatoes or halved or quartered small red potatoes; dry well. Place in a shallow baking dish and toss with 3 tablespoons olive oil. Season liberally with coarse salt and freshly ground pepper. Roast 35 to 40 minutes, turning several times, until the potatoes are nicely browned outside and tender to the center.

PINWHEEL VEGETABLE GRATIN

8 servings

Here's an easy, colorful vegetable side dish. The only hard part may be finding the appropriate pan to cook it in. I use a fifteen-inch paella pan. If you don't have one, make a striped gratin in a large baking dish or divide the ingredients and make two pinwheels in separate nine- or ten-inch glass or ceramic pie plates.

1/4 cup extra virgin olive oil
1 pound medium zucchini, thinly sliced
2 large tomatoes, halved and sliced
1 medium red onion, halved and thinly sliced
1 pound yellow squash, thinly sliced
2 tablespoons fresh lemon juice
1 1/4 teaspoons coarse salt
3/4 teaspoon coarsely cracked pepper
4 slices firm-textured white bread
1 medium shallot, quartered
2 garlic cloves, chopped
1/2 cup fresh basil leaves (optional)
1/3 cup parsley sprigs.

1. Preheat the oven to 400 degrees. Slice all the vegetables as directed above. Grease a large round paella pan or ovenproof platter with 1 tablespoon of the olive oil.

2. Arrange overlapping slices of the zucchini, tomatoes, red onion, and yellow squash in separate concentric circles in the pan, starting at the outer edge and repeating until all the vegetables are used. Sprinkle the lemon juice over the vegetables and season with ³/₄ teaspoon of the salt and ¹/₂ teaspoon of the pepper. Drizzle on 1¹/₂ tablespoons of the olive oil.

3. Tear the bread into a food processor. Add the shallot, garlic, basil if you have it, parsley, and remaining salt and pepper. Grind to crumbs. Sprinkle the herbed crumbs over the vegetables. Drizzle the remaining 1¹/₂ tablespoons olive oil over the gratin.

4. Bake the gratin for 25 minutes, or until the vegetables are tender and the topping is browned and crisp. Serve hot.

Stir-Fried Zucchini with Corn and Sweet Pepper

4 to 6 servings

Southwestern seasonings work just as well in the Northeast, I've learned. This is a recipe I make all year round, with fresh corn in summer and canned in winter. It is a quick, versatile vegetable, which goes well with any simply cooked meat.

> 1 medium onion, chopped
> 2 tablespoons olive oil
> 2 garlic cloves, minced
> 1 medium red bell pepper, cut into 1/2-inch squares
> 1 teaspoon ground cumin
> 1/4 teaspoon crushed hot red pepper flakes
> 3 medium zucchini, cut into 1/2-inch dice or thinly sliced
> 1/2 teaspoon salt
> 1 1/2 cups corn kernels—fresh, vacuum-packed niblets, or thawed frozen
> 1 tablespoon fresh lime or lemon juice

1. In a large skillet, cook the onion in the olive oil over moderate heat until it is softened and just beginning to color around the edges, about 3 minutes. Add the garlic and bell pepper. Cook, stirring frequently, until the pepper begins to soften, 2 to 3 minutes. Add the cumin and hot pepper and cook, stirring, for 1 minute.

2. Add the zucchini and season with the salt. Cook, stirring occasionally, until the zucchini is tender but still firm, 3 to 5 minutes. Add the corn and cook, stirring frequently, until hot, about 2 minutes. Sprinkle on the lime juice and serve hot or at room temperature.

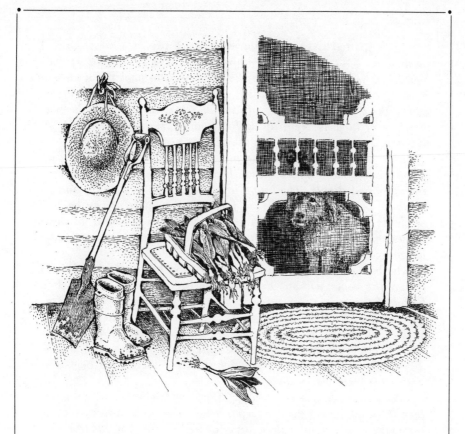

· RAMPS ·

The first time I encountered a ramp, it was raw, on someone else's breath, and despite his excitement, I wasn't sure the arrival of ramp season was such a blessing. If you've never had any, you should know that the scent of ramps is to that of garlic like the strength of a Mack truck to that of a Volkswagen Beetle.

Wild leek is the standard term for this potent allium, which grows indiscriminately in dense patches wherever there are moist, rich woodlands all up and down the East Coast, from Canada in the North to Georgia in the South. While they are not so popular inland, they can be found as far west as Minnesota and again in the Northwest. They are called wild leeks in my town, where digging for them is one of spring's early pleasures. (I'm convinced it says something about a community's character when its citizens pay attention to the edibles growing in their woods.)

(continued)

I first spotted wild leeks, however, in an urban market, labeled with their Southern name, ramps, and I like the sound of that word. To me it suggests both the tramping through the woods to find a patch, the forest-green lily-of-the-valley leaves unmistakable above the dead brown cover of last fall's leaves, and the wild exuberance of digging them up and whooping them home to cook up a batch. So excuse me if I use the two terms interchangeably.

In my experience, a spading fork is the best tool for digging up ramps, but some people use shovels, and one friend of mine swears by his forked dibble. The bulbs frequently grow in clumps, and as small as they are, the combined force of all their roots can be surprisingly tenacious. If there are rocks below, they'll cling to them like octopi. Of course, when the ground is soft and loamy it is easier going.

The best way to get at wild leeks is from below. The trick is to loosen the roots without breaking the bulbs, so you can grab a fistful of the purple stems near the ground and pull them up without tearing off the round white bulbs, which are about the size of shallots. Unearthed, the onions are covered with dirt and frequently clumped together, and the outer layer of the bulbs is usually mushy-soft and discolored. I just throw them in a bag as is and wash them off at home.

Cleaning ramps is not a lot of fun, but it's not hard work, either. Mozart helps. Besides separating them and cutting off the roots, there is usually a thin, slimy outer layer that needs to be removed. Underneath, the fresh bulbs are hard and a brilliant, almost luminous, pearly white. Depending upon how I'm using them, I may or may not detach the leaves. If I do, I cut them so that most of the purple stem (which turns greenish when cooked) remains attached to the bulb. The leaves, which need only a good rinsing, have a mild chivelike flavor and they quickly become tender when cooked.

Wild leeks are excellent stir-fried, pickled, and simmered in soups, sauces, and stews. The trick, as in animal training, is to tame them without breaking their spirit. Three to five minutes of cooking for the greens and ten to twenty minutes for the white bulbs mellows the flavor while leaving the distinctiveness of the wild leeks intact. Despite their raw strength, over half an hour on the stove can cause them virtually to disappear. That's why in recipes that cook for a longer time, I add the ramps close to the end.

RAMPED RICE

4 to 6 servings

Rice cooks the optimum time that ramps, or wild leeks do—twenty minutes —which makes them a natural pairing, though the distinctive onion/garlic/ leek flavor of the ramps makes them the dominant partner. This is a simple risotto-style rice, which goes well with just about any poultry, fish, or meat.

3 tablespoons unsalted butter
$^1/_2$ cup thinly sliced ramp bulbs (from about $^3/_4$ cup ramps)
$1^1/_2$ cups long-grain white rice
3 cups unsalted homemade chicken stock or reduced-sodium canned broth
1 teaspoon salt
$^1/_8$ teaspoon cayenne
$^1/_3$ cup minced ramp greens

1. In a heavy, medium saucepan, melt the butter over moderate heat. Add the sliced ramp bulbs and cook, stirring occasionally, until softened, 2 to 3 minutes. Add the rice and cook, stirring to coat the rice with butter, for about 1 minute, until the grains turn opaque.

2. Add the chicken stock, salt, and cayenne. Bring to a boil, stir once, and reduce the heat to very low. Cover and simmer for 20 minutes, or until the rice is tender and all the liquid is absorbed.

3. Stir $^1/_4$ of the minced ramp greens into the rice. Turn into a serving dish and sprinkle the remaining minced ramps over the top.

CREAMY BAKED RICE
WITH RAMPS AND CHEESE

6 servings

This delectable dish has a lot of the qualities of a Mexican baked rice—notably sour cream and cheese—but instead of the pungency of chiles, it is imbued with the aromatic flavor of ramps.

> Ramped Rice (page 169)
> 3/4 cup sour cream
> 1 cup shredded fontina or Monterey jack cheese (about 4 ounces)
> Salt and freshly ground pepper

1. Prepare the ramped rice as directed in the recipe. Preheat the oven to 375 degrees.

2. Stir the sour cream and 3/4 cup of the cheese into the rice. Season with salt and pepper to taste. Spoon the rice into a buttered baking dish or shallow casserole. Sprinkle the remaining 1/4 cup cheese over the top. (The recipe can be prepared to this point up to a day ahead. Cover and refrigerate.)

3. Bake the rice uncovered about 20 minutes, until it is piping hot throughout and the cheese on top is melted and beginning to brown.

CHESTNUT STUFFING WITH
APRICOTS AND PRUNES

Makes about 7 cups

This is my favorite stuffing for goose or wild turkey, because its richness complements the unctuousness of the meat. Actually, it is my favorite stuffing, period, so of course there's nothing wrong with using it for your

Thanksgiving turkey or even a large roasting chicken. If liver pâté is unavailable or unduly expensive at your market, you can substitute a quarter pound of chicken livers, trimmed, cut into half-inch pieces, and sautéed in a tablespoon or two of butter until just pink inside.

1¼ pounds chestnuts
5 ounces dried apricots, quartered
16 pitted prunes, quartered
2 tablespoons Cognac or brandy
4 tablespoons (½ stick) unsalted butter
2 medium onions, finely diced
2 celery ribs, finely diced
1 turkey, goose, or chicken liver trimmed and finely diced
2 ounces pâté de foie gras or canned liver pâté
1½ teaspoons salt
¾ teaspoon freshly ground pepper
1 tablespoon minced winter savory or 1 teaspoon dried savory or thyme leaves
4 cups cubed stale French or Italian bread
1 cup unsalted homemade chicken or turkey stock
2 eggs, lightly beaten

1. Preheat the oven to 375 degrees. Cut an X into the flat side of each chestnut. Spread out on a baking sheet and roast until the shells begin to curl back, about 20 minutes. As soon as the chestnuts are cool enough to handle, remove the shells and dark brown inner skins. Quarter the chestnuts.

2. Put the apricots and prunes in a medium bowl. Add the Cognac and 2 tablespoons hot water. Let stand at room temperature, tossing occasionally, for about 15 minutes, or until slightly softened.

3. Meanwhile, in a large skillet, melt the butter. Add the onions and celery and cook over moderate heat, stirring occasionally, until the onions are just beginning to turn golden, about 10 minutes. Add the diced liver and cook, tossing, until browned, 5 to 7 minutes. Remove from the heat and stir in the pâté. Season with the salt, pepper, and savory.

4. In a large bowl, combine the bread cubes and the apricots and prunes with their liquid. Scrape the vegetables and liver from the skillet into the bowl. Mix well. Toss with the stock and eggs until evenly moistened. If not used immediately, cover and refrigerate.

Mary Welch's Country-Style Bread Dressing with Sausage and Sage

Makes about 16 cups

Mary Welch is my neighbor Peggy Soden's mother and a fine cook. As she had nine children, she just naturally cooks in quantity; this is about one-fourth of the amount of stuffing Mary prepares for Thanksgiving. Everyone gets a pan to take home with them for the next day. No one makes it quite as well as Mary, but I tried.

This dressing reheats well and can be baked with or without the turkey next to it.

> 4 loaves (1 pound each) supermarket-style soft Italian bread,
>   broken into chunks and dried until stale
> 3 medium onions, chopped
> 1 pound bulk pork sausage
> 1 tablespoon plus 1 teaspoon poultry seasoning
> 1½ teaspoons celery seed
> ¾ teaspoon ground sage
> 1 tablespoon baking powder
> 1 tablespoon salt
> ½ teaspoon freshly ground pepper

1. Put the bread in a large roasting pan; a turkey roaster works well if you have one. Add 4 cups of water, allow to soak briefly, and knead the bread until it's mushy and soft like dough. Add up to 2 cups more water if necessary to achieve the proper consistency.

2. Add all the remaining ingredients and mix well (I use my hands) until the stuffing is the consistency of mashed potatoes. Divide the stuffing between two large shallow baking dishes. Let stand at room temperature for ½ hour.

3. Preheat the oven to 350 degrees. Bake the dressing uncovered for 1 hour. (If the dressing looks dry, drizzle up to ½ cup of water over each pan.) Cover with foil and bake for 30 minutes longer.

BED·AND·
BREAKFAST FARE

Morning has never been my best hour. I slept late until the fifth decade of my life. At work, I was frequently observed shuffling to my desk with a cup of coffee clenched between my lips, trying desperately to caffeine my way into consciousness before the first staff meeting of the day. On weekends, I slumbered, with tightly closed shutters, until the sun was high in the sky. Needless to say, when you sleep in and miss morning, breakfast is a superfluous meal.

All that changed when I came to the country. Perhaps it was the shock of the icy-cold air in the then-unheated upstairs that first winter in the old farmhouse that got me out of bed at sunrise. There were about thirty degrees of incentive to turn on the kitchen stove and add to the wavering warmth the patched furnace threw off. Shivering, I cradled the big, hot mug of coffee between my fingers, sucking in the steam, while swallowing soft, warm curds of silky egg or spoonfuls of gritty oatmeal, which supplied childishly simple delight. For extra warmth, I toasted bread in the oven under the broiler, as my Southern friend Frances had taught me to, slathering it with sweet butter before adding a thick dusting of sugar and cinnamon, which cooked to a thin, crackly caramel.

There was, of course, encouragement enough to wake up simply from the beauty of that sunrise, with the soft, early-morning mist rising above the meadows, floating, like a second landscape, just beneath the tips of the mountains, blue-gray streaked with pale peach, dissolving the world in a monochrome of white when it snowed. There existed always the possibility of sighting a big buck under the apple tree, hearing a caucus of crows on the fence lining the cow pasture, glimpsing a shy black bear trundling along the stone fence at the top of the field.

My postman, Hank, who has white hair and the local limpid blue eyes, delivers eggs. In winter they come in cartons wrapped in a thick blanketing of brown paper bag or newspaper to insulate them from the weather while he makes his rounds in his red pick-up truck. Sometimes bits of straw still cling to the tan shells, testifying to their freshness. Inside, the whites are clear, thick, and viscous, like a jellyfish; the yolks, yellow as goldenrod, are smooth and round.

When you crack four of these eggs into a skillet, they remain discrete. I fry them, scramble them, poach them, boil them, bake them. I make flat, firm American-style omelets; light, fluffy French-style omelets; and thick frittatas, loaded with potatoes, onions, and whatever fresh vegetables and bits of cheese happen to be on hand.

This is bed-and-breakfast country. Skiing, snowmobiling, summer camps, hunting, fishing, and the glorious changing of the leaves bring in tourists. Many of the best homes, built oversized in late Victorian years, trimmed with ornate gingerbread carving, appended with porches, have been converted into B&Bs. It was from my friends who ran these lodgings—Ginny and Bobi and Margaret and Mary—that I learned how far you could go with breakfast.

Of course, I knew about fried eggs and oatmeal and cereal and toast, but these hard-working women really knew how to compete—in the kitchen. They rose early, whipped up pancakes and muffins, pulled savory puddings out of their freezers, piled sausages and bacon on gaily painted plates. Eventually, after months of talking and tasting, I believe I caught their early-morning culinary enthusiasm.

Breakfast soon became the delightful meal I'd never known. It provided new opportunities for employing the night before's tasty leftovers. While no good cook ever condones waste, when the nearest market is miles away, and a treacherous trek in winter, using what you have in the refrigerator becomes more necessary than righteous. Roast turkey, chicken, and beef, along with whatever kind of gravy or sauce that accompanied them, became different kinds of hash. Leftover vegetables were added to savory pancakes; stale bread was prized for puddings, brunch casseroles, and, as a last resort, for fresh crumbs.

With good reason to warm up the oven, I followed the example of my bed-and-breakfast friends. Muffins and biscuits, easy coffee cakes, and quick breads were added to the morning menu. It's easy to rationalize when you love to eat. So much energy was needed to shovel that long, curving walkway, to haul those heavy stones out of the garden, to mow that endless lawn, I needed the nourishment. On came the hash browns, pancakes, sausages, homemade preserves, and juice. Many of these dishes are so substantial they might just as easily serve as a Sunday supper, when you've had your big meal at noon.

While my hours have altered to a schedule more in synch with the sun, and breakfast is a newfound feast, morning is still new to me, a somewhat delicate time of day. I take it gently, preferring to look about the land for a while and then slip into my writing, with serious cooking and heavy physical work saved for later in the afternoon. Consequently, you will find the recipes in this chapter a comfortable way to start the day, delicious and nourishing, I hope, but not at all demanding. You may need the time, after all, for an early-morning walk.

MILE HIGH THREE-GRAIN GRIDDLE CAKES

Makes 2 dozen 3-inch cakes

I've always found that pancakes sit like lead in my stomach. Maybe I've been making them wrong all these years. These are high—a full half inch—light, and tasty, with the nutty flavor of buckwheat and the inimitable tang of buttermilk. Cornmeal adds a nice gritty texture as well as a hint of sweetness, which is amplified with a touch of rich dark brown sugar.

If you're having company, or like me you're slow in the morning, you can make up the dry ingredients as far ahead as you like—a day, a week, or a month—and store them in a plastic bag. It's like having your own mix. With my crowd, people will realistically eat anywhere from a meager three to a generous six pancakes, depending partly on gender and activity level. So you can rely on this recipe to serve four to six. If you want to make pancakes for two or three, it's easier because of the measurements to mix up all the dry ingredients. Measure out a cup to use and store the remainder for another day. The other ingredients halve easily.

> 1 cup all-purpose flour
> 1/3 cup whole wheat flour
> 1/3 cup buckwheat flour
> 1/3 cup yellow cornmeal
> 2 tablespoons packed dark brown sugar
> 1 teaspoon baking powder
> 1 teaspoon baking soda
> 1/4 teaspoon salt
> 2 eggs
> 2 cups plus 2 tablespoons buttermilk
> 4 tablespoons (1/2 stick) unsalted butter, melted
> Maple or fruit syrup

1. In a medium bowl, combine the all-purpose flour, whole wheat flour, buckwheat flour, cornmeal, brown sugar, baking powder, baking soda, and salt. Whisk gently to blend well.

2. Heat a griddle or large cast-iron skillet over moderate heat for 2 minutes to heat evenly. Wipe with a greased paper towel and continue to heat over moderately low heat while you finish the batter.

3. In a small bowl, whisk the eggs until blended. Whisk in the buttermilk and beat until blended. Add the liquids to the dry ingredients. Pour the melted butter on top. Stir with the whisk until the batter is just barely mixed. Some lumps of flour should still be visible.

4. Scoop about 2 tablespoons of the batter at a time onto the griddle and cook over moderately low heat until small bubbles have formed on top of the cakes and the bottoms are nicely browned, 1½ to 2 minutes. Turn over gently and cook until the second side is browned and the cakes are dry throughout, 45 to 60 seconds longer. Grease the griddle as necessary to prevent sticking. Serve hot, with syrup on the side.

HASH BROWNS MY WAY

4 servings

Actually, I enjoy hash browns any way, but mine is nice, highly seasoned and with lots of onions. If you think of it, cook the potatoes the night before and just stick them in the fridge, to be peeled and cut up in the morning. The forethought will allow you to make a hearty breakfast quickly and with little fuss. If you want someone to fall in love with you, serve these with fried or scrambled eggs, the biscuit or muffin of your choice, homemade preserves, fresh orange juice, and good strong coffee.

> 2 medium onions, cut into ½-inch dice
> 2 to 3 tablespoons olive oil
> 4 medium red potatoes, cooked until tender, peeled, and cut into
>   ½-inch dice
> Salt and freshly ground pepper
> 3 or 4 dashes of Worcestershire sauce
> At least 5 dashes of Tabasco

1. In a large skillet, preferably well-seasoned cast iron, cook the onions in 2 tablespoons of the olive oil over moderate heat, stirring occasionally, until they just begin to color slightly around the edges, 3 to 5 minutes.

2. Add the potatoes and stir to mix them with the onions and oil. If the pan seems too dry, add the remaining 1 tablespoon oil. Season liberally with salt and pepper, and cook, turning fairly frequently with a wide spatula, until the onions are golden and at least one-third of the potatoes are brown and crisp, 7 to 10 minutes.

3. Taste and, if necessary, add more salt and especially pepper. The potatoes should be highly seasoned. Sprinkle on the Worcestershire and Tabasco and turn and stir with the spatula to mix in the flavorings. Serve the hash browns hot.

BARBECUED TURKEY HASH

4 servings

A savory hash like this is not a fussy dish. You can make it with leftover roast turkey—the most likely candidate—or poached turkey breast. The same recipe works well with leftover cooked chicken, as well.

4 medium potatoes, about 1¼ pounds total
2 tablespoons olive oil
2 medium onions, coarsely chopped
Salt and freshly ground pepper
2 cups diced cooked turkey
1 cup Tangy Barbecue Sauce (page 61), or use your favorite bottled brand
4 eggs (optional)

1. If you have leftover cooked potatoes, by all means use them. If not, place the potatoes in a large saucepan, cover with water, and bring to a boil. Continue to boil over moderately high heat for 15 to 20 minutes, until the potatoes are tender throughout and will drop from a knife inserted in the center; drain. Peel the potatoes when they're cool enough to handle and cut them into ½-inch dice.

2. In a large ovenproof skillet, preferably cast-iron, heat the olive oil. Add the onions and cook over moderately high heat, stirring often, until they soften, about 3 minutes. Add the potatoes, reduce the heat to moderate, and cook, turning occasionally with a spatula, until both the onions and the potatoes are lightly browned, 5 to 7 minutes. Season generously with salt and freshly ground pepper.

3. Add the turkey to the skillet and cook, turning with the spatula, until heated through and some pieces are crispy around the edges, about 5 minutes. Add the barbecue sauce and cook, turning, until mixed through and heated.

4. Serve the hash either as is or as follows: Preheat the oven to 400 degrees. Make 4 equidistant nests on top of the hash with a large spoon, drop an egg into each indentation, and set the skillet in the oven for 5 to 7 minutes, until the eggs are set and the hash is slightly browned on top.

SCRAMBLED EGGS WITH CREAM CHEESE AND TARRAGON

4 to 5 servings

This is my answer to making scrambled eggs for a group of guests some of whom may like them prepared harder and some softer. It goes both ways. The eggs are cooked slowly until they are firm and fully cooked, then they are stirred around with the cheese until it melts and coats them with a creamy smoothness, which simulates a softness with its rich touch. If you want to hold the eggs or keep them warm in a chafing dish at the table, be sure to undercook them just slightly before adding the cream cheese.

> *10 eggs*
> *1 teaspoon dried tarragon*
> *½ teaspoon salt*
> *⅛ teaspoon Tabasco*
> *5 tablespoons unsalted butter*
> *3 ounces cream cheese, cut into small bits*
> *¼ teaspoon freshly ground pepper*

1. Crack the eggs into a medium bowl and beat them together with the tarragon, salt, and Tabasco until the eggs are blended.

2. In a large heavy skillet, melt the butter over moderate heat. Pour in the eggs and reduce the heat to moderately low. Cook, scraping the bottom of the pan with a wooden or plastic spatula and folding the eggs over on themselves as they begin to form curds, until they are firm but still moist all over and runny in spots, about 3 minutes.

3. Add the cream cheese and season with the pepper. Cook, folding the eggs and cream cheese over the heat for about 15 seconds. Remove from the heat and continue to fold until the cream cheese is completely melted and coats the eggs. Serve at once.

Kitchen Sink Frittata

4 to 6 servings

When there's nothing in the house to cook and I feel like something really savory, this is the quick and easy recipe that comes to mind. It is a great brunch dish, also fine as a light supper or midnight snack.

2 or 3 red potatoes, peeled
3 tablespoons olive oil
Salt and freshly ground pepper
1 medium onion, cut into 1/2-inch dice
1/2 red or green bell pepper, cut into 1/2-inch dice
7 eggs
Several dashes of Tabasco
1/2 cup cooked broccoli florets
2 ounces cream cheese

1. Cut the potatoes into 1/4-inch-thick slices. In a well-seasoned 9-inch cast-iron or ovenproof nonstick skillet, heat 1 1/2 tablespoons of the olive oil. Add the potatoes, cover, and cook over moderate heat, turning them once or twice, until golden brown and tender, 6 to 8 minutes. Season generously with salt and pepper. With a slotted spatula, remove the potatoes to a plate.

2. Heat the remaining olive oil in the skillet, swirling to coat the sides of the pan. Add the onion and cook over moderate heat until softened and just beginning to brown, 3 to 5 minutes. Add the diced pepper and cook 2 to 3 minutes longer, until softened. Return the potatoes to the pan.

3. Beat the eggs with the Tabasco and a generous pinch of salt and pepper until blended. Pour into the skillet, tilting the pan so the egg covers the vegetables evenly. Reduce the heat to moderately low. Arrange the broccoli florets on top, pushing them gently partway into the frittata, and dollop the cream cheese on top. Cover and cook until the frittata is about three-quarters cooked and just set around the edges; the center will still be runny.

4. Preheat the broiler. Transfer the skillet to the broiler and cook about 4 inches from the heat for about 2 minutes, until the frittata is puffed and lightly browned on top. Serve hot, warm, or at room temperature.

Huevos Rancheros Casserole

8 to 10 servings

*E*ven though we don't have any Mexican restaurants in northeastern Pennsylvania, Mexican foods are very popular in the supermarkets. I have a weakness for huevos rancheros, and when I travel in Mexico, they are what I order almost every morning. This casserole version is easy and wonderful for brunch entertaining because you can make the whole thing the night before, refrigerate it, and bake it after everyone arrives in the morning.

> 2 tablespoons olive oil
> 2 medium onions, chopped
> 1 medium green bell pepper, finely diced
> 1 medium red bell pepper, finely diced
> 2 large garlic cloves, minced
> 1 teaspoon ground cumin
> 1/2 teaspoon oregano
> 1 can (14 ounces) Italian peeled tomatoes, coarsely chopped, with their juices
> 1 cup reduced-sodium chicken broth
> 3 pickled jalapeño peppers, minced, plus 1 tablespoon of their liquid
> 3/4 teaspoon salt
> 1/4 teaspoon freshly ground pepper
> 12 corn tortillas
> 1 can (16 ounces) refried beans
> 8 hard-cooked eggs, sliced
> 10 ounces Monterey jack or Cheddar cheese, shredded
> 1 cup sour cream

1. Heat the olive oil in a large nonreactive flameproof casserole or saucepan. Add the onions, cover, and cook over moderately low heat for 5 minutes. Uncover, raise the heat to moderate, and cook, stirring occasionally, until the onions are golden, 10 to 15 minutes.

2. Reserve about 1/4 cup of the red and green peppers for garnish. Add remaining peppers to the casserole and cook, stirring occasionally, until the

peppers are softened but still brightly colored, about 5 minutes. Add the garlic, cumin, and oregano and cook, stirring, for 1 minute. Add the tomatoes with their juices, the chicken broth, and the pickled jalapeño peppers with their liquid. Season with the salt and pepper. Bring to a boil, reduce the heat to moderately low, and simmer, stirring occasionally, until the sauce is slightly thickened, 15 to 20 minutes.

3. Meanwhile, wrap the tortillas in two batches of 6 in microwave-safe paper towels and microwave on High for 45 seconds each to heat through. In a small saucepan, heat the refried beans slowly, stirring, until smooth and hot. As soon as you can handle the tortillas, spread a thin layer of refried beans over 8 of the tortillas.

4. Spread a thin layer of the tomato sauce over the bottom of a 12-inch gratin or 9 × 13-inch baking dish. Put 4 of the tortillas, bean side up, in the dish to cover the bottom; tear to fit if necessary. Arrange half the sliced eggs on the tortillas and sprinkle one-third of the cheese over the eggs. Ladle on one-third of the sauce. Repeat with another layer of bean-coated tortillas, the remaining eggs, and half the remaining cheese and sauce. Top with the plain tortillas. Spread the remaining sauce over the tortillas to coat them and sprinkle on the remaining cheese. Dollop the sour cream over the casserole and sprinkle the reserved red and green peppers over the top. (The recipe can be prepared to this point up to a day in advance. Cover and refrigerate.)

5. To finish the casserole, preheat the oven to 375 degrees. Bake the casserole uncovered for 20 to 30 minutes, until bubbling and heated through.

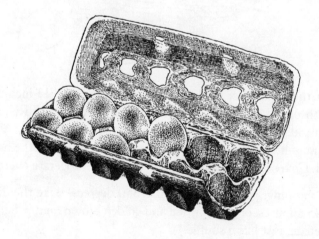

Savory Bread Pudding

6 to 8 servings

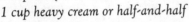

My friend Bobi, who runs a lovely bed-and-breakfast in the next town over, is always devising new recipes for her guests. This is one of her favorites. I like it because all the work, which is minimal to begin with, is done the night before.

½ pound French or Italian bread, torn into large chunks
¼ pound honey-baked ham, cut into ½-inch dice
¼ pound Swiss cheese, cut into ½-inch dice
6 eggs
1 cup milk
1 cup heavy cream or half-and-half
½ teaspoon salt
¼ teaspoon freshly ground pepper

1. Scatter the bread over the bottom of a buttered 9 × 13-inch rectangular baking dish or a 12-inch oval gratin. Sprinkle the ham and cheese evenly over the bread. In a medium bowl, beat the eggs until blended. Whisk in the milk, cream, salt, and pepper. Pour this custard gently over the ham, cheese, and bread. Cover the dish with plastic wrap and refrigerate overnight.

2. In the morning, preheat the oven to 350 degrees. Bake the dish, uncovered, for 45 minutes, or until puffed and golden brown on top. Serve at once. (It will deflate, just like a soufflé.)

BLUEBERRY CORN MUFFINS

Makes 12

*F*or a long while I only picked berries from my own tall, scrawny huckle-berry bush. They were small and tart, and some days the birds took so many there weren't enough for even a single serving. Finally I gave in and followed the signs to the "Pick your own blueberries" farm. Who would have dreamed? Full and lush, the branches of the broad bushes splayed out like fountains, bending gracefully, heavy with huge stone-blue marbles of full-flavored fruit. So much for the pleasures of the wild. In less than an hour, I'd grabbed something like fourteen pounds of berries, which cost me all of seven dollars. Needless to say, before I gave in and filled up the freezer, the next week was blueberry this and blueberry that, including these delectable cornmeal-piqued muffins.

> 1½ cups plus 1 teaspoon all-purpose flour
> ½ cup cornmeal
> 2½ teaspoons baking powder
> ½ teaspoon baking soda
> ⅛ teaspoon salt
> ¼ cup sugar
> 1 generous cup blueberries
> 1 egg
> 1 cup buttermilk
> 6 tablespoons unsalted butter, melted

1. Preheat the oven to 400 degrees. In a medium bowl, combine 1½ cups flour with the cornmeal, baking powder, baking soda, salt, and sugar. Whisk gently to combine. Toss the blueberries with the remaining 1 teaspoon flour.

2. Beat together the egg and buttermilk. Add to the dry ingredients along with the melted butter. Stir until just barely blended. The batter should be lumpy. Stir in the blueberries. Spoon into 12 lightly greased muffin cups.

3. Bake 22 to 25 minutes, or until the muffins are a deep golden brown.

VARIATION
Raspberry Corn Muffins—Substitute 1 cup raspberries for the blueberries.

GLAZED CINNAMON BUNS

Makes 2 dozen

As word worked its way around town that I was writing a cookbook, a number of people opened their hearts, their homes, and their heirloom cookbooks, filled with handwritten recipes in faded script, to me. One lovely surprise was to come home one evening to find a package of fragrant cinnamon buns waiting on the doorstep. There was no note. For a week, I wondered what kindly neighbor—and fine baker—had left the anonymous gift. Finally I received this note from Margaret Dickey, one of our town's most renowned bakers.

"This basic recipe was taken from an old 1930s Spry cookbook and adapted by me when I was a teenager. I made and sold these cinnamon buns to help with college expenses. Even today, some 60-odd years later, folks in my home town remember my tasty cinnamon buns."

If you prefer a more buttery flavor, as I do, feel free to substitute a stick of softened unsalted butter for the shortening in Step 1.

1 cup milk
2/3 cup sugar
1 teaspoon salt
1/2 cup solid vegetable shortening
2 envelopes (1/4 ounce each) active dry yeast
1/2 cup lukewarm water (105 to 115 degrees)
2 eggs, well beaten
4 1/2 to 5 cups all-purpose flour
8 tablespoons (1 stick) unsalted butter, at room temperature
2 cups packed brown sugar
1 1/2 cups chopped walnuts and/or pecans
2 tablespoons ground cinnamon
1 cup raisins

1. In a small saucepan, bring the milk just to a simmer. Remove from the heat and add the sugar, salt, and shortening. Stir to dissolve the sugar and shortening. Pour the milk mixture into a large bowl and let cool to lukewarm —105 to 115 degrees.

2. Meanwhile, add the yeast to the warm water. Let stand until foamy, 5 to 10 minutes. Add the dissolved yeast and eggs to the milk mixture and beat well. Gradually add 4½ cups of the flour and mix thoroughly.

3. Turn the dough out onto a floured countertop and knead, adding additional flour if necessary to prevent sticking, until smooth and elastic, 5 to 10 minutes. Form the dough into a ball, place in a greased bowl, and turn to coat. Cover with a towel and let rise in a draft-free place until doubled in bulk, about 1½ hours.

4. Meanwhile, in a small saucepan, combine 1 cup brown sugar, 4 tablespoons butter, and ½ cup water. Cook over moderate heat, stirring, until the butter and sugar melt and the syrup is smooth, 3 to 5 minutes. Spread the syrup evenly over the bottom of two 9 × 13-inch baking pans, preferably nonstick. Sprinkle the nuts over the syrup.

5. Divide the dough in half. Roll out one piece of dough to a 10 × 2-inch rectangle about ¼ inch thick. Spread it with 2 tablespoons of butter. Mix together the remaining 1 cup brown sugar, the cinnamon, and the raisins and sprinkle half the mixture evenly on top of the dough. Roll up the dough jellyroll fashion, starting with a long end; pinch the long seam to seal. Cut the dough into 1-inch slices and set, cut side up, in one of the prepared baking pans. Repeat with remaining dough and filling. Cover loosely with a sheet of lightly oiled plastic wrap and a kitchen towel. Let rise until doubled. Meanwhile, preheat the oven to 375 degrees.

6. Bake the cinnamon buns for 18 to 20 minutes, or until golden brown. Immediately invert onto a plate, glazed side up. Serve warm or at room temperature.

BUTTERMILK BANANA BREAD

Makes 1 loaf

If you live in the country, bananas are one of the few fruits you can depend on year round, at even the smallest local market. Bought with the best intentions—because they are there—the bunch may languish in a far corner of the kitchen, with the last bananas not infrequently ending up blackened and shriveled, crying out for the compost heap. It is at this point, when you question whether you feel like handling the peel with your bare hands, and not before, that this versatile fruit is, in fact, *perfect* for banana bread.

I experimented with so many different formulas to try and devise the best banana bread ever that I can no longer visit one of my close country friends without being offered all their over-the-hill bananas—a mixed blessing.

Another tip for baking perfect quick breads: Be sure you use a *metal* (but not cast-iron) loaf pan. Even though we all used heatproof glass for a million years, it is not the right material, and will yield heavy breads, overdone outside, soggy inside, and humped in the middle.

$1^{1}/_{2}$ to $1^{3}/_{4}$ *cups mashed overripe bananas*
   (3 small to medium or 2 large)
2 eggs
$^{1}/_{2}$ *cup granulated sugar*
$^{1}/_{2}$ *cup packed dark brown sugar*
$1^{1}/_{2}$ *teaspoons vanilla extract*
$^{1}/_{2}$ *cup buttermilk*
2 cups all-purpose flour
$^{1}/_{2}$ *teaspoon salt*
1 teaspoon baking soda
$^{1}/_{2}$ *teaspoon baking powder*
8 tablespoons (1 stick)
   unsalted butter, melted
$^{1}/_{2}$ *cup chopped pecans or walnuts*

1. Preheat the oven to 400 degrees. Butter and flour a 9 × 5 × 3-inch metal loaf pan.

2. In a medium bowl, combine the mashed bananas, eggs, granulated sugar, brown sugar, and vanilla. Beat with a wooden spoon until well blended. Beat in the buttermilk.

3. In a larger bowl, combine the flour, salt, baking soda, and baking powder. Whisk gently to mix. Add the banana mixture and the melted butter and beat until well blended. Stir in the nuts. Turn the batter into the prepared loaf pan.

4. Place the pan in the preheated oven and immediately reduce the temperature to 350 degrees. Bake for 1 hour and 15 minutes, or until the bread is risen, nicely browned, and beginning to pull away from the sides of the pan and a tester inserted in the center comes out clean. Let stand about 10 minutes, then invert onto a rack to unmold. Carefully turn the bread right side up and let cool before serving.

EASY APPLE COFFEE CAKE

9 to 12 servings

Because this cake is so moist, it keeps well for several days. I make it most often in the early fall, when my own apple trees are loaded with fruit. The recipe works well with any kind of baking apple that will hold its shape and not give off too much liquid. This is particularly good as a morning dessert or with coffee.

1 cup milk
1 tablespoon distilled white vinegar
8 tablespoons (1 stick) unsalted butter, softened
1 cup packed dark brown sugar
1/2 cup plus 3 tablespoons granulated sugar
1 egg
1 1/2 teaspoons vanilla extract
2 cups all-purpose flour
1 1/2 teaspoons baking powder
1/2 teaspoon baking soda
1/4 teaspoon salt
3 cups diced (3/4-inch) apples
1 1/2 teaspoons ground cinnamon

1. Preheat the oven to 350 degrees. Grease a 9 × 13-inch baking pan. In a glass measuring cup, combine the milk and vinegar, stirring to blend. Set aside; as it stands, the milk will "sour" and thicken.

2. In a large bowl, cream the butter. Add the brown sugar and 1/2 cup of the granulated sugar and beat until smooth and light. Add the egg and vanilla and beat well.

3. In another bowl, combine the flour, baking powder, baking soda, and salt. Stir well or whisk gently to blend. In several additions, alternately mix the dry ingredients and the sour milk into the butter mixture, beginning and ending with flour. Stir until the batter is just mixed.

4. Spread about two-thirds of the batter in the greased baking pan. Layer the diced apples over the batter and cover with the rest of the batter. Combine the remaining 3 tablespoons sugar with the cinnamon and sprinkle evenly over the top.

5. Bake 40 to 45 minutes, or until the cake is golden brown on top and beginning to pull away from the sides of the pan. A tester inserted in the center should come out clean. Let the cake cool in the pan completely before cutting into squares to serve.

BUTTERMILK BREAKFAST MUFFINS

Makes 12

Out here in the boondocks, we may not have access to brioche and crois-
sants nor the time to make them, but these simple buttery muffins offer much
the same pleasure in a fraction of the time. Enjoy them plain or serve with
your best preserves or apple butter.

> 3 cups all-purpose flour
> 1/3 cup sugar
> 1 1/2 teaspoons baking soda
> 3/4 teaspoon baking powder
> 1/2 teaspoon salt
> 2 eggs
> 1 1/2 cups buttermilk
> 8 tablespoons (1 stick) unsalted butter, melted and cooled to tepid

1. Preheat the oven to 425 degrees. In a large bowl, combine the flour,
sugar, baking soda, baking powder, and salt. Whisk gently to blend.

2. In a small bowl, beat the eggs. Blend in the buttermilk and melted butter.
Add the liquid ingredients to the flour mixture and stir with a wooden
spoon until just barely blended. The batter should be lumpy; do not overmix.

3. Turn the batter into 12 greased muffin cups, filling them about three-
quarters full. Bake 18 to 22 minutes, until the muffins are golden brown on
top and the edges are just beginning to pull away from the sides of the pan.

Bran Muffins with Molasses and Raisins

Makes 12

Lots of molasses, raisins, and wheat bran cereal make these muffins nutritious as well as delicious.

1¾ cups all-purpose flour
1¾ teaspoons baking powder
½ teaspoon baking soda
¼ teaspoon salt
1 cup wheat bran cereal
2 eggs
⅔ cup milk
½ cup molasses
3 tablespoons dark brown sugar
6 tablespoons butter, melted and cooled to lukewarm
⅔ cup raisins

1. Preheat the oven to 400 degrees. In a large bowl, combine the flour, baking powder, baking soda, and salt. Stir or whisk gently to blend. Stir in the bran cereal.

2. In a medium bowl, beat the eggs. Blend in the milk and then the molasses and melted butter. Add the liquid ingredients to the flour-bran mixture and stir with a few strokes until just barely blended. There will be lumps in the batter; do not overmix. Stir in the raisins.

3. Turn the batter into 12 greased muffin cups and bake for 20 to 25 minutes, or until the muffins are puffed and the edges are just beginning to pull away from the sides of the pan.

Banana-Nut Muffins

Makes 12

Since I found my house pretty much by potluck—I lacked a map and had no idea where the town was when I headed out to see it—was it just a coincidence that one of the few neighbors on my sparsely inhabited road turned out to be another cookbook writer? Anyway, my friend Peter Wynne is always experimenting with healthful ways to bake, and this is one of his lightest successes.

1½ cups all-purpose flour
⅔ cup granulated sugar
1½ teaspoons baking powder
½ teaspoon ground cinnamon
¼ teaspoon ground mace
½ cup chopped walnuts
⅔ cup mashed very ripe banana (1 large)
1 egg
¼ cup milk
¼ cup plus 1 tablespoon peanut oil or other flavorless vegetable oil
2 tablespoons dark rum
¼ cup rolled oats
1 tablespoon dark brown sugar

1. Preheat the oven to 350 degrees. In a large mixing bowl, whisk together the flour, granulated sugar, baking powder, cinnamon, and mace. Stir in the chopped walnuts and set aside.

2. In a medium bowl, beat together the mashed banana and the egg to make a fairly smooth paste. Beat in the milk, ¼ cup of the oil, and the rum.

3. In a small bowl, combine the rolled oats, brown sugar, and remaining 1 tablespoon oil. Stir to blend well. Set this topping aside.

4. Add the liquid banana mixture to the flour mixture and stir with a wooden spoon with as few strokes as possible just until everything is moistened. Don't worry about a few small lumps. Spoon the batter into 12 lightly oiled muffin tins. Sprinkle the topping evenly over the batter.

5. Bake 25 to 30 minutes, until the muffins are golden brown and slightly springy when poked on top. Let the muffins remain in the pan 3 to 4 minutes before turning out.

DATE-NUT MUFFINS

Makes 12

Dark brown sugar and a touch of vanilla add depth of flavor to these sweet muffins, which are perfect for breakfast or brunch, or as a snack with a cup of hot coffee or tea anytime of day or night.

2 cups all-purpose flour
1/4 cup sugar
2 teaspoons baking powder
1/4 teaspoon baking soda
1/4 teaspoon salt
2/3 cup chopped pitted dates
2/3 cup chopped pecans or walnuts
2 eggs
1 1/4 cups milk
6 tablespoons butter, melted and cooled to lukewarm
1/4 teaspoon vanilla extract

1. Preheat the oven to 400 degrees. In a large bowl, combine the flour, sugar, baking powder, baking soda, and salt. Whisk gently to blend. Add the dates and nuts and toss to coat them with the flour mixture.

2. In a small bowl, beat the eggs. Blend in the milk, melted butter, and vanilla. Add the liquid ingredients to the flour mixture and mix lightly until the batter is just barely blended. There will be lumps; do not overmix.

3. Drop the batter into 12 greased muffin cups and bake for 20 to 22 minutes, until lightly browned on top and the edges are just beginning to pull away from the sides of the pan.

Broiled Cinnamon Toast

6 servings

My dear friend, San Francisco poet Frances Mayes, is originally from Fitzgerald, Georgia. This is how she makes her toast. Crisp and buttery, crackling with its glazed cinnamony topping, it is infinitely superior to and more satisfying than an ordinary slice of buttered toast.

> 1 teaspoon ground cinnamon
> 1/4 cup sugar
> 12 slices firm-textured white bread
> 4 tablespoons (1/2 stick) unsalted butter, at room temperature

1. In a small bowl, combine the cinnamon and sugar and mix well. Set aside. Spread one side of each slice of bread with 1 teaspoon of the softened butter.

2. Preheat the broiler. Arrange the bread on a baking sheet in a single layer, buttered side down. Broil 6 to 8 inches from the heat for 2 to 3 minutes, until the bread is lightly toasted.

3. Turn the slices over and sprinkle the cinnamon sugar evenly over the bread. Broil 3 to 4 minutes, until the top is toasted and the butter and cinnamon sugar are melted to a thin crackly glaze.

Corny Buttermilk Mini-Muffins

Makes 36

Tiny muffins are great for nibbling with drinks, or as a bread with a meal. The miniaturized form is charming and much less crumb-producing than its larger counterpart, since it is bite-sized and doesn't need to be broken into pieces for eating. A couple of tins the proper size are well worth the small investment. If you only have two mini-muffin pans, make the last dozen in a second batch.

³/₄ cup yellow cornmeal
³/₄ cup all-purpose flour
2 tablespoons sugar
1¹/₂ teaspoons baking powder
¹/₂ teaspoon baking soda
¹/₂ teaspoon salt
Dash of cayenne
1 egg
1 cup buttermilk
4 tablespoons (¹/₂ stick) unsalted butter, melted and
*   cooled to lukewarm*
³/₄ cup corn kernels (I use vacuum-packed niblets)

1. Preheat the oven to 425 degrees. Butter 3 mini-muffin pans, each cup 1¹/₂ inches in diameter and between ¹/₂ and ³/₄ inch deep.

2. In a medium bowl, combine the cornmeal, flour, sugar, baking powder, baking soda, salt, and cayenne. Stir well or whisk gently to blend. Make a well in the center.

3. In a small bowl, beat the egg until blended. Beat in the buttermilk and the melted butter. Pour the liquid ingredients into the well in the dry ingredients. Add the corn kernels and stir just enough to blend the batter. Do not overmix; there should still be some lumps.

4. Quickly fill the muffin tins about three-quarters full with heaping teaspoons of the batter. Bake 15 minutes, or until the muffins are lightly browned on top and the edges are just beginning to pull away from the sides of the pan. Serve warm, or transfer to wire racks to cool and serve at room temperature.

BUTTERMILK DROP BISCUITS

Makes 10

These should be served piping hot, right out of the oven, and be forewarned —they go fast. If you are having more than four people at the table, make a double batch.

1 cup all-purpose flour
1 teaspoon baking powder
$^1/_4$ teaspoon baking soda
$^1/_8$ teaspoon salt
3 tablespoons unsalted butter
$^2/_3$ cup buttermilk

1. Preheat the oven to 450 degrees. In a medium bowl, combine the flour, baking powder, baking soda, and salt. Whisk gently to blend. With a pastry blender or two knives, cut in the butter until the mixture resembles coarse meal. (Or pulse in a food processor.)

2. Add the buttermilk and stir until just blended; do not overmix. Drop by heaping tablespoons about 2 inches apart onto a lightly greased cookie sheet. Bake about 12 minutes, until the biscuits are golden brown.

VARIATION

Cheddar Drop Biscuits—Prepare the biscuits as above, but add a generous pinch of cayenne and $^1/_4$ cup packed grated sharp (aged) Cheddar cheese to the dry ingredients.

ROLLED BAKING POWDER BISCUITS

Makes 9

Roslyn Lee, whom I see several times a week at my local market in the next town over, bakes these flaky, golden-brown biscuits in staggering quantities for her church's chicken and biscuit suppers. The recipe was handed down to her from her mother, who learned it from her grandmother, an English gentlewoman who lived on a great West Indian sugar plantation until her husband died of sunstroke.

There's a touch of irony—or something—here, because Roslyn's church is situated in a town that has a biblical name but that, because it is located high on a ridge looking out on a breathtaking panoramic view of the hills to the west, is locally referred to as "Sunset." Both lovers and ordinary people drive over just to stand in front of the church and watch the sun go down in all its glory.

> *2 cups all-purpose flour*
> *1 tablespoon baking powder*
> *1 teaspoon sugar*
> *1/2 teaspoon salt*
> *1/4 cup solid white vegetable shortening (Crisco)*
> *3/4 cup milk*

1. Preheat the oven to 425 degrees. In a large bowl, mix together the flour, baking powder, sugar, and salt. Cut the shortening into the dry ingredients until the mixture resembles cornmeal. Add the milk and stir gently until mixed. The dough is not kneaded, so the trick is to mix it enough to blend in the moisture but not to overmix it, so the biscuits will remain tender.

2. Handling the dough as little and as gently as possible, turn it out onto a floured board. Form it into a ball and either roll it out or do as Roslyn directs and pat it out, using the heel of your hand, to a disk 1/2 inch thick. Cut into rounds with a 3-inch biscuit cutter.

3. Set the biscuits at least 1 inch apart on a lightly greased cookie sheet and bake 15 to 20 minutes, or until golden brown.

SOUR CREAM RAISIN SCONES

Makes 12

Many's the morning I've wished I could just run out to a local bakery and buy something simple and slightly sweet to go nicely with an excellent cup of coffee. Alas, we don't even have a Dunkin' Donuts. That's why I welcome recipes that are so easy, like these scones, which are crumbly and barely sweet.

> 2 cups all-purpose flour
> 1½ teaspoons baking powder
> ½ teaspoon baking soda
> 1½ tablespoons plus 2 teaspoons sugar
> ½ teaspoon salt
> 5 tablespoons unsalted butter
> 2 eggs, 1 separated
> ½ cup sour cream
> 3 tablespoons milk
> ⅓ cup raisins

1. Preheat the oven to 425 degrees. In a large bowl, combine the flour, baking powder, baking soda, 1½ tablespoons of the sugar, and the salt. Whisk gently to blend.

2. Cut in the butter with a pastry blender or 2 knives until the mixture resembles oatmeal. Add 1 whole egg, 1 egg yolk, the sour cream, and the milk. Stir carefully until the flour is just moistened, then mix with a wooden spoon until a soft dough forms and masses together. Stir in the raisins.

3. Turn out the dough onto a lightly floured surface and knead lightly for 30 seconds. Roll out into a circle ½ inch thick and cut into 12 triangles.

4. Place the triangles about 2 inches apart on an ungreased cookie sheet. Lightly beat the remaining egg white and brush over the tops. Sprinkle with the remaining 2 teaspoons sugar. Bake for 12 to 15 minutes, or until light golden.

CHEESE TWISTS

Makes 48

If you have a gourmet take-out shop, you're probably aware that these breadsticks are addictive—and expensive. Since we don't, I devised an easy way to make them at a fraction of the cost at home. I like to serve them at brunch as well as for a nibble before dinner.

1 package (17¼ ounces) frozen puff pastry (2 sheets)
1 egg, beaten with 1 teaspoon water
⅛ teaspoon cayenne
1 cup plus 2 tablespoons freshly grated Parmesan cheese, about 5 ounces

1. Preheat the oven to 350 degrees. Thaw the puff pastry according to the package directions, usually 20 minutes. Do not let it stand out much longer, or it will be hard to work with. One at a time, roll out each pastry sheet on a lightly floured surface to a 12-by-12-inch square.

2. Brush the beaten egg all over the pastry squares. Toss the cayenne with the grated Parmesan cheese and sprinkle half over each pastry square. Press gently to help the cheese adhere.

3. Using a small sharp knife or a rolling cutter, cut each square of pastry in half and then into ½-inch-wide strips. Carefully pick up each strip, twist, and set on an ungreased baking sheet. (You may get all the twists on 2 sheets or you may need 3. Bake together or in batches accordingly.)

4. Bake the cheese twists in the preheated oven for 10 minutes, rotating the baking sheets after 7 minutes, until golden brown and crisp.

SMALL-BATCH PICKLES AND PRESERVES

Preserving represents country cooking at its best—at once down-to-earth and highly creative, frugal and generous, stretching the color and munificence of the harvest through the stingy, cold gray months of winter. To me, it is a magical art that can turn too much into not enough, bestow perpetual youth upon produce about to pass its prime, capture the essence of a season behind glass. Surely there must be some alchemy in reducing baskets of tart-sweet raspberries into a few precious jars of intense jam; transforming sullen, overgrown zucchini into manageable bottles of pickles; resurrecting juicy peaches, picked at their peak, in a complexly sliced chutney that sings of summer all year round. These kinds of culinary transmutations fascinate me.

But this is the chapter that could give me away. "City slicker!" they'll cry when they see the small number of pints my recipes yield. It's true, you'll have to look elsewhere for directions on putting up bushels of tomatoes, peppers, asparagus, cabbage, corn, and beans. I have never practiced large-scale canning. For one thing, my garden is small, intentionally planted for fresh eating in season. The long stretches of time required to wash, trim, peel, cut up, cook, and process fruits and vegetables in quantity does not suit my lifestyle, nor do I have room to freeze in volume.

But instead of tendering apologies, I would much prefer to extol the virtues of small-batch preserving, which, with its simplicity and speed, has made a convert out of me. Rather than being a disruptive day-long project, this type of preserving can easily become a quick, natural part of everyday cooking. Because only a few jars are produced at a time, designed to be eaten within several months, they can be stored in the refrigerator, which obviates the need for water-bath processing, that last extra step in canning which detours so many cooks. You don't need a large kitchen for production-line work, and except for the canning jars and lids, no special equipment is required.

In late June and early July, when the bees are cavorting over the privet hedge in bloom, the field across from my driveway and the clearing all the way up the road next to the edge of the woods are filled with raspberry bushes covered with fruit. With the hot sun, thorns, insects, and especially the bending, berry picking is much harder work than you might imagine, and I like the luxury of laboring for only an hour or so, while it's still enjoyable, and whipping up three or four half-pint jars of extravagantly lush preserves in less than fifteen minutes. If I'm lazy enough, I can even go to the store, buy a couple of pints of berries, and produce almost the same preserves.

Since longevity and room-temperature storage are not a consideration, I can add as little sugar as I like. Besides highlighting the flavor of the fruit, less sugar allows jam to thicken more effectively without added jelling agents. So I do it the old-fashioned way—naturally.

I've discovered that with small amounts of fruit—no more than six cups at a time—a minimum amount of sugar, and a large stainless steel skillet, you can make delicious jam in roughly ten minutes. Timing will vary depending on the ripeness and moisture content of your fruit, sugar-acid balance, etc., and making jam does take some practice. But once you get a feel for the thickening, this technique is so quick and easy you may never approach preserving any other way. Jams are good for at least six months, but jellies, especially high-acid jellies, should be used within three, because without added stabilizer, they will break down and liquefy over time.

Pickles, relishes, and chutneys, which are all safely tucked away in an acid bath, are even easier, and they will keep in the refrigerator for a year or more. Even a single jar of your own homemade raspberry or strawberry jam or cherry preserves can turn a simple breakfast of scrambled eggs and muffins into a culinary treat. Thick jams can be thinned with water or a liqueur and used as a sauce over fruit, ice cream, or pound cake. Roast turkey is roast turkey and baked ham is baked ham, but team either one with sweet green-tomato pickles, Blueberry Peach Chutney, Apple Cranberry Relish, or spicy Pickled Jerusalem Artichokes, and you've revitalized the meal.

PETE REMINGTON'S FIVE-MINUTE STRAWBERRY JAM

Makes 6 (½-pint) jars

Pete Remington is my friend Barbara's mother, and hails from Minneapolis, Minnesota. Pete's real name is Marguerite, after her Dutch grandmother, Margarita Peternella Van der Bies. When she was a young girl, the family began using her grandmother's middle name as an affectionate nickname, and Pete she's remained. Coincidentally, not long after she shared this recipe with me, I was leafing through a culinary journal that stretched from the early 1920s all the way up to 1942. It belonged to a woman who had evidently moved when she married from the Midwest to Santa Barbara, California. Near the end of the notebook, in 1941, were some memorabilia from Minnesota and next to them, in pencil, the exact same recipe for strawberry preserves.

> 4 cups strawberries, washed and hulled
> 4¼ cups sugar
> 2 teaspoons fresh lemon juice

1. In a large, wide saucepan or flameproof casserole, combine the berries with the sugar and lemon juice. Bring gradually to a boil over moderately low heat, stirring to dissolve the sugar.

2. Increase the heat to moderately high and keep at a full rolling boil without stirring for a good 5 minutes.

3. Ladle the jam into 6 hot, sterilized half-pint canning jars. Cover with the lids and screw on the bands loosely. Let stand at room temperature until the jars are cool and the lids are indented. Then tighten the bands and store in the refrigerator until ready to use.

· BERRY PICKING ·

I'm convinced that picking berries is one reason people used to have large families. All the local old-timers tell of being sent out with baskets on their arms, sacks tied around their waists, charged with picking so many quarts of berries for that night's pie or mother's special preserves. One of my antique cookbooks, **The New Encyclopedia of Domestic Economy,** published in 1872, addresses this matter directly. At the beginning of a recipe for blackberry jam, it reads: "In families where there are many children, there is no preparation of fruit so wholesume, so cheap and so much admired as this homely conserve."

Berry season starts discreetly sometime near the end of June, when the weather finally softens after a flickering series of frosts and false summer starts. It is a busy time. Beginning with the lilliputian wild strawberries, a parade of red raspberries, black caps, huckleberries and blueberries (one wild, the other tame), green gooseberries, rose-hued gooseberries, red currants, and thimbleberries ripen dizzily one after the other, ending early in September with bulging fat blackberries.

Almost shyly, the delicate three-pointed leaves of the wild strawberries throw off their miniature white blossoms, yellow centered, feminine to a fault. There's been a lot of rain this year, and they're all over the lower lawn. It occurs to me that if I didn't mow the lawn, a wealth of wild strawberries would carpet my yard. I try it, but it doesn't work. The grass grows so tall it chokes out the berries and provides safe haven for every garter snake in the county. You've heard the expression "snake in the grass"? They love it in the high grass. There is a constant trade-off between neat and nature.

I dress for berry picking with less regard for my appearance than for the dangers that come with the territory. I smear sunscreen all over my face, neck, hands, and forearms and don a straw hat with an exaggeratedly wide brim, which I bought in the local dime store for four dollars and gussied up with a new baby blue satin ribbon. Because of the way the hat is designed, the only place the ribbon will stay put is tied absurdly in a coquettish bow on the side of my face, but it does keep the hat on my head.

For at least minimal protection against Lyme disease—I am, after all, foraging in the brush—I put on a long-sleeved white shirt, buttoned at the wrists, long pants, and high bobby socks with tie sneakers. If the ground is damp, I wear rubber sailing boots. So armed, I venture forth to pick berries, with a woven rush basket swinging from my wrist. If I were picking in a commercial farm, where you can't grab enough fruit fast enough, I'd tie the basket to my belt, but speed is rarely a problem in the wild.

I always say berry picking is an existential experience. If you approach a bush from one point of view, you see the berries to go for. When you're through picking, you'd swear the plant was harvested clean. Then on the way back down the road, you approach the same bush from a different direction, and it looks untouched, loaded with ripe red fruit. I've experimented and have found the same goes for up and down. Somehow, the biggest, ripest berries are always just out of reach.

Picking berries is both exhilarating and exhausting. Sun, prickles, bugs, and bending make it seem athletic, if you're really doing your job. From wild bushes, it can take hours to accumulate enough berries for a pie, let alone the volume needed for preserves. That's why so many children were bred for the task.

QUICK BLACK RASPBERRY JAM

Makes 2 (½-pint) jars

*B*ecause black raspberries are so seedy, they really do have to be strained. If you have a food mill, this is a snap. If you don't, use the sieve method described below; it is a bit tedious, but if you adore black raspberries, it is well worth it.

> 4 cups black raspberries
> 1 cup sugar
> ¼ cup water
> 1 tablespoon fresh lemon juice

1. In a 10-inch stainless steel skillet, combine the black raspberries, sugar, water, and lemon juice. Bring to a boil over moderate heat, stirring to dissolve the sugar and pressing with a large spoon to crush the berries. Boil for 3 minutes.

2. Pass the raspberries and syrup through the fine disc of a food mill. Alternatively, puree everything in a food processor and strain through a food mill or sieve—medium, not fine-mesh—in two or three batches, working the pulp and seeds against the strainer with a spoon or plastic spatula and scraping the bottom of the sieve periodically to extract as much of the fruit as possible.

3. Return the raspberry puree to the skillet and boil over moderately low heat for 5 to 7 minutes, until it thickens and jells lightly on a cold saucer. A spoon drawn across the bottom of the pan should leave a trail for a moment or two.

4. Ladle the hot jam into 2 hot half-pint jelly jars, cover with lids, and screw on the bands loosely. Let stand at room temperature until the jam cools and the lids depress. Then tighten the bands and store in the refrigerator.

Red Red Jam

Makes 2 (½-pint) jars

All the old country cookbooks contain at least one recipe for raspberry and red currant jam, because before the days of commercial pectin, farmhouse cooks saw the wisdom of fortifying red raspberries, which are exceptionally low in pectin, with red currants, which are extremely high in pectin, for the best combination of texture and flavor in the least cooking time. The almost lemony tartness of the currants is extremely pleasing with the lush flavor of raspberry, and the jam boasts a beautiful burgundy color.

3 cups red raspberries
2 cups red currants
1½ cups sugar
½ cup water

1. In a 10-inch stainless steel skillet, combine the raspberries, currants, sugar, and water. Bring to a boil slowly over moderate heat, stirring to dissolve the sugar and pressing with a large spoon to crush the berries. Boil for 3 minutes.

2. In two batches, puree the berries and syrup in a food processor. Strain through a food mill or sieve—a medium, not fine-mesh sieve—to remove the seeds. Return to the skillet and boil over moderate heat for 5 to 7 minutes, or until the jam will jell lightly on a cold saucer. When you draw a spoon across the bottom of the skillet, it should leave a trail for a moment or two.

3. Ladle the hot jam into 2 hot half-pint jelly jars, cover with lids, and screw on the bands loosely. Let stand at room temperature until the jam cools and the lids depress. Then tighten the bands and store in the refrigerator.

LEMON PLUM CONSERVE

Makes 4 (½-pint) jars

Because both prune plums and lemons are loaded with pectin and there is little moisture in these preserves, I make this conserve in a saucepan rather than a skillet to minimize evaporation. The combination of flavors, blended with the almond, is subtle and sophisticated, and this makes a delightful spread on any simple muffin or bread.

> 2½ to 3 pounds prune plums
> 1 lemon
> 2 cups sugar
> ½ cup slivered blanched almonds, coarsely chopped
> ⅜ teaspoon almond extract

1. Rinse the plums well. Quarter them and remove the pits but leave the skin on.

2. Wash the lemon well. Seed and chop the lemon, peel and all, into small dice.

3. In a medium nonreactive saucepan, combine the plums, lemon, and sugar. Bring to a boil over moderate heat, stirring to dissolve the sugar. Reduce the heat to moderately low and cook uncovered for about 1 hour, or until the mixture is thick and a few drops on a cold spoon jell.

4. Remove from the heat and stir in the almonds and almond extract. Fill 4 sterilized half-pint jelly jars with the conserve to within ¼ inch of the top. Cover with lids and screw the bands on loosely. Let stand until the lids are sucked down (you'll notice they're concave rather than flat). Tighten the bands and store in the refrigerator for up to a year.

Sweet and Sour Cherry Preserves

Makes 4 (½-pint) jars

Sweet and sour here doesn't mean sugar and vinegar, but a mix of sweet cherries and sour cherries. The combination gives a lovely, complex flavor. Since some of the cherries are left luxuriously whole and some are pureed to add body, this is partially a preserve and partially a jam.

> 4 cups sour cherries (about 1⅓ pounds)
> 2 cups sweet cherries (about 1 pound)
> 1⅔ cups sugar
> ½ cup water
> 2 tablespoons lemon juice
> ⅜ teaspoon almond extract (optional)

1. Pit the cherries over a bowl to catch the juices. If it makes them easier to pit, cut the sweet cherries in half.

2. In a large stainless steel skillet, combine the cherry juices that have collected in the bowl with the sugar and the water. Bring to a boil, swirling to dissolve the sugar. Boil over moderately high heat for 3 to 5 minutes, until the syrup begins to thicken.

3. In a food processor, puree about one-third of the cherries with ½ cup of the syrup. Add to the skillet along with the remaining cherries and any more juice that has collected in the bowl. Reduce the heat to moderate and boil, stirring occasionally, for 10 to 15 minutes, until the syrup jells on a cold saucer.

4. Stir in the lemon juice and almond extract and ladle the jam into 4 hot, sterile half-pint jelly jars. Cover with the lids and loosely screw on the bands. Let cool until the lids compress. Then tighten the bands and refrigerate the jam.

BLUEBERRY-PEACH CHUTNEY

Makes about 5 (½-pint) jars

Another product of my blueberry picking on a commercial farm. Keep this in your refrigerator for a couple of months before you open it, and the flavor will improve greatly. It's a deep, dark chutney that goes beautifully with Indian food, with simple roast birds, and with ham.

2 pounds blueberries (about 5 cups or 2 pints)
2 pounds firm, ripe peaches (about 8 medium)
1 pound tart green apples (3 or 4 medium)
1 cup raisins
2 medium onions, chopped
1 tablespoon finely chopped garlic
3 cinnamon sticks, split lengthwise in half
1 tablespoon mustard seeds
1 teaspoon powdered ginger
½ lime, chopped (peel and all)
½ teaspoon crushed hot red pepper flakes
1 tablespoon coarse salt (or 1½ teaspoons regular salt)
1 bay leaf
1 teaspoon black peppercorns
8 whole cloves
1 cup packed light brown sugar
¾ cup cider vinegar

1. Rinse the blueberries and drain in a colander. Pick them over to remove any woody stems or bruised berries.

2. Peel the peaches by plunging them into a large saucepan of boiling water for 30 to 60 seconds, until the skins split. Rinse under cold water and remove the skins. Halve the peaches, remove the pits, and cut the peaches into ½-inch dice.

3. Peel the apples and cut into ½-inch dice.

4. In a large stainless steel or enameled pot, combine half the blueberries with the apples, raisins, onions, garlic, cinnamon sticks, mustard seeds, ginger, chopped lime, hot pepper flakes, and salt. Tie the bay leaf, peppercorns, and cloves in cheesecloth and add to the pot. Add the brown sugar and vinegar.

5. Bring to a boil over moderately high heat, stirring frequently. Reduce the heat to moderate and boil gently until the onions are soft, about 15 minutes. Add the peaches and remaining blueberries and cook until the peaches are tender and the chutney is thickened, 10 to 15 minutes longer. Remove and discard the spice bag.

6. Ladle the hot chutney into 5 sterilized half-pint jars with self-sealing lids. Set the lids on top and let stand at room temperature until the chutney is cooled and the lids are slightly depressed in the center. Tighten the screw tops and store in the refrigerator for up to a year. The chutney improves with age.

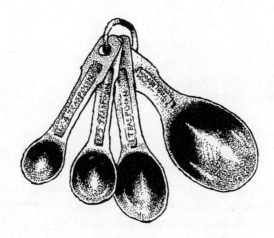

CRANBERRY APPLE CHUTNEY

Makes 5 pints

This recipe makes a bit more than usual, because so much of it disappears between Thanksgiving and Christmas. If I'm not the one doing the cooking, I bring a jar as a gift, a piece of gingham cloth wrapped around the cap and tied with a grosgrain ribbon.

2 medium onions, chopped
2 garlic cloves, crushed through a press
1½ cups sugar
1½ cups water
1 cup cider vinegar
Zest and juice from 1 lemon or lime
2-inch piece of fresh ginger, peeled and minced
5 cinnamon sticks
2 teaspoons ground cinnamon
2 teaspoons ground coriander
½ teaspoon freshly ground pepper
¼ teaspoon grated nutmeg
¼ teaspoon ground cloves
¼ teaspoon salt
6 flavorful apples, peeled, cored, and cut into ½-inch dice
2 bags (12 ounces each) fresh cranberries, rinsed and picked over

1. In a large stainless steel pot or enameled cast-iron casserole, combine the onions, garlic, sugar, water, vinegar, lime zest and juice, ginger, cinnamon sticks, ground cinnamon, coriander, pepper, nutmeg, cloves, and salt. Bring to a boil, stirring to dissolve the sugar. Reduce the heat and simmer for 15 minutes.

2. Add the apples and simmer for 10 minutes, or until almost tender. Add the cranberries and simmer until the berries begin to pop, 5 to 7 minutes longer.

3. Ladle the chutney into 5 sterilized pint jars, adding 1 cinnamon stick to each jar. Cover loosely with self-sealing lids. Let stand until the chutney is cooled and the lids are slightly indented in the center. Tighten the screw bands and store the chutney in the refrigerator. Let ripen at least 1 week before serving.

RHUBARB GINGER JAM

Makes about 3 cups; 3 (½-pint) jars

You'll be hard put to find a more old-fashioned or, to my taste, more delicious preserve than this one. The bite of the fresh ginger paired with the tartness of the rhubarb, both softened with just the right amount of sugar, creates an exceptionally good jam.

2 pounds trimmed fresh rhubarb, cut into ¾-inch pieces (to yield 6 cups)
2¼ cups sugar
⅓ to ½ cup peeled and finely diced fresh ginger (see Note)

1. In a large stainless steel skillet, combine the rhubarb, sugar, and ginger. Cover and cook over moderately low heat until the sugar melts and the rhubarb begins to give off its juice, about 5 minutes. Uncover and boil over moderate heat for 10 to 15 minutes, or until the ginger is tender and the jam is thickened.

2. Ladle into 3 hot, sterilized half-pint jars. Set on the lids and screw on the bands loosely. Let stand at room temperature until the jars are cooled and the lids compressed. Tighten the bands and store the jam in the refrigerator.

NOTE: If you happen across very young ginger, especially the Hawaiian variety, which has a thin ivory-colored skin tinged with pink, peel it, and slice it paper thin. You can use up to ¾ cup if you like a distinctive ginger flavor, as I do.

CRANBERRY-LIME CONSERVE WITH TOASTED WALNUTS AND PEARS

Makes 4 pints

Because fruit conserves and chutneys are so easy to make and so versatile, I often find myself experimenting with new combinations. Here lime and pear add an interesting twist to the more usual cranberry-apple pairing, while a generous addition of walnuts contributes to the texture.

> 2 packages (12 ounces each) fresh cranberries
> 2 limes
> 1 pound flavorful sweet-tart apples, such as Winesap or Northern Spy, peeled and cut into 1/2- to 3/4-inch dice
> 1 pound firm, ripe pears, peeled and cut into 1/2- to 3/4-inch dice
> 2 1/4 cups sugar
> 4 cinnamon sticks
> 8 whole cloves
> 1 1/2 cups broken walnut pieces (about 6 ounces)

1. Preheat the oven to 350 degrees. Rinse the cranberries and pull off any stems you see. Throw away any soft, bad berries. Put the cranberries into a large nonreactive saucepan or flameproof casserole.

2. Slice off and discard the ends of the limes down to the pulp. Thinly slice the limes, put them in a food processor, and mince. Add to the pot. Add the apples, pears, sugar, cinnamon sticks, and cloves. Mix well. Cover and cook over moderate heat for 10 minutes, stirring occasionally. Uncover and cook for 10 minutes longer.

3. Meanwhile, spread out the walnuts on a baking sheet and bake, shaking the pan once or twice until the nuts are lightly toasted, about 5 to 7 minutes. Add to the conserve and mix well.

4. Spoon the conserve into 4 hot pint jars, making sure there is 1 cinnamon stick in each jar. Cover and let cool. Refrigerate for at least 3 days and up to 3 weeks before serving.

WILD RASPBERRY JAM

Makes 4 (½-pint) jars

While I love the intense flavor and sunny aroma of wild berries, along with the torturous pleasure involved in picking them, they are seedy, and this recipe will work perfectly well with the berries you find in your market. Because it's such a small-batch recipe, you'll also be able to afford to make it.

> *2½ pounds red raspberries (about 5 cups), preferably freshly picked*
> *1¼ pounds sugar*

1. Rinse and drain the berries and place them in a large stainless steel skillet. Bring to a boil over moderate heat. Boil, stirring and crushing the berries with the back of a spoon, until the juices are all released and they have reduced by at least half, about 10 minutes.

2. Add the sugar, stirring until dissolved. Boil 5 to 10 minutes, or until the mixture is reduced to a jam consistency. To test, spoon a few drops onto a saucer and set it in the freezer for a couple of minutes.

3. Ladle the hot jam into 4 sterilized half-pint jars. Cover with lids and screw on the bands loosely. Let cool to room temperature. Tighten the bands and refrigerate.

RED CURRANT JELLY

Makes 2 (½-pint) jars

If you've ever picked and then picked over currants, you'll know why I made such a small quantity of this jelly. Since I use it mainly as a flavoring in sauces and as a glaze, this small amount gets me through most of the year. The actual cooking is a snap, since currants contain such a lot of pectin.

4 cups red currants
¾ cup sugar

1. In a medium nonreactive saucepan, cook the currants over moderate heat, crushing the berries with the back of a spoon to release all the juice, for about 10 minutes.

2. Strain through a double layer of dampened cheesecloth into a 2-cup measure and let drip for 15 minutes to catch as much of the liquid as you can. Do not squeeze the pulp or your jelly will be too tannic.

3. Pour the currant juice into a small nonreactive saucepan. Add the sugar and stir to dissolve. Bring to a boil and cook until jelled, about 10 minutes. Pour into 2 sterilized half-pint jars. Cover loosely with the lids and let cool to room temperature. Tighten the bands and refrigerate.

FRESH TOMATO KETCHUP

Makes 3 cups

Next to soup, this is the best use I know for garden-ripe tomatoes just a tad past their prime. Because of the high acid content of the tomatoes and vinegar, be sure to cook this in a pot that is neither iron nor aluminum.

4 pounds very ripe tomatoes, peeled, seeded,
  and coarsely chopped
1 large onion, chopped
2 garlic cloves, minced
2/3 cup cider vinegar
2 tablespoons dark brown sugar
1 1/2 teaspoons salt
1 teaspoon ground cinnamon
3/4 teaspoon powdered mustard
1/2 teaspoon ground coriander
1/4 teaspoon ground allspice
1/4 teaspoon freshly ground pepper
1/8 teaspoon ground cloves
1/8 teaspoon cayenne
1 bay leaf

1. Combine all the ingredients in a large stainless steel saucepan. Bring to a boil, reduce the heat to moderately low, and simmer, partially covered, stirring often, for 1 hour. Remove and discard the bay leaf.

2. In batches if necessary, puree the ketchup in a blender or food processor until smooth. Return to the saucepan and simmer over low heat, uncovered, stirring frequently to prevent scorching on the bottom, until thickened, 20 to 30 minutes.

3. Ladle the ketchup into 3 hot, sterilized half-pint canning jars. Set the lids on top and screw on the bands loosely. Let stand until the jars are cooled to room temperature and the lids are compressed. Tighten the bands and refrigerate. The ketchup keeps well in the refrigerator for up to 6 months.

PICKLED JERUSALEM ARTICHOKES

Makes 4½ to 5 pints

If you grow Jerusalem artichokes, you are guaranteed to have too many of them, and this is a great way to use up the surplus. For some reason, these tubers never lose their crispness, and the sweet-hot brine makes them irresistible. I put these pickles out with assorted hors d'oeuvres before dinner parties in the winter and on the picnic table with the hot dogs and hamburgers in summer.

> 3 pounds Jerusalem artichokes
> ⅔ cup coarse (kosher) salt
> 1 medium onion, sliced
> 5 garlic cloves, bruised
> 3½ cups cider vinegar
> ⅔ cup sugar
> 1 tablespoon yellow mustard seeds
> 1½ teaspoons whole coriander seeds
> ½ teaspoon whole allspice berries
> ½ teaspoon crushed hot red pepper flakes
> 5 very small bay leaves

1. Scrub the artichokes thoroughly with a stiff new vegetable brush. Cut them into ¼-inch slices. In a large stainless steel bowl or pot, dissolve the salt in 2 quarts of cold water. Add the artichoke slices and let stand 8 to 12 hours. Drain the artichokes into a nonaluminum colander. Return to a clean bowl of cold water, swish around with your hands to rinse, and drain well.

2. Lower 5 clean pint canning jars into a large pot of boiling water to cover for 3 to 5 minutes. Remove with tongs and set on a kitchen towel. Divide the artichokes, onion slices, and garlic cloves among the hot jars. The last pint may be a little slim, and if it seems appropriate, use a half-pint instead.

3. In a large enameled or stainless steel saucepan, combine the vinegar with 1½ cups water. Add the sugar, mustard seeds, coriander seeds, allspice berries, hot pepper flakes, and bay leaves. Bring to a boil, stirring to dissolve the sugar. Reduce the heat to moderately low and simmer for 5 minutes.

4. Ladle the hot pickling syrup and spices into the jars, making sure a piece of bay leaf gets into each. Be sure the vegetables are entirely covered with syrup and leave about ½ inch space at the top of the jars. If you see any air bubbles or suspected bubbles, run the handle of a clean stainless steel fork or spoon around the inside of the jar. Cover with canning lids that have been dropped into simmering water for a couple of minutes. Set bands over the lids and let stand until the lids compress in the center. Tighten the bands and refrigerate for at least 2 weeks and up to a year before serving.

Mrs. Lewis's Bread 'n' Butter Pickles

Makes 4 pints

This is a local recipe that's been handed down so many times it has something of a history. I've put my own imprint on it by reducing the turmeric to suit my personal taste and by quartering the recipe so that it remains "small batch" and manageable. Know, however, that if you have a garden full of cucumbers, it can be, and originally was designed to be, made in volume. The one-step procedure is particularly easy to assemble.

My friend, writer Jan Quackenbush, shared the recipe with me. He writes: "I refer to this as 'Mrs. Lewis's' because she passed it on to me. She was a sweet, white-haired gal in her eighties who had lived for years at ——— Lake, where I first enjoyed these sliced cukes. To her credit, she in turn referred to the recipe as 'Hub Yost's' since she got it from him. Hub, too, lived at the lake. He was a large, red-faced man, an ex-Justice of the

(continued)

Peace, who had given my father his driver's license in the thirties when my dad was only 14, a mild overlooking of the law until my dad soon afterwards drove a horse-drawn haywagon team off a narrow bridge into ——— Creek, whereupon my dad was constrained from further driving and, furthermore, had to pay back the farmer by working all summer on his farm."

4 cups sliced cucumbers
4 cups sliced onions
1/2 red bell pepper, thinly sliced (optional)
3/4 cup distilled white vinegar
3/4 cup sugar
1 tablespoon mustard seeds
2 teaspoons canning or coarse (kosher) salt
1 1/2 teaspoons turmeric
3/4 teaspoon powdered mustard

1. Combine all the ingredients in a large nonaluminum saucepan. Bring just to a boil and immediately remove from the heat.

2. Pack the vegetables into 4 hot, sterilized pint canning jars. Pour the hot vinegar mixture over them. If any pieces are not covered, top off the jar with a little extra vinegar. Cover with lids and screw on the bands loosely. Let stand until cool. Then tighten the bands and store in the refrigerator for up to a year.

COOKING FROM A COUNTRY FARMHOUSE

Josie Soden's Sweet Green Tomato Pickles

Makes 4 pints

Crisp and sweet, green tomato pickles are decidedly country, from the North to the South. These are from a very old farmhouse recipe from the third-generation Soden dairy farm just down the road.

2½ pounds green tomatoes
3 cups water
2 cups sugar
1½ cups cider vinegar
4 cinnamon sticks, split lengthwise in half
2 teaspoons whole cloves

1. Wash tomatoes well. If your tomatoes are reasonably small, simply cut them into ¼-inch-thick rounds. If they are on the large side, first cut in half and then slice. Soak the tomato slices in a bowl of heavily salted water (use coarse or pickling salt if possible) for at least 6 hours, or overnight. Drain the tomato slices.

2. In a large stainless steel or enameled saucepan, combine the water with the sugar, vinegar, cinnamon sticks, and cloves. Bring to a boil, stirring to dissolve the sugar. Reduce the heat to low and simmer for 10 minutes.

3. Add the tomato slices, increase the heat to moderate, and cook for 2 minutes only. Immediately transfer the tomato slices to hot, sterilized canning jars. Divide the syrup among the jars and set 2 pieces of cinnamon stick in each. Cover loosely with self-sealing lids and let stand until the pickles are cooled and the lids are slightly indented in the center. Screw the bands tightly closed and refrigerate the pickles for at least a week and up to a year before opening.

PICKLED RAMPS OR SHALLOTS

Makes 2 pints

Because these aren't cooked, the ramps remain crisp and pungent, something like small white cocktail onions. Serve them as you would pickles. They are especially good with cheese, with pâté, and with potted pork.

24 ramp bulbs (see page 167) or small shallots (about 1 pound)
1 cup cider vinegar
1 cup water
1/4 cup sugar
1/2 teaspoon black peppercorns
1/2 teaspoon whole allspice berries
1/2 teaspoon mustard seeds
4 blades of mace (optional)
1/2 teaspoon coarse salt

1. Peel off the soft outer layer of the ramp bulbs or the brown skin from the shallots. Trim off the roots. Rinse the ramps and drain well. Divide the ramps or shallots between 2 sterile pint canning jars.

2. In a medium stainless steel saucepan, combine the vinegar, water, sugar, peppercorns, allspice, mustard seed, mace, and salt. Bring to a boil, stirring to dissolve the sugar. Reduce the heat to very low and simmer 2 minutes. Pour the hot liquid and spices into the jars, dividing evenly. Cover with the lids and screw on the bands loosely. Let stand until the jars are cool; then tighten the bands and store in the refrigerator for at least 2 weeks before using.

PAULINE'S CHERRY BOMB

Makes 2 quarts

My friend Pauline Ross has a pair of the most glorious sour cherry trees I've ever seen. They are so roundly pruned and the cherries are such a brilliant scarlet that when they are covered with ripe fruit you'd swear they were made of silk. I'm always tempted to pin a bunch of the cherries to my hat. While this tantalizing nectar tastes like pure essence of cherry, sweetened just enough to appear innocuous, don't be fooled—Pauline doesn't call it a bomb for nothing.

> 4 cups sour cherries
> 1/2 gallon vodka
> 1 cup honey, preferably wildflower

1. Wash the cherries well, drain, and spread on paper towels to dry. Remove any stems. Put the cherries in a large clean gallon crock or jar. Pour the vodka over the cherries. Cover and let stand at room temperature 4 to 6 weeks, until the cherries turn white.

2. Pour 1/2 cup honey into each of 2 clean quart jars—I like to use canning jars. Drain the vodka from the cherries into the jars, dividing evenly. Stir until the honey is dissolved. Cover and set aside in a cool dark place. Serve as a liqueur, chilled if you like. The bomb gets even better after a couple of months.

COUNTRY DESSERTS

Everyone I know seems to have a sweet tooth. In the country, we talk about it a little bit differently from the way they do in the city. We say, "I'd like to have a big piece of that apple pie"; they say, "I think I'd like a thin wedge of that apple tart." We say, "I'll have a thick slice of that delicious-looking chocolate cake"; they say, "I'll just have a sliver of that flourless chocolate torte." We spoon up puddings; they swallow pots de crème. If you ask me, it's all the same.

Also, if you ask me what is the quintessential country dessert, I would have to answer—pie. Bob Dylan didn't reveal it to the world in *Nashville Skyline,* but he vocalized about it awfully nicely. Anyone who has ever visited a state fair, attended a church social bake sale, or walked into a farmhouse kitchen on a crisp fall morning knows the peculiarly pleasurable sight of that flaky phenomenon—apple, peach, blueberry, cherry, rhubarb, custard, lemon, or lime. Country pies are generous, heaped high in the center, loaded with fruit, sweetened to a flaw. Their success hinges largely on the artistry of the pastry, forked, fluted, or braided around the rim. There are probably as many different crusts as there are farmhouse cooks. I've included two of my favorites here: a marvelously flaky sour-milk-and-Crisco pastry given to me by a transplanted Pennsylvania Dutch woman and a crisp, tender butter and buttermilk crust of my own.

Cakes and cookies may be a close second. Probably because there are no bakeries out here, everyone seems to bake their own. At any holiday, birthday, or other occasion, you'll always find a homemade cake or a platter of freshly baked cookies on the table. I like good-keeping cookies, either raw in the freezer, to be baked up fresh on the spur of the moment—Chocolate Pecan Icebox Cookies, for example—or long-lasting cookies, like Sugar

Cookies and Molasses Gingersnaps, lavishly spiced, which hold well for as long as you like stored in an airtight tin and which even improve with age.

When I first came to the country, I made a pilgrimage twice a week half a mile down the road to get milk from my neighbors; they raise prize-winning Holsteins, which produce milk with a butterfat content that averages over 5 percent. Fresh unpasteurized milk is thick and sweet, with a clean, subtle scent, a different beverage entirely from the thin, pallid fluid that streams vapidly from paper containers and plastic bottles. The first time I attended a local county fair, my neighbor's eleven-year-old son showed me how to milk a cow by hand, and the warm white liquid that squirted directly into my cupped fingers tasted as sweet as candy.

That milk, paired with Hank the postman's spanking fresh eggs, make it easy to see just why puddings and custards and ice creams have such a generous quality out here. Of course, unless you have access to a certified farm, there are serious health hazards associated with drinking raw milk, so as a substitute, I've used a blend of ordinary pasteurized milk and some sort of cream to add body to the recipes in this book. The compromise works, though don't think for a moment it is as good as the original.

Fruit desserts are the other hands-down favorites. Apples are perennially popular, especially when they are falling from the trees. Actually, apple harvests can be sparse out here, when a not-uncommon, wacky late frost hits the trees in late April or even early May, just as the blossoms are forming. But this year, early spring was wet and warm, the trees bloomed luxuriantly, and everyone has too many apples: Northern Spy, Macs, Ida Reds, Macouns, Empires. You often bump into your neighbors hauling huge bags of battered apples down to the old cider mill.

When I cook with apples, I like to use two kinds, for more complex flavor and texture. Sometimes I'll blend my own Northern Spies with some Greenings or Granny Smiths from the store. Berries, rhubarb, and currants are the other prolific fruits, with sour cherries, a few late peaches, and some stolid types of pears. Besides pies and preserves, cobblers, crisps, fruit-laden coffee cakes and frozen desserts put most of these fruits to best use.

Brown Sugar Apple Pie

6 to 8 servings

You can't have too many recipes for apple pie, especially if you have your own trees. This one has a slightly caramelized flavor from the dark brown sugar and is redolent of cinnamon.

> 6 large baking apples
> 1 tablespoon lemon juice
> ³/₄ cup packed dark brown sugar
> 1¹/₄ teaspoons cinnamon
> 1¹/₂ tablespoons instant tapioca
> Sour Milk Flaky Pastry (page 239) or
>   Buttermilk Butter Crust (page 236)
> 2 tablespoons unsalted butter

1. Preheat the oven to 400 degrees. Peel and core the apples and cut them into ¹/₂-inch wedges. In a bowl, toss the apples with the lemon juice, brown sugar, cinnamon, and tapioca.

2. Divide the pastry into 2 unequal halves. On a lightly floured surface, roll out the larger half into a circle about 11 inches in diameter and ¹/₈ inch thick. Ease the pastry into a 9-inch pie pan without stretching the dough. Pour and scrape the apples and seasonings into the pie shell.

3. Roll out the remaining pastry into a circle about ¹/₈ inch thick and set it on top of the pie. Trim both layers of dough to leave a ¹/₂-inch overhang. Fold the doubled edge under and crimp decoratively to seal. Prick the top of the pie with a fork or cut several steam vents in it with the tip of a knife.

4. Bake the pie for 50 minutes, or until the juices are bubbling up and the crust is a light golden brown. Check the pie 10 to 15 minutes before it is done and if the edges of the pie look as if they are browning too much, cover the rim with strips of aluminum foil.

LEMONY BLUEBERRY PIE

6 to 8 servings

Be forewarned: I do not care for my desserts overly sweet, so the tartness of the lemon, to my palate, makes this pie just perfect. If you are of the majority party, however, feel free to add a few more tablespoons of sugar to the filling. The last time I made this pie it was for a good friend and his son. As it was coming out of the oven, another close friend dropped by, one of my writer compatriots. She is quite concerned with healthful eating and professes to avoid sugar. Nevertheless she took one look at that blueberry pie, and there was no stopping her. I finally had to pull the pie plate away from her, to save a couple of slices for the boys.

> 5 cups blueberries
> 3/4 cup plus 2 teaspoons sugar
> Grated zest of 1 lemon
> 1 tablespoon lemon juice
> 2 tablespoons instant tapioca
> Sour Milk Flaky Pastry (page 239) or Buttermilk Butter Crust (page 236)
> 1 egg white, lightly beaten, or 1/2 tablespoons milk

1. Preheat the oven to 425 degrees. Rinse the berries and drain well in a colander. Pick over to remove any woody stems and bruised berries.

2. In a large bowl, combine the blueberries, 3/4 cup sugar, the lemon zest, lemon juice, and tapioca. Toss to mix well, but be gentle to avoid breaking the berries. Set aside at room temperature while you roll out the pie crust. Toss the berries a couple of more times as you work.

3. Divide the pastry almost in half, leaving one piece slightly bigger than the other. On a lightly floured surface, roll out the larger piece until it forms a circle a little more than 1/8 inch thick. If rolling out dough tends to give you trouble, or if you find it sticking because of the weather, an easy trick is to roll out the dough between two sheets of waxed paper or plastic wrap. Fit the dough into a 9-inch metal pie pan, easing it down into the bottom and pressing it gently against the sides without stretching the dough, which would cause it to shrink while being baked. Store the pie shell in the refrigerator while you roll out the smaller piece of dough to make a top crust.

4. Remove the bottom crust from the refrigerator. Give the berries a final gentle toss and mound them in the pie pan. Moisten all around the rim of dough with a damp finger or a pastry brush and lay the second round of dough loosely on top, leaving plenty of room over the berries. Press the two pieces of dough together around the rim of the pie pan to seal. Trim the edges to about ½ inch of overhang. Fold the doubled edge under and crimp decoratively. Brush the egg white or milk over the top crust and sprinkle on the remaining 2 teaspoons sugar. Cut five slits or thin petal-shaped pieces in the top crust to allow steam to escape.

5. Bake the pie for 15 minutes at 425 degrees. Reduce the oven temperature to 350 and bake 35 to 45 minutes longer, or until the crust is golden and the juices from the berries bubble up in a thick syrup. Let cool before serving.

FOURTH OF JULY CHERRY PIE

Makes a 9-inch pie

If you only make fresh cherry pie once a year, Independence Day is the holiday to do it. In late June and early July, sour cherries are ripe on your trees, on your neighbor's trees, or in your farmer's market, and sweet cherries are at their best—and their lowest price—in supermarkets. I like the depth of flavor you get with a blend of the two kinds of cherries.

While pitting cherries is not actually fun, it is busy work that can be accomplished while you listen to the radio, watch television, or talk on the phone. I can pit a pound of cherries in fifteen to twenty minutes, and I don't own a cherry pitter. Any reasonably sharp object you can insert into the stem end will serve; just work it around the pit, squeeze, and the pit will pop out. Be sure to work over a bowl to catch all the juices.

In this version of the all-American classic, the pitted cherries are macerated overnight with the sugar, so that they give off their juices, which are

(continued)

reduced and thickened before being added to a partially baked pie shell. This solves the technical problem so prevalent with any juicy fruit pie—soggy bottom crust. As perfect as this cherry pie turns out, it is intense and tastes best, in my opinion, à la moded with a scoop of vanilla ice cream.

4 cups sour cherries (about 1⅓ pounds)
2 cups sweet cherries (about 1 pound)
¾ cup plus 3 tablespoons sugar
Buttermilk Butter Crust (page 236)
3 tablespoons all-purpose flour
1 tablespoon kirsch (optional)
2 tablespoons unsalted butter

1. Wash the cherries well; remove any stems (or do so as you pit the cherries). Pit the sour cherries over a bowl to catch the juices. Work with a cherry pitter or by inserting a sharp, narrow object into the stem end, working it around the pit, and squeezing the cherry gently until the pit pops out. As you pit them, drop the cherries into the bowl. Over the same bowl, cut the sweet cherries in half with a small stainless steel knife, cut out the pit with the tip of the knife, and drop the cherries into the bowl. Add ¾ cup plus 2 tablespoons sugar to the bowl, stir to mix with the cherries, cover with plastic wrap, and let stand at room temperature, stirring once or twice, for at least 6 hours and preferably for up to a day.

2. Make the Buttermilk Butter Crust. Divide the dough in half, leaving one half a bit larger than the other. Wrap in waxed paper and refrigerate for at least 30 minutes.

3. While the dough is chilling, drain the cherries, reserving the juice. Measure out and set aside ¼ cup of the cherry juice. Pour the remainder into a medium-sized stainless steel saucepan and boil over moderately low to moderate heat until the sweetened cherry juice is reduced by half. (There will only be 1 to 1¼ cups of juice to begin with, but the syrup really boils up, so choose a large enough pan.) Set the reduced cherry syrup aside.

4. Preheat the oven to 400 degrees. Roll out the larger piece of pie dough on a lightly floured surface to an 11-inch circle about ⅛ inch thick. (I always find it's easier to roll out dough without any problems if you do it between floured sheets of waxed paper or plastic wrap.) Fit the dough without stretching into a 9-inch metal pie pan. Trim the edges to a ½-inch overhang, fold the edges under, and crimp to seal. Prick the pastry all over with a fork at 1-inch intervals.

5. Set the bottom pie shell in the oven and bake for 5 minutes. Prick any large bubbles that have formed with a fork and continue baking for 7 minutes longer. Remove from the oven but leave the oven on. While the pie shell is baking, roll out the top crust from the second piece of dough.

6. Bring the reduced cherry syrup to a boil over moderate heat. In a small bowl, combine the reserved ¼ cup cherry juice with the flour to form a slurry. If more juices have collected in the cherry bowl, add a couple of more tablespoons to the flour slurry and the remainder to the saucepan. Stir the kirsch into the slurry, mixing until it is smooth and there are no small lumps of flour. Stir the flour slurry into the boiling cherry syrup. Boil, stirring, for 2 minutes, or until smooth and thickened.

7. Pour and scrape the thickened cherry syrup into the bowl with the cherries and stir to mix. Turn the filling into the warm pie shell. Dot with the butter. Set the top crust over the pie and press onto the rim of the bottom crust, trimming away any excess as you work around the pie; the raw dough will stick to the warm baked pastry. Cut 5 slits in the top pastry to allow steam to escape. Sprinkle the remaining 1 tablespoon sugar over the crust.

8. Return the pie to the oven and bake 30 to 35 minutes longer, or until the juices are bubbling up and the top crust is a light golden color. After about 20 minutes, if the rim of the pie starts to brown too deeply (and it usually does), cover that part of the crust with strips of aluminum foil. Let cool on a wire rack for at least 30 minutes before serving warm or at room temperature.

BUTTERMILK BUTTER CRUST

Makes enough for 1 double-crust 9-inch pie or 2 tarts

Buttermilk produces a light, crisp, delicate crust, perfect for all kinds of fruit pies and tarts. The butter and nutty tang of the buttermilk lend a luxurious effect. Making this in the food processor is easy and efficient, but to keep the pastry tender, mix only until crumbly; the dough should not form a ball in the machine.

Tip: If you make the pastry as directed and roll it out between two sheets of lightly floured plastic wrap, you'll never shy away from making your own, all-from-scratch pies and tarts.

> 2 cups unbleached all-purpose flour
> 1 tablespoon sugar
> 1/4 teaspoon salt
> 12 tablespoons (1 1/2 sticks) cold unsalted butter
> 1/3 cup buttermilk

1. In a food processor, combine the flour, sugar, and salt. Run the machine briefly to blend the dry ingredients. Cut the butter into tablespoons and drop them on top of the flour. Pulse the machine or turn it quickly on and off 10 to 12 times, until the butter is cut into pieces about the size of small peas.

2. Measure out the buttermilk. Turn the machine on and pour in the buttermilk through the feed tube. Process only until the liquid is mixed and the pastry is blended to the consistency of coarse sand; do not allow it to form a ball. Turn out onto a sheet of waxed paper or plastic wrap and lift up the paper to press the pastry together. Without overworking it, turn and press the dough until it forms a mass. Then press together with your hands into a disk, or better yet, two disks, dividing equally or as directed by your recipe.

3. Wrap the pastry disks in waxed paper or plastic wrap and refrigerate for at least 30 minutes before rolling out. The pastry can be prepared a day before you bake it, but I prefer the dough freshly made. If it is chilled until very firm, let it stand at room temperature for 5 to 10 minutes, until malleable, before working with it, so it doesn't crack easily as you roll it out.

BANANA SPLIT PIE

8 servings

Kitsch is just as popular in the country as it is in the city. In fact, judging from all the fake wooden geese, beribboned lambs, and bonneted little lasses on front lawns, perhaps more so. All this by way of introducing this rather kitschy but exceptionally delicious pie that is guaranteed to win popularity contests at potluck suppers and dessert parties with young and old alike.

Depending upon the sophistication of your audience and the time you have available, you can use a ready-made prebaked crust, a graham cracker crust, a chocolate wafer cookie crust, or a halved recipe of any of your favorite pastries in this book, fitted into a nine-inch pie plate, pricked all over, and baked at 375 degrees for 16 to 18 minutes.

6 tablespoons sugar
3 tablespoons cornstarch
2 cups milk
2 egg yolks
3 tablespoons unsalted butter
1¼ teaspoons vanilla extract
½ cup mini chocolate bits
2 to 3 bananas
1 prebaked 9-inch pie shell
½ pint strawberries, hulled and sliced lengthwise
1 cup (½ pint) heavy chilled cream
2 tablespoons confectioners' sugar
⅓ cup chopped walnuts
1 maraschino cherry (optional)

1. In a medium saucepan, combine the sugar and cornstarch. Gradually whisk in the milk until blended. Set over medium heat and cook, stirring frequently, until the mixture comes to a boil and thickens, about 5 minutes.

2. In a small bowl, whisk the egg yolks. Gradually whisk in ½ cup of the hot thickened milk. Whisk the egg yolk mixture into the remaining milk in the saucepan. Boil the custard, whisking, for 1 minute. Remove from the

(continued)

heat and whisk in the butter, 1 tablespoon at a time, until melted. Blend in 1 teaspoon of the vanilla. Set aside, whisking occasionally, until cooled to room temperature. Cover with a sheet of waxed paper directly on the custard and refrigerate until chilled, about 1 hour. Whisk again to smooth out and then stir in the chocolate bits.

3. Peel the bananas and slice fairly thinly crosswise on the diagonal. Line the bottom and sides of the pie shell with the banana slices. Pour in the chocolate chip custard and smooth the top. Arrange the strawberry slices on top of the custard in concentric circles.

4. Whip the cream lightly. Beat in the confectioners' sugar and the remaining ¼ teaspoon vanilla. Beat until stiff. Spread the whipped cream decoratively over the top of the pie. Sprinkle the chopped walnuts on top and set the cherry in the center. Refrigerate until serving time.

VERNA DEY'S STRAWBERRY RHUBARB PIE

Makes a 9-inch double-crust pie

I met Verna Dey when I went to visit Roger Hess, her son-in-law, who raises Jersey cows. These small brown bovines are not common in this region, but their rich yellow milk is fabulous for cooking. Verna, by reputation an extraordinary cook, is a large, shy woman, who came north from Pennsylvania Dutch country. When I asked her for a couple of recipes, she hesitated at first, doubting the exactness of her measurements, but after I asked a couple of the right questions, she relaxed, and we spent a wonderful afternoon together.

Strawberries and rhubarb are often paired, because the pectin in the rhubarb is very helpful to the juicy berries, and their flavors balance together beautifully. While orange and ginger can be added to the mix, this recipe is pure country, simple and sweet.

Verna Dey's Sour Milk Flaky Pastry (recipe follows)
3 cups diced rhubarb
3 cups halved strawberries
2½ tablespoons instant tapioca
1¼ cups sugar

1. Preheat the oven to 400 degrees. On a lightly floured surface, roll out the larger pastry disk into a round about ⅛ inch thick. Fit it into a 9-inch metal pie pan.

2. In a medium bowl, toss the rhubarb and strawberries with the tapioca and sugar. Pile into the pastry shell.

3. Roll out the second piece of pastry into a circle about ⅛ inch thick and center it over the pie. Trim the edges with scissors to allow an overhang of about ½ inch. Fold the edges of the pastry under and crimp to seal. With the tip of a knife, cut 5 slits or decorative cutouts in the top crust to allow steam to escape.

4. Bake the pie in the preheated oven for 10 minutes. Reduce the heat to 350 degrees and bake for 45 minutes longer, or until the fruit is bubbling and the crust is pale brown.

VERNA DEY'S SOUR MILK FLAKY PASTRY

Makes 1 double crust

In the old days, milk that was not pasteurized spoiled easily; the acid produced by the bacteria gave baked goods a very tender crumb. Mixing milk with vinegar produces much the same results; you won't taste the vinegar in the crust. I've never been particularly fond of solid vegetable shortening in pastries, but this crust is exceptional—tender and flaky. I like the way it holds its shape naturally after the pie cools, forming a generous-looking crenellated dome on top.

(continued)

$1^1/_2$ teaspoons distilled white vinegar
$1/_2$ cup milk
$2^1/_3$ cups all-purpose flour
$1/_2$ teaspoon salt
$3/_4$ cup Crisco

1. Stir the vinegar into the milk and let stand at room temperature while you prepare the dry ingredients. The milk will thicken slightly as it "sours."

2. In a medium to large bowl, combine the flour and salt. Cut in the Crisco with 2 knives or a pastry cutter until the mixture resembles coarse meal. Drizzle the soured milk over the pastry while tossing with a fork to moisten evenly. Mix just until barely blended.

3. Gather the pastry into a ball, pressing any loose pieces together. Divide in half, giving slightly more pastry to the half that will become the bottom crust. Flatten both pieces into thick disks, wrap in plastic wrap, and refrigerate for at least 30 minutes before rolling out.

LEMON BUTTER PIE

6 to 8 servings

I usually serve this delightfully tart pie covered with a swirled mound of slightly sweetened whipped cream flavored with vanilla, as indicated below. The garnish of candied strips of lemon peel adds extra color and more lemon flavor, but it is not an essential ingredient. When I have raspberries on hand, cultivated or wild, I cover the top of the pie with a single layer and pass the whipped cream on the side.

$1/_2$ recipe Buttermilk Butter Crust (page 236)
3 whole eggs
2 egg yolks
$3/_4$ cup plus 2 tablespoons sugar

Finely grated zest of 1 lemon
1¼ teaspoons cornstarch
½ cup fresh lemon juice (see Note)
8 tablespoons (1 stick) unsalted butter, cut into tablespoons
1 cup heavy cream
1½ tablespoons confectioners' sugar
½ teaspoon vanilla extract
Candied Lemon Zest (page 242), optional

1. Preheat the oven to 375 degrees. On a lightly floured surface—or better yet, between two sheets of lightly floured plastic wrap—roll out the pastry into an 11-inch circle. Invert into a 9-inch pie plate. Ease the pastry into the bottom and against the sides of the pan. Trim the excess pastry to ½ inch, fold under and crimp decoratively. Cover with a sheet of lightly buttered aluminum foil (buttered side-down) and fill with pie weights or dried beans.

2. Bake the crust for 8 minutes. Remove the weights and foil, prick the bottom of the shell with a fork, and return the crust to the oven. Bake for 8 to 10 minutes longer, or until the shell is dry throughout and very lightly colored. Set on a rack and let cool completely. (The crust can be baked up to a day ahead, as long as the weather is not too humid.)

3. In a heavy nonaluminum saucepan, beat the whole eggs and the yolks together until blended. Gradually beat in the sugar and whisk until light and fluffy. Add the grated lemon zest. Dissolve the cornstarch in the lemon juice and beat into the mixture. Cook over moderate heat, whisking frequently, until the mixture comes to a simmer, 3 to 5 minutes. Reduce the heat to low and whisk in the butter, about 2 tablespoons at a time, until blended and smooth. Immediately remove the lemon curd from the heat and scrape into a bowl. Place a sheet of plastic wrap directly on the surface and allow to cool. Refrigerate, whisking once or twice, until chilled, about 2 hours.

4. About 1 to 2 hours before serving, fill the baked shell with the lemon curd. Whip the cream until soft peaks form. Add the confectioners' sugar and vanilla and beat until stiff. Dollop on top of the pie and swirl decoratively with the back of a spoon. Garnish with candied lemon zest, if desired, and refrigerate until serving time.

NOTE: If you plan to make the candied lemon zest, remove the zest from 2 or 3 of the lemons before you juice them.

CANDIED LEMON ZEST

Remove the zest of 2 or 3 lemons with a zester to yield 3 tablespoons of thin strips. If you don't have a zester, peel off the yellow part of the skin only—not the white pith—with a swivel-bladed vegetable peeler and cut the zest into very thin strips with a stainless steel knife. Place the strips of lemon zest in a small saucepan half-filled with cold water. Bring to a boil and drain into a sieve. In the same saucepan, combine ⅓ cup sugar with ⅓ cup water. Bring to a boil, stirring to dissolve the sugar before the water bubbles. Add the lemon zest and boil over moderate heat about 7 minutes, until the strips of zest are tender and the syrup is thickened. If made ahead, store the zest in the syrup in a jar in the refrigerator. Before using, remove the strips with a fork and let drain on a sheet of waxed paper. Separate them from clumping, if necessary, while they are still moist.

BUTTERMILK FUDGE FROSTING

Makes about 2 cups, enough to frost a 9-inch double-layer cake

Fudge frostings are not difficult as long as you can restrain yourself from stirring them. It is the stirring that causes crystallization and gives fudge that granular sugary consistency. Don't worry about a bit of separation initially; the mixture comes together when you beat it. Sweet fanciers adore this frosting, and it has a professional-looking glossy sheen. The extra bit of chocolate at the end is not traditional, but I prefer my chocolate fudge really chocolatey.

2 squares (1 ounce each) unsweetened chocolate
1¾ cups sugar
1 cup buttermilk
2 tablespoons light corn syrup

COOKING FROM A COUNTRY FARMHOUSE

4 tablespoons unsalted butter, at room temperature
1 ounce semisweet or bittersweet chocolate, chopped
1 teaspoon vanilla extract

1. In a large saucepan, combine the unsweetened chocolate, sugar, buttermilk, and corn syrup. Bring to a boil over moderate heat, stirring early on to dissolve the sugar. Reduce the heat to moderately low and boil *without stirring* for 15 minutes, or until the mixture reaches 225 to 230 degrees on a candy thermometer.

2. Remove from the heat and scrape into a mixing bowl. Beat in the butter and let stand 15 minutes. Add the chopped chocolate and vanilla and beat with an electric mixer for 3 to 5 minutes, until completely smooth. Let the frosting stand, stirring occasionally, until it begins to set up, 10 to 15 minutes. Use at once. If the frosting gets too hard, set the bowl in a larger bowl of hot water and stir until loosened, or microwave on Medium for about 30 seconds, stirring every 10 seconds.

Quick Chocolate Cream Icing

Makes enough to frost a 9-inch double-layer cake

6 ounces semisweet chocolate bits
1/2 cup sour cream
1 1/2 cups heavy cream

1. Place the chocolate in a 1-quart glass or ceramic bowl. Microwave on High for 2 to 3 minutes, until the chocolate looks shiny and is melted and smooth when stirred. Whisk in the sour cream until well blended.

2. In a large chilled bowl with chilled beaters, whip the cream until it mounds softly. Scrape the chocolate mixture into the whipped cream and beat again until stiff enough to spread.

BAKE-SALE
CHOCOLATE LAYER CAKE

Makes a 9-inch double-layer cake

*P*icture a classic two-layer chocolate cake filled and iced with fudgy frosting, the kind of picture-perfect dessert grandmothers made from scratch and many mothers whipped up from a mix when we were children. An extra egg and a mixture of butter and oil make this a rich chocolate cake with a moist, tender crumb.

The secret of its extra goodness is the buttermilk, which adds tangy flavor and moisture with very little fat. If buttermilk is not available in your market, mixing milk and distilled white vinegar will give you the equivalent of sour milk, a classic combination with chocolate. Low-fat or two-percent milk can be used without affecting the results.

When I make the Buttermilk Fudge Frosting, I like to ice this cake neatly and stick a maraschino cherry in the center, so that it looks like a bakery cake. If that's not your idea of humor, chopped nuts or a single flower blossom provide more elegant decoration. Or simply swirl the frosting with the back of a spoon.

> 2 cups all-purpose flour
> 1 cup unsweetened cocoa powder, preferably Dutch processed
> 1½ teaspoons baking soda
> ½ teaspoon baking powder
> ¼ teaspoon salt
> 4 eggs
> 2 cups sugar
> 1 teaspoon vanilla extract
> 8 tablespoons (1 stick) unsalted butter, melted and cooled to lukewarm
> ½ cup vegetable oil
> 1⅓ cups buttermilk or 1¼ cups milk blended with
>   1½ tablespoons distilled white vinegar
> Buttermilk Fudge Frosting (page 242) or
>   Quick Chocolate Cream Icing (page 243)

1. Preheat the oven to 350 degrees. Grease and flour two 9-inch cake pans. In a medium bowl, combine the flour, cocoa powder, baking soda, baking powder, and salt. Sift together or whisk to blend and remove any lumps.

2. In a large bowl, beat the eggs with an electric mixer until blended. Gradually beat in the sugar and add the vanilla. Scrape down the sides of the bowl. Beat on high speed 2 to 3 minutes, until the mixture thickens and forms a slowly dissolving ribbon when the beaters are lifted.

3. In a medium bowl or large glass measure, whisk together the melted butter, oil, and buttermilk. With the mixer on medium, beat a third of the flour mixture into the butter and sugar and then a third of the buttermilk mixture. Beat in another third of the flour and half the remaining buttermilk. Beat in half the remaining flour and all the remaining buttermilk mixture. Beat in the remaining flour, mixing until thoroughly blended. Scrape the batter into the prepared pans.

4. Bake 25 to 30 minutes, or until a cake tester inserted in the center comes out clean and the edges of the cake are just beginning to pull away from the sides of the pan. Do not overbake, or the cake may dry out. Let the pans cool on wire racks for 10 minutes; then unmold the cakes onto the racks. Let cool completely before frosting.

BUTTERMILK BUTTER CAKE

Makes a 9-inch double-layer cake that will serve 8

Here's more of my love affair with buttermilk. This is a classic, basic yellow cake that, when frosted with dark fudge frosting, looks just like the archetypal layer cake in a children's storybook. Because it uses leaveners and requires no separate beating and folding of the egg whites, it's easy to make with an electric hand-held mixer. If you use a stationary, heavy-duty model, reduce the mixing times a bit.

After baking, be sure to let the cake layers cool completely before frosting. I learned the hard way it's important, not just to apply the icing at the proper temperature, but to let gases from the baking powder and baking soda dissipate. As with many cakes, I prefer this one the day after it is baked; the

COOKING FROM A COUNTRY FARMHOUSE

layers freeze well, too. Frost this cake with Buttermilk Fudge Frosting (page 242) or with your favorite icing. Technically, the cake easily makes enough for ten, but when I serve it with fudge frosting, everyone has seconds, so eight is a safer call.

2¼ cups sifted cake flour
2½ teaspoons baking powder
½ teaspoon baking soda
¼ teaspoon salt
12 tablespoons (1½ sticks) unsalted butter, at room temperature
1¼ cups sugar
4 eggs, at room temperature
1½ teaspoons vanilla extract
1¼ cups buttermilk

1. Preheat the oven to 375 degrees. Grease the bottoms of two 9-inch cake pans. Line each with a round of waxed paper; butter and flour the paper.

2. In a medium bowl, combine the flour, baking powder, baking soda, and salt. Whisk gently to blend.

3. In a large bowl, and using an electric mixer, beat the butter until light and fluffy. Gradually beat in the sugar, blending well as you go so that it is all incorporated before you shake on the next addition. After all the sugar is added, beat on high speed for a full 2 minutes. Beat in the eggs, one at a time, beating well after each addition. Blend in the vanilla.

4. With the mixer on medium speed, add the flour and buttermilk alternately in thirds, beginning and ending with flour and beating well after each addition. Beat the batter for 30 seconds. Scrape down the sides of the bowl and beat for 30 seconds longer. Turn the batter into the prepared cake pans. Smooth the tops gently with a rubber spatula.

5. Bake the layers 35 to 40 minutes, until the cake is golden brown on top, springs back lightly when touched, and has begun to pull away from the sides of the pan. Transfer the pans to a wire rack and let cool 5 minutes. Then unmold the cakes unto the rack, peel off the waxed paper and let the layers cool completely before frosting.

WILMA COOPER'S COALMINER'S CAKE

Makes a 13 x 8-inch sheet cake

Wilma's husband Charlie does beautiful woodwork. The Shaker-style coat rack hanging on my kitchen wall—the house didn't have a single closet when I moved in—displays his skill. Wilma is known for her baking, and this easy recipe of hers is one I turn to whenever I need a birthday cake on the spur of the moment.

> *2 cups all-purpose flour*
> *2 cups sugar*
> *2 teaspoons baking soda*
> *1 teaspoon baking powder*
> *³⁄₄ unsweetened cocoa powder, preferably Dutch-processed*
> *1 cup milk*
> *1 teaspoon vanilla extract*
> *1 cup strong brewed coffee*
> *1 cup flavorless vegetable oil*
> *2 eggs*
> *Coffee Buttercream Icing (recipe follows)*

1. Preheat the oven to 350 degrees. Lightly grease a 9 x 13-inch Pyrex baking dish or half-sheet pan. In a large bowl, combine the flour, sugar, baking soda, baking powder, and cocoa. Whisk gently to blend.

2. Add the milk, vanilla, coffee, oil, and eggs. Beat until well blended. Pour and scrape the batter into the pan and bake for 30 to 35 minutes, or until a cake tester inserted in the center comes out clean. Let stand for 10 minutes, then unmold onto a wire rack and let cool.

3. Using a long, narrow metal spatula, frost the top and sides of the cooled cake with coffee buttercream icing.

Coffee Buttercream Icing

Makes about 2 cups

Because it has no eggs to bind it, this frosting tends to separate. If it does that to you, whip it well, chill slightly, and beat again to smooth it out.

> 8 tablespoons (1 stick) unsalted butter, at room temperature
> 2 cups confectioners' sugar
> 1 teaspoon vanilla extract
> 1/4 cup strong brewed coffee

In a medium bowl, beat the butter with a whisk or an electric hand mixer on medium speed until it is fluffy. Beat in the sugar gradually, then add the vanilla and coffee and continue to beat until light, fluffy, and smooth. If necessary, cover and refrigerate the icing for 10 to 15 minutes to help it set up before using to frost a cake.

Gina Upright's Melt-in-Your-Mouth Blueberry Cake

6 servings

I am indebted to Gina and her husband Carl for many things, this delectable cake among them. Because Gina would rather be outside walking, naming all the wildflowers and the birds, you can be sure this recipe is easy and quick. It's perfect for breakfast or a snack with tea or coffee any time of day.

> 2 eggs, separated
> 1 cup plus 1 tablespoon sugar
> 8 tablespoons (1 stick) unsalted butter, at room temperature,
>   or ½ cup solid vegetable shortening
> ¼ teaspoon salt
> 1 teaspoon vanilla extract
> 1½ cups all-purpose flour
> 1 teaspoon baking powder
> ⅓ cup milk
> 1½ cups fresh or frozen blueberries

1. Preheat the oven to 350 degrees. Beat the egg whites until soft peaks form. Gradually beat in ¼ cup sugar and continue beating until stiff and glossy. Set aside.

2. In a large bowl, cream the butter or shortening. Add the salt and vanilla. Gradually beat in ¾ cup sugar. Add the egg yolks and beat until light and fluffy.

3. Remove 2 tablespoons flour to a small bowl. Sift together the remaining flour and the baking powder. Alternately mix the dry ingredients and milk into the butter mixture, beginning and ending with dry ingredients and beating until blended before each addition. Stir in ¼ of the egg whites to lighten the batter. Gently fold in the remaining egg whites.

4. Toss the blueberries with the reserved 2 tablespoons flour. Fold into the batter. Turn into a greased 8-inch square metal baking pan. Sprinkle the remaining 1 tablespoon sugar over the top.

5. Bake 50 to 55 minutes, or until a tester inserted in the center comes out clean. Let cool before serving.

PEACH CHERRY COBBLER

6 servings

Peaches are not local around these parts, but they do come into the markets in volume about the same time the sour cherries ripen, and the two together make a delightful pairing, the sassy tartness of the cherries adding a lilt to the lush mellowness of the peaches. Both are juicy fruits, so they must be treated with due consideration to avoid a soggy dessert.

Store-bought peaches trucked in hard as nails from their far-off tree of origin used to cause me despair until I learned that peaches, like avocados, can be made to ripen nicely at home. Choose fruit that is already as ripe as possible. A golden yellow cast—as opposed to greenish—is more important than the amount of red on the skin. Let the peaches stand at room temperature for one to three days, until fragrant and slightly soft. You'll be surprised at how good they taste.

Cobblers should be eaten fresh, warm or at room temperature, the day they are made, preferably with a scoop of good vanilla ice cream plopped on top.

> ³/₄ *pound sour cherries, pitted (over a bowl to catch the juices)*
> 1¹/₂ *pounds firm, ripe peaches, peeled and cut into ¹/₂-inch wedges*
> ¹/₂ *cup sugar*
> 2 *tablespoons flour*
> ¹/₂ *cup sliced almonds*
> 2 *tablespoons unsalted butter*
> *Sweetened Buttermilk Biscuit Dough (page 253)*

1. In a medium bowl, combine the cherries, peaches, and sugar. Stir gently to mix. Let the fruits macerate with the sugar for 3 to 6 hours.

2. Preheat the oven to 400 degrees. Drain the fruit, reserving the juices. Immediately return the fruit to the bowl. Set aside ¹/₄ cup of the juices. Boil the remaining juices over moderate heat for 5 minutes, or until reduced to ³/₄ cup. More juices will collect in the bowl; add them to the saucepan.

3. Add the flour to the reserved ¹/₄ cup juices and stir until blended and smooth. Stir this slurry into the boiling juices. Boil, stirring, for 1 to 2 minutes, until thickened and smooth. Add this thickened syrup to the fruit

and stir gently to mix. Pour the fruit and syrup into a shallow 2½-quart ceramic baking dish. Sprinkle on the sliced almonds. Dot with the butter.

4. Make the sweetened buttermilk biscuit dough as directed. Drop by heaping teaspoons onto the fruit. Leave a 1-inch border all around the edges and don't worry about spaces between the dough. It will expand to cover the dessert. Do not spread the dough or press it into the fruit.

5. Bake the cobbler for 30 to 35 minutes, until the juices are bubbling and the biscuit crust is dry throughout and golden brown on top. Serve warm or at room temperature.

SWEETENED BUTTERMILK BISCUIT DOUGH

Makes enough for 12 biscuits or to cover a cobbler that serves 6

The food processor makes the quickest, easiest biscuit dough. If you don't own one, cut in the butter in whatever manner you're accustomed to, with two knives or a pastry blender. If the dough is used to make individual biscuits, bake in a 450-degree oven for 12 minutes.

1¼ cups all-purpose flour
1½ tablespoons sugar
1¼ teaspoons baking powder
¼ teaspoon baking soda
4 tablespoons (½ stick) cold unsalted butter
½ cup plus 1 to 2 tablespoons buttermilk

1. In a food processor, combine the flour, sugar, baking powder, and baking soda. Whirl briefly to blend. Add the butter, cut into tablespoons, and process, pulsing or turning the machine quickly on and off 8 to 10 times, until the dough looks like coarse meal.

2. Turn out into a bowl, add ½ cup of the buttermilk, and stir briefly until almost blended. Working the dough as little as possible, add the remaining 1 to 2 tablespoons buttermilk to make a soft dough that will drop from a spoon.

BOURBON PEACH SHORTCAKE

6 servings

Here is a wonderful alternative to strawberry shortcake. The flavor combination of peaches, brown sugar, bourbon, and almond is sublime, especially when paired with vanilla whipped cream and the slight nuttiness of the cornmeal-based shortcake biscuits that follow.

>   6 large peaches
>   3 to 4 tablespoons packed dark brown sugar
>   2 tablespoons bourbon whiskey
>   1/2 teaspoon almond extract
>   1 cup heavy cream
>   1 tablespoon confectioners' sugar
>   1/2 teaspoon vanilla extract
>   Cream Shortcake Biscuits (page 255)

1. Plunge the peaches into a large saucepan of boiling water and boil for 30 to 60 seconds, until the skins just begin to loosen. Lift out with a slotted spoon and transfer to a colander. Rinse under cold running water. Slip off the skins and cut the peaches into slices about 1/2 inch thick in the center. As you cut them, place the slices in a medium glass or ceramic bowl.

2. Add the brown sugar, bourbon, and 1/4 teaspoon of the almond extract to the peaches and toss gently. Let stand for at least 1 hour and up to 3 hours, stirring occasionally.

3. In another medium bowl, whip the cream until soft peaks form. Add the confectioners' sugar, vanilla, and remaining 1/4 teaspoon almond extract. Beat until fairly stiff. Cover and refrigerate if not using immediately.

4. Assemble the shortcakes just before serving: Split each biscuit. Place the bottom of a biscuit on a dessert plate. Drizzle some of the peach juices over the biscuit and add a couple of spoonfuls of peaches. Set the top of the biscuit over the peaches, cover with a large dollop or two of the whipped cream, and top with a spoonful of peaches. Repeat to make 6 shortcakes.

CREAM SHORTCAKE BISCUITS

Makes 6

Don't be alarmed if your biscuits are only about half an inch high: that's the way they're supposed to be. When you split them, you'll see how tender and light they are. The addition of cornmeal adds a pleasing grittiness to the texture as well as a nutty sweetness to the flavor.

> 1 cup all-purpose flour
> 1/2 cup cornmeal
> 2 1/2 tablespoons sugar
> 2 teaspoons baking powder
> 1/4 teaspoon salt
> 5 tablespoons cold unsalted butter
> 1/2 cup heavy cream

1. Preheat the oven to 450 degrees. In a food processor, combine the flour, cornmeal, sugar, baking powder, and salt. Pulse briefly to mix. Cut the butter into tablespoons and drop them on top of the flour. Pulse 10 to 12 times, until the butter is cut into bits the size of a pea. Turn on the machine and quickly add the cream through the feed tube. Process just until blended—do not allow the dough to form a ball.

2. Turn out the dough onto a lightly floured surface and pat into a 7-inch square about 1/2 inch thick. With a 3-inch biscuit cutter, cut out 4 circles. Push the remaining dough scraps together and cut out 2 more biscuits.

3. Arrange the biscuits on a lightly buttered baking sheet and bake 10 to 12 minutes, until lightly browned on top. Remove to a rack and let cool slightly before serving.

DESSERT-FIRST
STRAWBERRY SHORTCAKE

6 to 8 servings

Plenty of strawberry shortcakes abound, but "dessert first" deserves an explanation. My neighbor, seventy-two-year-old dairy farmer Bill Soden, related to me how his mother sent him and his brothers out to pick berries in the late spring and early summer. "Ordinarily," said Bill, "when we sat down to supper, we had to finish all our meat and potatoes before Mother would give us dessert. But once or twice a year, when we'd come back with baskets of wild strawberries, those tiny little ones the size of your fingernail, she'd make a huge strawberry shortcake and serve it first."

2¼ cups flour, preferably 1¼ cups all-purpose flour and 1 cup soft-wheat flour, such as White Lily
1¼ teaspoons baking soda
¼ teaspoon salt
3 tablespoons unsalted butter
2 tablespoons solid vegetable shortening
1 egg, separated
1 cup buttermilk
About ⅓ cup granulated sugar
2 pints strawberries, wild if you have them
1 cup heavy cream
2 tablespoons confectioners' sugar
1 teaspoon vanilla extract

1. Preheat the oven to 425 degrees. In a large bowl, combine the flour, baking soda, and salt. Whisk gently to blend. Cut in the butter and shortening with a pastry blender or 2 knives until the mixture resembles coarse meal. Beat the egg yolk with 1 cup of the buttermilk. Add to the dry ingredients and stir until blended. If the dough is too dry, add more buttermilk 1 tablespoon at a time.

2. On a lightly floured surface, roll or pat out the dough ¾ inch thick. Trim to an 8-inch round. (Or cut into 3-inch biscuits. Press the scraps together and cut out more biscuits. There should be enough dough to make 8 to 10.) Lightly beat the egg white and brush over the dough. Sprinkle ½ teaspoon sugar over the top of each biscuit.

3. Set the dough on a lightly greased cookie sheet and bake 20 to 25 minutes, until risen and golden brown. Let cool on a wire rack.

4. Meanwhile, halve, quarter, or slice the strawberries. Toss with 3 table-spoons sugar. Taste and add another spoonful or two if they need it; it will depend upon the sweetness of the berries. Let stand 30 to 60 minutes, tossing occasionally.

5. Shortly before serving, beat the cream until soft peaks form. Beat in the confectioners' sugar and vanilla. Split the shortcake in half and place the bottom on a platter. Spoon some berries and juice onto the shortcake and cover with the top. Spoon a generous dollop of cream over the shortcake and top with more berries.

STRAWBERRY TRIFLE

8 servings

Where life is a little rugged, a pretty treat is greatly appreciated, as long as it's not fussy. This dessert looks like a lot of work, but it's not. Traditionally trifle is made with a stirred custard that takes some time over the stove and can curdle if hurried. I like to use a foolproof light vanilla pudding, which can be whipped up in five minutes. If you really need to shave seconds, you could substitute a packaged mix, but the flavor will not be the same.

Depending on the season, blueberries or raspberries can be substituted for the strawberries, or for a really spectacular look, use a mix of all three.

2 pints strawberries, quartered or thickly sliced, plus 5 to
    7 berries for garnish
¼ cup granulated sugar
2 tablespoons Grand Marnier or orange juice
1 pound cake (14 to 16 ounces)
6 tablespoons raspberry jam, preferably seedless
Vanilla Pudding (page 259)
1 cup heavy cream
2 tablespoons confectioners' sugar
1 teaspoon vanilla extract or 1 tablespoon Grand Marnier

1. In a medium bowl, toss the strawberries gently with the granulated sugar and Grand Marnier or orange juice. Let stand at room temperature, tossing occasionally, for at least 30 minutes.

2. Meanwhile, cut the cake lengthwise into 6 slices about ½ inch thick. Spread 2 tablespoons of the raspberry jam over every other slice to coat 3 slices of cake evenly to the edges. Sandwich together a jam-covered slice with a plain slice of cake so there are 3 sections of cake layers filled with jam. Cut each section crosswise into slices ¼ to ⅜ inch thick.

3. Cover the bottom of a 3- to 4-quart glass trifle dish or reasonably straight-sided bowl with a layer of cake pieces. Arrange more pieces standing up around the sides.

4. Drain the strawberries, reserving the juices; there will be about ¼ cup. Drizzle 2½ to 3 tablespoons of the juices over the cake pieces in the bowl. Place half the strawberries in the bottom. Cover with half the vanilla pudding. Place the remaining cake pieces on top. Drizzle with the remaining juices and cover with the remaining berries and pudding. Cover and refrigerate until serving time.

5. Shortly before serving, beat the cream with the confectioners' sugar until fairly stiff. Beat in the vanilla. Spread the whipped cream over the top of the trifle and garnish with the whole berries.

Vanilla Pudding

Makes about 2 cups

 2 tablespoons cornstarch
 6 tablespoons sugar
 2 cups milk
 2 egg yolks
 2 tablespoons unsalted butter
 1½ teaspoons vanilla extract

1. In a heavy medium saucepan, combine the cornstarch and sugar. Gradually whisk in the milk until blended. Set over medium heat and bring to a boil, whisking frequently; this will take 3 to 5 minutes. Boil, whisking, for 30 seconds. Remove from the heat.

2. In a small bowl, whisk the egg yolks to break them up. Gradually whisk in about ½ to ¾ cup of the hot custard. Whisk the egg yolk mixture back into the remaining custard in the pan. Cook over medium heat, whisking, for 1 minute.

3. Remove from the heat and whisk in the butter until melted. Blend in the vanilla. Let stand until cooled slightly, whisking several times. Cover with a sheet of wax paper placed directly on the pudding and refrigerate until chilled. Whisk briefly before using to loosen slightly.

Mapled Apple Crisp
with Oatmeal and Walnuts

8 servings

Maple and walnuts are a natural combination, but be sure the nuts are very fresh. If you have an opened package, store it in the refrigerator or, better yet, in the freezer. As with all my apple desserts, for a more complex flavor I like to use two varieties of the fruit if they are easily available.

To save time and labor, instead of coring each apple, simply cut the wedges right off the central core.

> 8 tart-sweet baking apples, peeled and cut into 1/2-inch wedges
> 1/4 cup maple syrup, preferably amber
> 1/2 teaspoon ground cinnamon
> 1/2 cup very coarsely chopped walnuts
> 1/2 cup all-purpose flour
> 1/4 cup whole wheat flour
> 2/3 cup packed dark brown sugar
> 6 tablespoons unsalted butter, cut into bits
> 1/2 cup rolled oats

1. Preheat the oven to 375 degrees. In a 9 x 13-inch baking dish, toss the apples with the maple syrup and 1/4 teaspoon of the cinnamon. Sprinkle the walnuts over the apples.

2. In a medium bowl, combine the all-purpose flour, whole wheat flour, brown sugar, remaining 1/4 teaspoon cinnamon, and the butter. Pinch and rub between your fingers until the mixture is blended to the consistency of very coarse meal. Add the rolled oats and mix well with your fingers. Pinch together bits of this topping and scatter it over the apples.

3. Bake 45 minutes, or until the apples are tender and the topping is browned and crisp.

CINNAMONY APPLESAUCE

6 servings

Apple season is a little like tomato season. All of a sudden, there is so much largesse you don't know what to do with it. There are apples everywhere—on the tree, on the ground, in baskets, in the basement, on your porch, on your neighbor's porch. Apple butter, apple cider, and apple pie are of course, ideal solutions to this abundance, but applesauce should not be overlooked. It is not just a childish pleasure. I like making applesauce because the apples don't have to look picture perfect to be usable, and the more kinds you throw in, the more complex the flavor.

This version, with a strong presence of lemon and lots of cinnamon, goes particularly well with the Sausage and Mashed Potato Loaf on page 96. But with a splash of heavy cream, it could serve just as well for dessert. The directions that follow yield a chunky sauce, which is my preference. If you like yours smooth, simply add all the apples at the start.

2½ pounds apples (about 8), preferably a mix of 2 or 3 kinds; the varieties
    do not matter as long as they are flavorful
2 tablespoons fresh lemon juice
⅓ cup granulated sugar
¼ cup packed dark brown sugar
¾ cup unsweetened apple cider, preferably fresh, or water
1 teaspoon ground cinnamon
1 tablespoon unsalted butter

1. Peel all but 2 of the apples and cut them off the core into large chunks. In a large nonaluminum pot, combine the apples with the lemon juice, granulated sugar, brown sugar, cider, and cinnamon. Cover and cook over moderately low heat, stirring occasionally, 12 minutes.

2. Peel the remaining apples and cut them into ½- to ¾-inch chunks. Add them to the sauce and continue to cook, partially covered, until the apples are reduced to a thick sauce with chunks, 15 to 20 minutes longer. Stir in the butter until melted. Let cool slightly before serving. Serve warm, at room temperature, or cold.

CHOCOLATE CHOCOLATE CHIP PUDDING WITH CHOPPED WALNUTS

5 servings

Puddings are so easy and foolproof I don't understand why they are not more popular. Perhaps the "instant" products on the market have led cooks to believe that scratch puddings were time-consuming and difficult. In fact, you can throw this dessert together in little more than five minutes. Because of the cornstarch thickener in the base, the added egg can be cooked over direct heat with no danger of curdling. Just be sure to use a heavy saucepan, keep the heat moderate, and reach all parts of the bottom of the pan with your whisk to prevent scorching.

2 tablespoons cornstarch
2 tablespoons unsweetened cocoa powder, preferably Dutch processed
1/3 cup sugar
2 cups milk
1 egg
1/2 cup mini chocolate chips
1 1/2 tablespoons unsalted butter
1/2 cup chopped walnuts
Whipped cream (optional)

1. In a heavy 1½-quart saucepan, combine the cornstarch, cocoa powder, and sugar. Gradually whisk in the milk. Set the pan over moderate heat and cook, whisking frequently and being sure to cover the entire bottom of the pan, until the custard comes to a boil, 4 to 5 minutes. Cook, whisking constantly, for 30 seconds.

2. In a small bowl, whisk the egg until blended. Gradually whisk in about ½ cup of the hot custard. Whisk the mixture back into the pan and cook over moderate heat, whisking, for 1 minute. Remove from the heat.

3. Add ¼ cup of the mini chocolate chips to the hot custard and whisk until melted and smooth. Add the butter and whisk until melted and smooth. Cover the custard with a piece of waxed paper set directly on the surface and refrigerate for 30 minutes.

4. Whisk the custard until smooth and light, cover again, and refrigerate for 30 minutes longer, or until cooled to room temperature. Whisk the custard again until smooth and light. Then stir in the remaining ¼ cup chocolate chips and ⅓ cup of the chopped walnuts. Spoon the custard into 5 ceramic ramekins or glass dessert dishes. Cover with plastic wrap and refrigerate until serving time.

5. To serve, top each custard with a dollop of whipped cream, if you like. Sprinkle the remaining walnuts on top.

· R H U B A R B ·

Rhubarb is an old-fashioned plant with confused gender. Like the tomato, one of my favorite vegetables, which experts insist is really a fruit, rhubarb, which masquerades as a fruit, is really a vegetable—so they say. In the nineteenth century, all this confusion was avoided by calling rhubarb "pie plant," a no-nonsense name that made its raison d'être absolutely clear.

Many people are either unfamiliar with rhubarb or they are sick of it, because you either have none or you have too much. Since it is not sold in cans and is only occasionally seen frozen, rhubarb is a highly seasonal ingredient, alien to many modern cooks. Yet once planted, it can take root for up to a century, and grows without care, easily doubling each year. Though gardening books say the roots like to be mulched with a rich composted material, I have always found rhubarb thrives even upon neglect.

Rhubarb is not a pretty plant. It is something of a dinosaur in the garden, with its tall, gawky stalks and crinkly, elephantine leaves. Most people plant it in an out-of-the-way spot or along a wall, because they know it will be there, bigger and more ungainly, year after year.

I've moved mine three times. It now thrives in what I hope will be its permanent home, just outside the fence at the southwestern corner of the garden. Its first resting place seemed perfect, in a small plot next to the attached shed at the back of the house. It took root and grew robustly early on; I had pie on my mind for weeks, even though they say you shouldn't harvest the first year.

I soon noticed, however, that the rhubarb was not alone. Just behind it on the left was a large, newly dug hole, which extended deep under the shed's crawlspace that abuts the basement to the house. Woodchuck, my neighbors diagnosed; they clucked their tongues and recommended the local cure—lead poisoning. No way.

I piled heavy rocks and old firestones on top of the entranceway, but the next day, the weighty stones had somehow been pushed slightly to one side, and new loose dirt was scattered all over the rhubarb and adjacent daffodils. After consulting the mayor, a mature, square-jawed man with wide-ranging practical skills, I took another humane approach: mothballs. I stuffed boxes of them down the hole and covered it over again with rocks. My furry nemesis stayed away for a week or two, or maybe he just used another entrance. During that time, the rhubarb reached maturity—enough, I thought, to taste just a sample, the first produce from my own land. I bent down, mulling over in my mind which stalk to snip, and lo and behold, they all smelled like mothballs. Thus began the plant's migration.

As a child I loved the rhubarb that came from my grandparents' garden, though my grandmother stewed it with so little sugar the astringency stung my mouth. Later I carried a sentimental affinity for rhubarb because the plant survived long after my grandfather died and the garden went to seed. Now I enjoy cooking with the fruit, and I appreciate the grownup freedom of adding as much sugar as I like, so that while not cloying, the tartness is at least tamed to the tongue.

What will surprise those who finally attempt to cook rhubarb, whose stalks look very much like a bunch of reddened celery, is how easy and quick it is to prepare. All you have to do is trim off the green leaves, which are toxic (and are usually removed in markets before it is sold), and rinse the stalks. Trim the ends if needed; there's no stringing or peeling or blanching. Stewing takes all of ten minutes.

Rhubarb stalks hold so much water there's never any need to add extra liquid. I've always found thickening it for pies to be a trifle tricky. Though I usually prefer instant tapioca to turn out a fruit pie that is juicy but still holds together, rhubarb requires that

(continued)

old-fashioned thickener, flour, and a good deal of it, about one-third cup for an average size pie.

Rhubarb has an affinity for orange, and I love the way it pairs with fresh ginger. It makes marvelous puddings and preserves. The only challenge is in balancing that wonderful tartness, which is rhubarb's glory, with just enough sugar to remove any unpleasant astringency, while leaving enough zing to keep its character intact.

Two pounds of rhubarb, which cooks down to a little over three cups, will take anywhere from one to one and one-fourth cups of sugar. You really do have to taste and decide how much sugar is needed, because the older strains of rhubarb, which are often green, can be exceedingly sour—though they say color is not always an accurate determiner of sweetness—while some new, redder varieties require considerably less sugar. Of course, personal preferences range from a pleasing pucker to childishly sweet, but I always add the minimum, let the sugar melt down and cook with the fruit a minute or two, taste, and then decide how much more is needed.

P.S. When I renovated the house, we removed the floor of the shed and underneath was the woodchuck's nest, a perfect doughnut about three feet in diameter, made up of every kind of scavenged material you can imagine, bits of string and paper and fabric and twigs, all woven together with mechanical perfection. Carl, my carpenter, patiently cleared it out, though we all marveled at the craftsmanship and precision of the work, and we felt a little sad at destroying someone's home. We needn't have worried. Next spring, as the daffodils next to the shed began to push up out of the ground, each day they were covered with a little more earth, and behind them, in the exact same spot, appeared the front door to the woodchuck's house.

STEWED RHUBARB

Makes about 3 cups

This old-fashioned recipe is wonderfully adaptable. Stewed rhubarb makes a marvelous breakfast fruit or snack, doused with a splash of chilled cream to soften its sassiness. For dessert, I like to layer it with sliced bananas and rice pudding or tapioca, which turns it into a tutti-frutti parfait.

> 2 pounds trimmed rhubarb, cut into ½-inch dice (8 cups)
> 1 cup plus 2 to 4 tablespoons sugar

1. Place the rhubarb in a stainless steel or enamel saucepan with 1 cup sugar. Cover and cook over moderate heat about 5 minutes, until the rhubarb gives up its juice.

2. Uncover, stir gently, and cook, stirring once or twice, 5 to 7 minutes, until the rhubarb is tender and the liquid has thickened slightly. Taste and add 2 to 4 tablespoons more sugar to taste.

Ruth Smith's Icebox Butter Cookies

Makes 7 to 8 dozen

Ruth Smith's grandparents were the first in her family to settle in this area. Given the fact that Ruth is now eighty-one and the town was founded in 1853, that makes them pioneers in these parts. These delicate sugar cookies are her mother's recipe, but while her mother rolled out the dough and cut the cookies the traditional way, Ruth's suggestion, which I give here, is to form the dough into large rolls, freeze them, and cut them into cookies as you need them. As she says, "The freezing and slicing was my own idea, as I don't like the mess of rolling out the dough, and I can't see but what the cookies are just as good if not better." I agree.

> 1/2 pound (2 sticks) unsalted butter, at room temperature
> 2 cups sugar
> 3 eggs
> 3/4 teaspoon baking soda
> 1 teaspoon vanilla extract
> 3 2/3 cups all-purpose flour
> 2 teaspoons baking powder
> 1/2 teaspoon salt
> 3/4 cup chopped walnuts (optional)

1. In a large bowl, cream the butter until fluffy and gradually beat in the sugar. Beat in the eggs one at a time until well blended. Add the baking soda and vanilla. Beat well. Sift together the flour, baking powder, and salt. Add to the butter mixture and blend well. Stir in the walnuts if you're using them. Cover and refrigerate the dough until it is firm.

2. Form the dough into 2 or 3 logs as big in diameter as the size of the cookie desired—3 inches works well. Wrap the logs well and freeze.

3. Preheat the oven to 375 degrees. Cut the frozen dough logs with a large sharp knife into slices about 3/8 inch thick and place 1 inch apart on a buttered cookie sheet. Bake the cookies until lightly browned, 10 to 12 minutes. Cool on a rack.

PECAN SPICE COOKIES

Makes 3½ dozen

Nuts and spice seem to address the fall woods and smoke-tinged air. Pecans, like all nuts, lack an oxidizing agent, so they turn rancid quickly. For sweet, fine-tasting cookies, be sure yours are fresh or were stored in the freezer.

2 cups all-purpose flour
1 teaspoon ground cinnamon
½ teaspoon freshly grated nutmeg
¼ teaspoon ground cloves
½ teaspoon salt
½ teaspoon baking soda
1½ teaspoons distilled white vinegar
½ cup milk
8 tablespoons (1 stick) unsalted butter, at room temperature
1 cup packed dark brown sugar
2 eggs, well beaten
1 cup coarsely chopped pecans
Granulated sugar

1. Preheat the oven to 375 degrees. In a medium bowl, combine the flour, cinnamon, nutmeg, cloves, salt, and baking soda. Whisk to blend. In a small bowl or cup, stir the vinegar into the milk; let stand. The milk will thicken as it "sours."

2. Meanwhile, in a larger bowl, cream the butter until light. Gradually beat in the brown sugar until smooth and fluffy. Add the eggs and beat well. Blend in the flour mixture alternately with the soured milk, beginning and ending with flour and beating until smooth after each addition. Stir in the pecans.

3. Drop the dough by teaspoonfuls onto an ungreased cookie sheet, spacing the cookies 2 inches apart. Flatten gently with a glass dipped in granulated sugar. Bake the cookies for 10 to 12 minutes, until firm and just beginning to color around the edges. Cool on a wire rack.

Old-Fashioned Baked Rice Pudding

6 to 8 servings

No dessert is simpler, more comforting, or more typical of country cooking than rice pudding, with its simple cupboard ingredients. If you happen to have access to raw whole milk, by all means use four cups of it for this recipe and omit the cream. Cooked, it is perfectly safe, and yields fantastic results in puddings and custards. While this one does take a bit of stirring, the rich, slightly caramelized results are well worth the attention.

> 1/4 cup long-grain white rice (not converted)
> 6 tablespoons sugar
> 3 1/2 cups milk
> 1/2 cup heavy cream
> 1 1/2 teaspoons vanilla extract

1. Preheat the oven to 325 degrees. Pour the rice, sugar, milk, and cream into a 3-quart glass or ceramic baking dish about 3 inches deep. Stir to dissolve the sugar. Microwave on High 2 minutes to warm the milk.

2. Transfer the dish to the preheated oven and bake 1 hour, stirring every 20 minutes. Cook 45 minutes longer, stirring every 15 minutes.

3. Stir in the vanilla and cook without stirring 30 to 40 minutes longer, until the pudding thickens and a light brown skin forms on top. Let cool to room temperature, then refrigerate until chilled before serving.

PEGGY'S EASY RICE PUDDING

6 to 8 servings

My friend and neighbor Peggy Soden has taught me a lot about living in the country. Married to Dave, who's gorgeous and a third-generation dairy farmer, she's a no-nonsense woman with an incredible mind for detail, a gift for story-telling and a great sense of humor. Here's her no-attention version of the previous baked rice pudding. They're both good, but surprisingly different; try the two and see which you prefer.

2 quarts milk
1 cup long-grain white rice (not converted)
1 cup sugar
1 cup raisins
2 teaspoons cinnamon (optional)

1. Pour the milk into a large saucepan. Stir in the rice and bring to a simmer over moderate heat. Reduce the heat to low, cover, and simmer for 1½ hours, or until most of the milk is absorbed and the rice is very soft.

2. Stir in the sugar. Add the raisins and the cinnamon if you like it. Let cool, then serve.

BLACK RASPBERRY
ICE CREAM

Makes about 5 cups

Of all the wild berries, black raspberries, which we call black caps, are hands down my favorite. They have an inky intensity and velvety deep flavor that is subtle and refined. Unfortunately, they are full of small seeds, which makes them hard to work with. I think ice cream, jam, and sauce put them to the best use.

1½ cups black raspberries
⅔ cup sugar
1 cup milk
1 cup heavy cream

1. Rinse the berries and drain in a colander. Handling them gently, pick over to remove any badly bruised or buggy fruit.

2. Place the berries in a heavy, medium saucepan made of stainless steel or enamel so they will not react. Set over moderate heat and warm the berries, crushing them with the back of a spoon, until they exude most of their juice, 2 to 3 minutes.

3. Stir in the sugar and cook, stirring, for 3 to 5 minutes, until a light syrup forms. Press berries and syrup through a medium mesh strainer into a bowl, working the seeds back and forth to extract as much juice and fruit as possible. Cover the berry extract and refrigerate or freeze until thoroughly chilled.

4. Whisk the milk and cream into the berry extract. Scrape into an ice cream maker and freeze according to the manufacturer's instructions. Serve at once or transfer to a covered container and freeze for up to 3 days.

RED RASPBERRY ICE CREAM

Makes about 1 pint

I like to make ice cream with wild raspberries, both because they are free and because their flavor is so sweet and so intense. Since the wild bushes ripen at different rates, depending upon their location in full sun, against a stone fence, or under some trees, the picking is usually good for up to a month. Of course, the biggest, best, ripest berries are always just out of reach, but depending upon your skill and how intent you are on just picking, you can gather enough for ice cream in under an hour. Or you can drive to the supermarket and pick up a pint of Driscoll or other good raspberries.

In addition to the usual water-and-salt models, I have one of those small insulated machines that make ice cream with a few turns in under half an hour. I like to use it because it is so easy, and most homemade ice cream is best eaten in a day or two.

> *2 cups red raspberries*
> *²/₃ cup sugar*
> *¹/₂ cup water*
> *1 cup heavy cream*
> *¹/₂ cup milk*

1. In a 2¹/₂- to 3-quart stainless steel saucepan, combine the raspberries with the sugar and water. Bring to a boil, stirring to dissolve the sugar. Boil over moderate heat for 5 minutes. Strain through a sieve or pass through the fine blade of a food mill to remove the seeds. (The berries will be very liquid, and this is not a lot of work.) Measure the juice; there will probably be about 1¹/₄ cups, but don't dilute it if you have less.

2. Return the berry juice to the saucepan and boil, again over moderate heat, until the syrup is then reduced to ³/₄ cup. Pour the raspberry syrup into a bowl and let cool for about 15 minutes. Stir in the cream and the milk, cover, and refrigerate until well chilled, at least 2 hours.

3. Freeze the mixture in an ice cream maker. Transfer to a covered container and place in the freezer until firm, usually at least 3 hours, before serving.

CHOCOLATE PECAN ICEBOX COOKIES

Makes 7 to 8 dozen

Cookie monsters thrive everywhere, but home-baked cookies belong to the country. Do-ahead icebox recipes provide the luxury of immediate gratification whenever you're in the mood. And double chocolate—unsweetened baking chocolate and cocoa—makes these an intense treat, a brownie in a wafer.

2 squares unsweetened chocolate
2 tablespoons strong brewed coffee or water
8 tablespoons (1 stick) unsalted butter, at room temperature
1½ cups sugar
1 egg
1 teaspoon vanilla extract
1⅔ cups all-purpose flour
2 tablespoons unsweetened cocoa powder, preferably Dutch processed
1 teaspoon baking powder
¼ teaspoon baking soda
¼ teaspoon salt
¾ cup finely chopped pecans

1. In a small heavy saucepan over very low heat or in a glass bowl in a microwave, melt the unsweetened chocolate in the coffee, stirring until smooth. Let stand until cooled to lukewarm.

2. In a large bowl, cream the butter until soft. Gradually beat the sugar into the butter until light and fluffy. Beat in the egg and continue beating until the mixture is pale in color and fluffy, about 2 minutes. Beat in the vanilla and the cooled melted chocolate.

3. In a medium bowl, combine the flour, cocoa, baking powder, baking soda, and salt. Stir well or whisk gently to blend. Add the dry ingredients to the chocolate-butter mixture and blend well. Stir in the pecans. The dough will be very thick.

4. With your hands, form the dough into 3 logs about 6 inches long and 2 inches in diameter. Wrap in plastic wrap and refrigerate until thoroughly chilled and set, at least 6 hours or overnight, or freeze for up to 2 months.

5. To bake the cookies, preheat the oven to 350 degrees. With a large, very sharp knife, cut as many of the logs as you wish into 1/8-inch-thick slices and set them 1 inch apart on a buttered cookie sheet. Bake 13 to 15 minutes, or until firm. Transfer to a wire rack and let cool before serving.

Rolled Sugar Cookies

Makes about 5 dozen

Soured milk, more vanilla, and less butter and sugar create a sturdier, more mellow cookie than the Icebox Butter Cookies. Try both and see which you prefer. I use this country classic to make my Christmas cookies every year, cutting the dough into animal shapes and sprinkling red and green crystal sugar over the tops. They keep beautifully for weeks if stored in an airtight tin.

> 3¼ cups all-purpose flour
> 1 teaspoon baking soda
> ½ teaspoon salt
> 1½ teaspoons distilled white vinegar
> ½ cup milk
> 12 tablespoons (1½ sticks) unsalted butter, at room temperature
> 1½ cups granulated sugar
> 1 egg
> 1½ teaspoons vanilla extract
> Crystal sugar, for sprinkling

1. In a medium bowl, combine the flour, baking soda, and salt. Whisk gently to blend. In a small bowl or cup, stir the vinegar into the milk; set aside. It will thicken slightly as it "sours."

2. In a large bowl, cream the butter with a wooden spoon until light. Gradually beat in the sugar until light and fluffy. Add the egg and vanilla and beat well.

Cooking from a Country Farmhouse

3. Add ¼ of the flour mixture to the butter mixture and beat until smooth. Add ⅓ of the sour milk and beat until smooth. Repeat 2 more times, beating after each addition. Work in the remaining flour. Cover and refrigerate the dough for at least 2 hours.

4. Preheat the oven to 350 degrees. On a lightly floured board, roll out the dough between ⅛ and ¼ inch thick. Cut with a 3-inch round floured cookie cutter or into other desired shapes. Transfer to a lightly greased cookie sheet, arranging the cookies 1 inch apart, and sprinkle sugar over the tops. Gather together the scraps of dough, roll out, and cut more cookies. Repeat to use up all the dough.

5. Bake the cookies for 10 to 12 minutes, until pale golden and just beginning to color around the edges. Let cool on a wire rack. Then store in an airtight tin.

Molasses Gingersnaps

Makes about 5 dozen

There's nothing wimpy about these cookies. Assertively flavored and crisp as a fresh apple, they are good keepers and actually improve with a little age. Store in an airtight tin as soon as they are cooled, to prevent softening.

3⅓ cups all-purpose flour
1½ teaspoons baking soda
½ teaspoon salt
2½ teaspoons ground ginger
¾ teaspoon ground cinnamon
12 tablespoons (1½ sticks) unsalted butter, at room temperature
½ cup sugar, plus additional for sprinkling
1 egg
¾ cup molasses

1. In a medium bowl, sift together the flour, baking soda, salt, ginger, and cinnamon.

2. In a large bowl, cream the butter until soft. Gradually add the ½ cup sugar and beat until light and fluffy. Add the egg and blend well. Mix in the molasses.

3. Gradually stir in the flour mixture, beating until smooth. Cover and refrigerate until the dough is chilled and stiff enough to roll out.

4. Preheat the oven to 375 degrees. Work with the dough in 3 or 4 batches; keep the remainder chilled. On a lightly floured board, roll out the dough ¼ inch thick. Cut with a 2½-inch floured round cookie cutter, preferably crinkled. Sprinkle with sugar and set 1 inch apart on a lightly greased cookie sheet.

5. Bake the cookies for 12 to 14 minutes, until firm. Remove to racks and let cool. Then store in an airtight tin.

ICED CURRANT RING
WITH BERRIES AND PEACHES

6 servings

Almost everyone who lives in the country has a currant bush or two or three somewhere on their property, and in good years, they are heavy bearers. For the same reason that currants make such good jelly—they are very rich in pectin, natural fruit gelatin—they produce an excellent, easy ice that requires no special processing. The tartness of currants provides a refreshing alternative to lemon ice, and with its lovely deep rose color, this recipe is a very pretty way to serve it. Pass a bottle of iced vodka or Cointreau to splash on top if you like.

> 2 cups red currants
> 1 cup water
> 1 cup sugar
> 1½ cups blueberries and raspberries, or any other berry
>   combination of your choice
> 2 ripe peaches, cut into ½-inch dice
> Fresh mint leaves, for garnish (optional)

1. In a medium stainless steel saucepan, combine the currants, water, and sugar. Bring to a boil over moderate heat, stirring to dissolve the sugar. Boil for 2 minutes. Remove from the heat and let cool slightly. Puree in a food processor, then strain into a bowl through a sieve to remove the seeds. Let cool to room temperature.

2. Pour the currant syrup into a 3-cup ring mold or other decorative shape. Freeze for at least 3 hours. or until set; the ice will never become hard as a rock, which is why you don't need to freeze it in an ice cream maker.

3. To serve, run a knife around the edge of the mold and dip the outside into a bowl of hot water for a few seconds to loosen. Unmold onto a serving platter. Toss together the berries and peaches and fill the center of the ice with them. If there is any fruit left, scatter it around the rim. Garnish the platter with the mint leaves if you have them.

·INDEX·